THE FALL OF THE OLD COLONIAL SYSTEM

The Fall of the

Old Colonial System

A STUDY IN BRITISH FREE TRADE
1770-1870

ROBERT LIVINGSTON SCHUYLER

Gouverneur Morris Professor of History
Columbia University

OXFORD UNIVERSITY PRESS

London   NEW YORK   *Toronto*

1945

PREFACE

THIS STUDY has to do with a major achievement of British liberalism that was of prime importance in the history of the British Empire. Had British statesmanship not outgrown the mentality of the Old Colonial System, the emergence of the present British Commonwealth of Nations would have been impossible. British colonies might conceivably have obtained complete self-government in the nineteenth century in spite of the old system, but this could not have come to pass within the Empire. It could have come about only by secession from the Empire, and secession could have come only through successful rebellion, as in the case of the Thirteen Colonies in the eighteenth century. To have permitted colonies to withdraw from the Empire in peace would have been wholly contrary to the ruling spirit of the old system.

British liberals, to whatever political party they belonged, believed intensely in the vitalizing virtues of individual liberty and free economic enterprise, and totally rejected the old mercantilist conceptions of society, state, and empire. From the days of Adam Smith to those of Goldwin Smith some of them—an increasing number as time went on—were avowed anti-imperialists who were convinced that the breakup of the Empire, by peaceful means they hoped, would be beneficial to the mother country, the colonies, and the world at large. They believed that it would promote peace, prosperity, and progress. With the emergence of new conditions in Britain toward the close of the nineteenth century, among

v

them a new collectivism and a new imperialism, it came to be the fashion to look back on the Mid-Victorian liberals and all their works with amused contempt and even with moral reprobation. At best they were visionaries, dreaming of permanent world peace and the brotherhood of man; at worst they were crass materialists, hopelessly lacking in appreciation of the higher things of life, including the greater glory of Britain and her Empire. Reflection on the fruitage of collectivism and imperialism in the totalitarianism of other countries may give us a new respect for them. The Mid-Victorian liberals have things to say to us today if we will but listen to them.

The title of this book calls for a word of explanation. In considering the Old Colonial System and its fall I have intentionally limited myself to colonial commerce and defense, and even in those fields no attempt has been made to describe the administrative machinery by which effect was given to imperial regulations. It did not seem necessary, therefore, to deal in the introductory chapter with the subject of the enforcement of the acts of trade, important as this obviously was. Nor has the constitutional side of the old system been included in the scope of this inquiry. I have not entered upon what has become the subject of an extensive literature—the governmental changes that were involved in the grant of responsible government to the more politically advanced of Britain's colonies in the middle decades of the nineteenth century. I am fully conscious, however, that colonial commerce, colonial defense, and colonial government were closely interrelated and that changes in any one of them affected the others.

I must be explicit, also, regarding another limitation. The research on which this book is based has been confined to

printed materials. Investigation of the state papers in the
British Public Record Office in London, especially the records of the Colonial Office and the Board of Trade, would
no doubt have yielded additional grist to my mill, but my
prospects of being able to examine these sources in the near
future are not bright. In any event, this limitation is less
serious than it would be if a great deal of important archive
material had not found its way into that vast accumulation
of printed sources, the Parliamentary Papers.

I have exhumed some articles of mine from their resting
places in the files of the *Political Science Quarterly* and the
American Historical Review and incorporated the substance
of them in Chapters II, IV, VI, and VII. I am grateful to the
editors of those journals for graciously permitting this dis-
interment and reincarnation to take place.

R. L. S.

Columbia University
February 1945

CONTENTS

I

INTRODUCTION

COMMERCIAL AND MILITARY ASPECTS OF THE OLD COLONIAL SYSTEM

THE old British colonial system was essentially commercial. It depended for its justification upon the doctrines of mercantilism, that politico-economic complex of principles, policies, regulations, and practices which existed in Europe between the late medieval period and the age of *laissez-faire*. In England some of the elements of mercantilism can be discerned at least as early as the fourteenth century, long before English colonies had come into existence overseas. A recent writer on English mercantilism remarks that 'the old colonial policy was merely the familiar doctrines of mercantilist economics applied to the new imperial situation.' [1] So long as mercantilist doctrines prevailed in England, colonies were valued because of the benefits which the mother country was supposed to derive from their trade, regulated by herself and primarily in her own interest—benefits which, it was believed, more than compensated her for the responsibilities and burdens of empire.

Like many other terms used by students of human affairs, past and present, the word mercantilism lacks definiteness. The subject for which it stands has been approached from different points of view, its aims have been variously conceived, and agreement has not been reached in regard to its content or peculiar characteristics. The expression 'mercan-

3

tile system' was first given currency by Adam Smith, who devoted approximately one-fourth of his great treatise to a discussion of the subject. He regarded as the basic doctrine of the mercantile system the popular notion that wealth consists in money, or in gold and silver; and as its chief objectives, an increase in the quantity of money and precious metals within a country by a favorable balance of trade and, connected with this, the encouragement of domestic industry by protecting it from foreign competition in the home market. The Oxford Dictionary defines the mercantile system as 'a term used by Adam Smith and later political economists for the system of economic doctrine and legislative policy based on the principle that money alone constituted wealth.' For a long time Adam Smith's interpretation was generally accepted. Desire for money and the precious metals has not, of course, been peculiar to mercantilism, and, on the other hand, many instances are to be found in mercantilist writings in which a distinction was made between money and wealth. Adam Smith knew this, but he said that those who recognized the distinction often lost sight of it in the course of their arguments: 'Some of the best English writers upon commerce,' he remarked, 'set out with observing that the wealth of a country consists, not in its gold and silver only, but in its lands, houses, and consumable goods of all different kinds. In the course of their reasonings, however, the lands, houses, and consumable goods seem to slip out of their memory, and the strain of their argument frequently supposes that all wealth consists in gold and silver, and that to multiply those metals is the great object of national industry and commerce.'

In the course of time, however, Adam Smith's interpretation came to be challenged. Gustav Schmoller, a leading exponent of the historical school of economics which flourished in Germany after its unification under Prussian leadership, took an entirely different view of the essence of mercantilism. In an essay published in 1884, *Das Merkantilsystem in seiner historischen Bedeutung,* he expounded the thesis that mercantilism was at bottom a phase of state-making, that it aimed primarily at the substitution of centralized economic policy and control for that previously exercised by local authorities.[2] Generalizing largely from events in Prussian history, he said:

The essence of the system lies not in some doctrine of money, or of the balance of trade; not in tariff barriers, protective duties, or navigation laws; but in something far greater:—namely, in the total transformation of society and its organization, as well as of the state and its institutions, in the replacing of a local and territorial economic policy by that of the national state.

To Schmoller, mercantilism signified essentially a system of unification.

The English economic historian William Cunningham, a contemporary of Schmoller, drawing his facts from English history, laid chief stress on mercantilism as a system of power, the external power of the state, that is to say, in relation to other states. The first edition of his *Growth of English Industry and Commerce* was published in 1882. Before the days of Adam Smith, according to Cunningham, 'the main object, which publicists who dealt with economic topics had had before their minds, was the power of the country; they set themselves to discuss the particular aspects of industry and commerce which would conduce to this end, according to the circumstances of different countries.' In Cunningham's opinion, navigation laws intended to promote English sea power were quite as characteristically mercantilist as measures designed primarily to secure a favorable balance of trade.

The broadest treatment of mercantilism is to be found in Eli F. Heckscher's historical treatise, *Mercantilism*.[3] The author, who has studied mercantilist writings long and deeply and looks at his many-sided subject from various points of view, deals with mercantilism as a unifying system, as a system of power, as a system of protection, as a monetary system, and as a conception of society.

From what has been said there would appear to be propriety in distinguishing between historical mercantilism and Adam Smith's 'mercantile system.' Maitland once humorously suggested that Sir Henry Spelman, the seventeenth-century legal antiquary, introduced the feudal system into England.[4] There is at least equally good reason for regarding Adam Smith as the creator of the mercantile system. He was concerned, as the title of his great work indicates, with the wealth of nations. He wrote as an economist, or, as he would have said, as a political economist, and political economy meant to him 'a branch of the science of a statesman or legislator' which had as its objects 'to enrich both the people and the sovereign.' [5] He did not see historical mercantilism whole. He concentrated, with brilliant analytical acumen, on its economic phases, those in which the objective was the wealth of nations. His mercantile system was not a system of power, and it was therefore not inconsistent that his celebrated eulogy of the Navigation Act, which mercantilists had been lauding for a hundred years, went hand in hand with the most formidable and effective indictment of mercantilism considered as a system of wealth that has ever been penned. His classic dictum that 'defence is of much more importance than opulence' could have been uttered by any good mercantilist, and as a matter of fact countless statements can be found in mercantilist writings defending and extolling the Navigation Act as the palladium of English sea power and security.[6] Mercantilists, however, praised the Navigation Act as promoting both national power and national wealth; Adam Smith saw in it a legitimate and praiseworthy sacrifice of wealth to power. The fact that he did not conceive of power as one of the basic objects of mercantilism explains the seeming paradox that neo-mercantilists have been able to appeal to the authority of the great opponent of the mercantile system in justification of their propaganda.

Probably the most helpful comprehensive view of mercantilism is that in which it is regarded as the economic phase of state-making, state-maintaining, and state-aggrandizing in the period when that many-sided movement which we call for convenience the Commercial Revolution was profoundly, though gradually, altering the conditions of European economic life and economic ideas. Mercantilism has often been called the economic phase of nationalism, and it is permissible to think of it as such if we remind ourselves that it flourished before the full-grown nationalism of our own times had come into existence. The collective entity with which mercantilists concerned themselves was the state, and most of the important states of Europe in the age of mercantilism included more than a single national element. The state, in mercantilist eyes, ought to be administered as an economic unit, and its interests ought to be promoted by the central government, in England the crown and its administrative agents and parliament. Mercantilists believed that the interests of the various classes in society could be resolved into a general harmony, but only by a system of wise governmental regulation. They did not believe, as Adam Smith did, that an 'invisible hand' led the individual, in pursuing his own self-interest, to promote the public interest.[7] There was nothing new about collective regulation of economic life, but in the Middle Ages the regulating authorities had been local—merchant and craft gilds, municipal authorities, and manorial courts. In the mercantilist régime the central government concerned itself increasingly with the whole range of economic life—commercial, agricultural, industrial—and thereby greatly expanded the sphere of the state. Its object was to encourage economic activities that were considered to be beneficial to the state and to discourage those regarded as injurious. As Cunningham remarks, 'Any scheme of controlling economic affairs for the public good must involve an interference with private interests. Some of them may be favoured, and some may be injured, but it is inevitable that very many should be affected in one way or another.' Private interests grew up under the fostering care of government, and it was to be expected that each of them would look upon its own prosperity as essential to the state's welfare, that there would be disagreement among them on questions of policy, and that they would not be backward in bringing to bear on the government such influence as they were able to exert in favor of measures which they deemed to be advantageous to themselves.[8]

In general, the state was idealized and thought of as something other than a mere aggregation of private interests and something quite different from the sum total of its inhabitants. Mercantilists were not interested in human welfare as such. Unlike medieval economic thinkers, they were not concerned with ethical considerations or spiritual values, and unlike later humanitarians, utilitarians, and socialists, they were not concerned with secular human happiness. Mercantilist writers were usually businessmen or politicians, distinctly not representatives of the 'lower orders,' who, as yet, had no place in the body politic; the state, as they conceived of it, could prosper and be strong though the great majority of its inhabitants were poverty-stricken and ignorant; indeed, it would scarcely be an exaggeration to say that it could not, in their eyes, prosper otherwise. 'It was the fate of the workers to be poor that the nation might be rich, and to be ceaselessly diligent that the nation might be powerful.' [9] In England the slave trade, with all the human misery it involved, was looked upon with great favor as one of the cornerstones of national prosperity and power. 'The necessity of kidnapping cargoes of slaves on the coast of Africa,' William Huskisson reminded the House of Commons twenty years after the abolition of the British slave trade, 'was, at that time, as coolly defended, on the score of encouragement to our marine, as the taking of cod-fish on the Banks of Newfoundland could be at the present day.' Child labor, too, was highly commended. Defoe, for example, in his *Plan of the English Commerce* (1728), spoke with approval of the fact that in parts of England infants of five, six, or seven years of age were earning their own livings.

Power was the primary concern of the state, the power of the state was thought of as the ultimate objective, and mercantilism, in Heckscher's words, would have had 'all economic activity subservient to the state's interest in power.' It was a system 'for forcing economic policy into the service of power as an end in itself.' The economic resources of the world, moreover, were conceived of as fixed in quantity, and ·

what one state gained, others were supposed to lose. To impoverish and weaken rival states was as important and laudable, in mercantilist eyes, as to increase the wealth and power of one's own; in fact, it was an indirect means of accomplishing this very purpose. This thought was clearly expressed by the English East India Company in 1641: 'The safety of the Kingdom consists not onely in its own strength and wealth but also in the laudable and lawful performance of those things which will weaken and impoverish such powerful Princes, as either are, or may become our Enemies.' [10]

It is not surprising, therefore, that the age of mercantilism was a period of chronic warfare between states. Europe as a whole was never at peace for any length of time, and the individual states, when they were not actually fighting, were preparing to fight. Mercantilism, indeed, was in large measure a system of military preparedness. The medieval ideal of Christian universalism had never been realized, and there had been plenty of fighting in the Middle Ages, but universalism had at least been cherished as an ideal. In the age of mercantilism the ideal had faded away. Its principal institutional expressions had been the 'Universal Empire' and the 'Universal Church,' and by the sixteenth century the former had become a hollow sham, and the latter had ceased to be universal.

Mercantilism, in its pursuit of state power, regulated economic activities in order to secure specific objects, the increase of the mercantile marine or of rural population, for example. It also strove to develop by regulations the general economic resources of the country so that the state, by taxation, would be able to obtain what it needed for defense or offense, and thus 'considerations of power became a motive for stimulating the general economic prosperity of the country, for this was considered the best guarantee for ensuring a powerful state.' [11]

*

*   *

In the late sixteenth and early seventeenth centuries, when the English Government was beginning to take an active interest in oversea colonization, the main lines of English mercantilism had been laid down, and colonies fitted nicely into the mercantilist scheme of things. They would contribute in various ways, it was believed, to the wealth and power of England. The arguments in favor of colonization as a public policy were set forth in contemporary English writings, and all of them of any importance can be found in Richard Hakluyt's remarkably interesting tract, *A Particular Discourse concerning . . . Western Discoveries,* written in 1584 though not published till 1877.[12] There are excellent lucid discussions of them in George Louis Beer's *The Origins of the British Colonial System* and Klaus E. Knorr's *British Colonial Theories,* 1570-1850. Nothing will be said here of the arguments corresponding to what Beer called the 'subsidiary motives' for colonization, though some of them were for a time decidedly influential and served to win support for the colonial movement.

Treasure as wealth and as a means of power was a commonplace in all mercantilist thinking. 'There are few mercantilist writings,' says Heckscher, 'that are not mainly preoccupied with what is usually known in English works as *"treasure,"* which was without exception synonymous with money or precious metals.' [13] The proud position held by

Spain under Philip II was commonly attributed to the treasure she derived from the mines of Mexico and Peru, and why might not England find similar fortune if she established colonies of her own in the New World? The belief that the eastern coast of North America abounded in precious metals died hard, as is shown by the persistence of provisions in royal charters to colonial proprietors and colonizing companies reserving to the crown a proportion of precious metals mined in the colonies.

Concurrent with this belief, and lasting long after it had been reluctantly abandoned, was the hope that colonies would contribute in another way to England's stock of treasure. The favorable balance of trade doctrine held a foremost place in all mercantilist planning for the promotion of national wealth and power. Generally speaking, this doctrine called, of course, for decreasing the importation and increasing the exportation of commodities so that there would be an inflow of money and bullion. Perhaps its best-known English exposition is in Thomas Mun's *England's Treasure by Forraign Trade,* written during the 1630's. 'The ordinary means . . . to encrease our wealth and treasure,' Mun said, 'is by Forraign Trade, wherein wee must ever observe this rule: to sell more to strangers yearly than wee consume of theirs in value.' [14] England, however, required imports, for there were important commodities that she needed and could not produce for herself: naval stores, for example, which she obtained from the countries of the Baltic and Russia; sugar and dried fruits, as well as silk and wine, from Mediterranean lands; spices, dyes, and other products of the Far East, from Portugal and afterwards from the Dutch. Would it not be possible to free her from the necessity of importing such commodities from foreigners by establishing colonies of her own in North America and opening up direct commercial intercourse with the Far East? Elizabethans and Jacobeans speculated hopefully on this prospect. According to Hakluyt:

> The countries . . . of America whereunto we have just title . . . being answerable in climate to Barbary, Egypt, Syria, Persia, Turkey, Greece, all the islands of the Levant sea, Italy, Spain, Portugal, France, Flanders, High Almayne [Germany], Denmark, Eastland, Poland, and Muscovy, may presently or within a short space afford unto us, for little or nothing, and with much more safety, either all or a great part of the commodities which the aforesaid countries do yield us at a very dear hand and with manifold dangers.

These dangers, which Hakluyt described in some detail, resulted mainly from the existing international situation and the depredations of the Barbary pirates. 'This desire to free England from the necessity of purchasing from foreigners,' says Beer, 'formed the underlying basis of English commercial and colonial expansion; it led directly to the formation of the East India Company and to the colonization of America.' [15] It was in the light of this predominant motive for colonization that the value of colonies was mainly to be judged; 'the ideal colony was one which would have freed England from the necessity of importing anything from her competitors.' [16]

Imports from colonies would evidently have to be paid for in commodities or in money, and England had no mind to ship money to her colonies. 'The theory that the colony was to be a source of supply implied . . . that it was also to be a market for English produce. One conception was the natural corollary to the other, and consequently the value of colonies as an outlet for the mother country's manufactures was by no means ignored.' [17] The hopeful Hakluyt, quite ignorant, of course, of conditions among the native peoples of North America, looked forward to a great market there for English woolen cloth. 'Now if her majesty take these western discoveries in hand, and plant there, it is like that in short time we shall vent as great a mass of cloth in those parts as ever we did in the Netherlands, and in time much more.' Though such expectations were not fulfilled, the utility of colonies as markets was never lost sight of.

One of Hakluyt's arguments in favor of colonization was that it would lead to an increase of English shipping and naval strength and give employment to many mariners. He assumed, in accordance with a generally accepted principle of European policy, that the trade of any colonies that might be established would be confined to the shipping of the mother country. The encouragement of native shipping was a well-established national policy in England at the beginning of the colonial era. The defense of the realm depended primarily upon sea power, and sea power depended upon a prosperous mercantile marine and an adequate supply of mariners to man it, upon both of which the navy could draw in time of war. Various means had been resorted to for building up the mercantile marine.[18] Navigation acts had been passed for the purpose of protecting English shipping from foreign competition, bounties had been given to promote English shipbuilding, alien duties had been levied on goods imported into and exported from the country in foreign ships in order to discourage the use of such ships in England's trade, and efforts had been made to foster English fisheries as the best possible nursery of seamen. These last are a good illustration of the lengths to which a mercantilist government was prepared to go in interfering in the life of its people. What came to be known as 'Political Lent' was first introduced in 1549 and was maintained until about the middle of the seventeenth century. Under this institution the use of meat was prohibited on certain days in order to stimulate a demand for fish. At a time, however, when fasting was looked upon by the Church of England as a 'popish superstition,' it was deemed expedient to make it quite clear that these political fast days had no religious purpose.

From what has been said it should be inferred that the ideal empire in the eyes of mercantilists would be economically self-sufficing, commercially independent of the outside world. Colonies would supply the mother country with what she needed but was unable to produce for herself; they, in turn, would obtain what they needed from her or through trade with one another; and all trade within the empire would be carried on in English or English colonial vessels. No such result could be hoped for without an extension of mercantilist regulations to the trade of the colonies. 'All Colonies and foreign Plantations,' said Sir Josiah Child, writing toward the end of the seventeenth century, 'do endamage their Mother-Kingdom, whereof the Trades of such Plantations are not confined to their said Mother-Kingdom by good Laws and severe Execution of those Laws.' [19] Such a monopolistic outlook, it should be understood, was not peculiar to English mercantilism. As stated in one of the English acts of trade, it was 'the usage of other nations to keep their plantations trade to themselves.' The mercantilist ideal of empire was never fully realized, but we should have it in mind as we survey summarily the main commercial phases of England's old colonial system. In the words of the late Professor Charles M. Andrews, 'According to this idea of the self-sufficing empire . . . the mother country, the sugar and tobacco colonies, the provision or bread colonies, the fisheries, and Africa formed a single economic and commercial whole, made up of widely scattered but coöperative members, each of which contributed something to the strength and profit of the whole. The ultimate advantage, however, went by design to the mother state, the kingdom or realm of England.'

Colonial policy began to take form in regulations relating to colonial trade, especially the Virginia tobacco trade, made during the reigns of James I and Charles I.[20] The ensuing period of civil war in England, however, was one of extreme decentralization in the nascent empire, and the beginnings of colonial policy lapsed. The execution of Charles I and the establishment of the Puritan Commonwealth in 1649 led to an imperial disruption; for the colonies, with the exception of the Puritan colonies of New England, repudiated the authority of the revolutionary Commonwealth Government. But they were soon reduced to obedience, and the Age of Cromwell, which was a time of imperial recovery and commercial and colonial expansion, was followed by the establishment of the old colonial system under Charles II.

The Restoration swept away all the innovations in church and state that had been made during the Puritan régime. All parliamentary enactments to which the royal assent had not been given, and this meant all the ordinances and acts passed after the outbreak of the Civil War in 1642, were treated as null and void, and the reign of Charles II was regarded as having begun at the moment of the 'murder' of his father in 1649. But whatever lawyers might say, or not say, about it, men could not forget the past. The high place among the nations which England had taken under Cromwell appealed powerfully even to those who detested everything he had stood for in religion and government, and there was no disposition to reverse his commercial and colonial policies. The new king was very greatly interested in trade and colonization, as were many of his courtiers, ministers, and officials. Charles himself and other members of the royal family invested in commercial ventures such as the East India Company, the Hudson's Bay Company, and the Royal African Company, and his brother James, Duke of York, became the proprietor of the province of New York, conquered from the Dutch in 1664. Many old Cromwellians— Anthony Ashley-Cooper, created Earl of Shaftesbury by Charles II, is a conspicuous example—made their peace with the new monarch, remained in public life, and carried on the Cromwellian tradition of commercial and colonial expansion. Merchants and colonial experts were frequently consulted by the government, and greater weight than ever before was given to mercantile considerations in the framing of national policies. Among influential officials Sir George Downing deserves particular mention. An office-holder and diplomat under Cromwell, he held various government positions under Charles II and probably had more to do with shaping colonial policy in commercial matters than anyone else. 'To him, far more than to any other individual,' says Beer, 'is due the commercial system which was elaborated during the Restoration era for the regulation of the Empire's trade.' [21]

*

* *

A summary sketch of the old colonial system on the side of commerce and defense is all that will be attempted in this introductory chapter. The subject has been dealt with in a number of historical works. Detailed accounts can be found in Beer's well-known treatises published a generation ago—*The Origins of the British Colonial System* and *The Old Colonial System*—and in Knorr's recent *British Colonial Theories,* 1570-1850, a work based upon extensive research in contemporary writings and replete with quotations from them. The organs and agencies of government, whether in England or in the colonies, that were responsible for administering the laws referred to will not be described. This is not, of course, because the subject of the administration and enforcement of the laws was not important. It was obviously of vital importance, but administration has been deliberately excluded from the scope of the present study.

The basic statute of the old system was the famous Navigation Act of 1660. Passed, in its own words, 'for the increase of shipping and encouragement of the navigation of this nation, wherein, under the good providence and protection of God, the wealth, safety and strength of this kingdom is so much concerned,' it introduced no new principles. English navigation acts went back as far as the fourteenth century, and the provisions of the Act of 1660 relating to the trade of the colonies were anticipated in regulations made under James I and Charles I and during the Interregnum. This particular act, however, was quickly followed by a spectacular enlargement of the English mercantile marine, which seems to have approximately doubled between 1660 and 1688, and it soon came to be revered as the sheet anchor of England's sea power and defense. Men spoke of it as 'the' Navigation Act *par excellence.* It was passed at a time of intense and bitter commercial hostility between England and the Dutch, a hostility that had already led to a war between the rivals in Cromwell's day and was soon to bring on two more. The Cromwellian war of 1652-4 had gone in favor of the English, but the Dutch still enjoyed by far the greater part of the carrying trade of Europe, still monopolized the more valuable branches of trade with the Far East, still held a commanding position in the African slave trade and the fisheries of northern Europe, and still maintained colonial establishments in the New World from which the English sought to oust them. A Navigation Act of 1651, passed during the Commonwealth period, had aimed at the exclusion of Dutch vessels from England's foreign and colonial trade, but that was one of the enactments on which the ban of nullification fell at the Restoration, and a new statute was obviously called for.

As to the colonial trade, with which we are particularly concerned here, the Navigation Act of 1660 forbade importation into and exportation from any English possession in Asia, Africa, or America except in ships belonging to the people of England, Ireland, Wales, or Berwick-on-Tweed (hereafter designated as English ships), or in ships built in those possessions and belonging to the people thereof (hereafter designated as colonial ships), such ships to be navigated by an English master and a crew of which at least three-fourths of the members were English. Penalty for breach of this law was forfeiture of ship and cargo.[22] Scottish ships were excluded from trade with the English colonies until the Union of England and Scotland in 1707. In order to qualify for the colonial trade colonial ships, it will be noted, had to be colonial-built as well as colonial-owned, though English ships need not be English-built. Two years later, however, by a statute known as the Act of Frauds, it was provided that foreign-built ships bought after 1 October 1662 should not enjoy the privileges of English ships but should be deemed alien and as such subject to duties to which alien ships were liable.[23] By excluding foreign shipping from the colonial trade, the Navigation Act gave protection to colonial as well as to English ships engaged in this trade, and ship-building became an important industry in the New England and middle colonies. The question of the extent to which colonial shipping was benefited by the elimination of Dutch competition in the colonial trade has received a good deal of attention. Professor Lawrence A. Harper thinks that the benefit was not very great. He points out that colonial ship-ping had attained considerable proportions in competition with the Dutch before 1660 and believes that even if Dutch ships had not been excluded, the small colonial vessels would have had an advantage over the larger Dutch ocean-going ships in the colonial coasting trade.[24]

A provision of the Act of 1660 for which there was no parallel in any earlier navigation act was the prohibition placed upon the exportation of certain colonial products to foreign countries.[25] These 'enumerated articles,' as they came to be called, were sugar, tobacco, cotton, indigo, ginger, and fustic and other dyeing woods, which henceforth could be exported from any English colony only to England, Ire-land, Wales, Berwick, or to some other English colony. Ex-cept for tobacco, none of these commodities could be pro-duced in England. The principle of 'enumeration' remained an essential part of the old colonial system, and from time to time other articles were added to the original list.[26] Some exceptions, however, were made in favor of particular articles previously enumerated. In 1739, for example, sugar was per-mitted to be exported from the British West Indies directly to Europe south of Cape Finisterre.

Being a general navigation act, the Act of 1660 was not

confined, of course, to regulations relating to the colonial trade. It was concerned with all branches of England's commerce. As regards trade between different parts of the British Isles (other than Scotland, which was regarded as a foreign country for commercial purposes until its union with England in 1707), England, Ireland, Wales, Berwick, and the Channel islands of Guernsey and Jersey were treated as a closed commercial area, within which trade was confined to English ships.[27] Commodities of the growth, production, or manufacture of foreign countries or colonies in Asia, Africa, or America could be imported into the British Isles only in English or colonial ships, and only from their places of production or usual ports of shipment.[28] Products of continental Europe could, in general, be imported into the British Isles in foreign ships without restriction, subject to the payment of alien duties, but various European commodities were specified that could be imported only in English ships or in ships built in the country in which the commodities were produced or in the port of usual shipment; and if any such commodities were imported in such foreign ships they were subject to the payment of alien duties. The list of specified commodities included all products of Russia and the Ottoman Empire, timber, pitch, tar, hemp, flax, olive oil, grain, wine, and brandy.[29] It has been calculated that the specified commodities constituted in weight a little more than half of England's imports from the continent, and in value a little less than half.[30] The Act of Frauds (1662), aimed principally at the Dutch, prohibited the importation of many commodities from the Netherlands or Germany in any ships.

The second major statute of the old system was the so-called Staple Act of 1663.[31] Under the Navigation Act, products of foreign European countries could be shipped directly to the English colonies if transported in English or colonial vessels. It was feared that this would lessen the consumption of English manufactures in the colonies, deprive English merchants of business, tend to weaken the political ties between the colonies and the mother country, and increase the number of colonial trade routes to be guarded by the English navy from foreign enemies in time of war and from pirates at all times. Accordingly the act prohibited, with a few exceptions, the importation of European products into any English possession in Asia, Africa, or America, unless those products had been laden and shipped in England, Wales, or Berwick (Ireland was not included) and carried directly, in English ships, to their destination. The purposes of the law were stated to be 'the maintaining a greater correspondence and kindness' between the colonies and England, keeping them 'in a firmer dependence upon it,' rendering them 'yet more beneficial and advantageous unto it in the further employment and increase of English shipping and seamen, vent of English woollen and other manufactures and commodities,' making the navigation to and from the colonies 'more safe and cheap,' and 'making this kingdom a staple, not only of the commodities of those plantations, but also of the commodities of other countries and places, for the supplying of them.' [32]

With these two basic acts of the old system, a third has often been associated, known as the Plantations Duties Act of 1673. The commodities enumerated in the Act of 1660 could lawfully be exported from the colonies where they were produced to other English colonies as well as to England. In this event, however, colonial consumers would enjoy an advantage not given to English consumers, since the commodities if shipped to England would be liable to substantial customs duties, while if sent to other colonies, they would pay either no duties at all or only such low ones as those colonies might levy. Complaint was made, moreover, that tobacco exported to New England was then illegally taken to foreign countries to the injury of the English customs revenue. By the Act of 1673, accordingly, duties were laid upon the enumerated commodities when exported from any colony, unless bond was given that they would be taken to England, Wales, or Berwick (Ireland was not included).[33] This law registered no new commercial policy, nor was it intended to yield any substantial revenue. It was essentially an administrative measure, designed to check violations of the enumeration provision of the Act of 1660, but it marks an important step in the development of imperial control over the colonies. The Commissioners of the Customs in England were made responsible for the collection of these new plantation duties,[34] and they appointed subordinate customs collectors and surveyors. 'Thus there was established in the colonies a comprehensive system of customs officials, who not only were absolutely independent of the authorities in the charter and proprietary colonies, but also were in a great measure free from control by the royal governors, since they were directly responsible to the higher authority of the Commissioners of the Customs.'[35]

These three acts of parliament have been called the economic framework of the old colonial system. A comprehensive navigation act passed in 1696 was important from the standpoint of administration and law enforcement, but it added nothing new in principle. It should be evident that these basic acts were thoroughly mercantilist in spirit and object. By excluding foreign ships from the colonial trade, prohibiting the exportation of the enumerated articles from the colonies to foreign countries, and limiting colonial imports, in general, to goods shipped from England, the English Government sought to increase English shipping and sea power, free the mother country from the need of importing from foreigners commodities which she could not produce, give English manufactures a virtual monopoly of the colonial market by discouraging colonial consumption of foreign goods, subjected, as they were, to payment of customs duties and transshipment charges in England and to higher freight charges due to indirect voyages, and improve England's trade balance. Other purposes also, it was hoped, would be served.

The primary function of the colony was to foster the development of English sea power, commerce, and industry. But, apart from its economic aims, it was realized that this system of regulating imperial trade possessed other distinct advantages. It inevitably led to the limitation of commerce to a few well-defined routes, and thus greatly facilitated the task of protection. Furthermore, it was perceived that the closer the commercial relations between colony and metropolis, the more firmly knit would become the political ties binding them together.[36]

English colonies were His Majesty's 'possessions,' but they were also 'foreign plantations,' which meant, for one thing, that they were outside England's customs system, and therefore her imports from and exports to them were, with few exceptions, subject to the payment of duties. The enumerated articles and any other colonial products that might be imported into England paid duties, as did goods imported from Europe. There was thus a fiscal motive for making England the staple for the trade of the colonies. In general, however, import duties were partially refunded upon re-exportation. In a comprehensive tariff act of 1660,[37] later known as the 'Old Subsidy,' the general rule was that half of the duty imposed by the act should be refunded. This 'drawback' system applied to all goods passing through England in transit, both colonial products destined for foreign European consumption and foreign European products destined for colonial consumption, and it was thus an important part of the old colonial system.

Another characteristic and very important feature of the old system was the preferential treatment of English imports from the colonies. This principle goes back to the beginnings of English colonization.[38] In the Old Subsidy of 1660 all of the enumerated articles received such favored treatment. Colonial tobacco, for example, was required to pay only twopence a pound as against sixpence charged on foreign tobacco. In the case of unrefined sugar, the duties were, respectively, 1s. 6d. and 4s. a hundredweight. The effect of these differential duties was to give colonial tobacco and sugar a virtual monopoly of the English market. In the year 1687-8 approximately 15,000,000 pounds of English colonial tobacco were entered at the London customhouse and only 16,000 pounds of Spanish tobacco.[39] It was quite in accord with mercantilist principles to encourage the importation of exotic products from colonies and discourage their importation from foreign countries, but the colonial preferences of 1660, confined as they were to the enumerated articles, seem to have been intended also as a partial compensation to the colonial producer for the restrictions imposed upon him by the enumeration policy. Many changes were made by parliament in the British customs duties, but the principle of colonial preference, embodied in the Old Subsidy of 1660, was retained and came to be extended to other colonial products than those enumerated; it was retained, as we shall see later, even after the principle of enumeration was abandoned in

1822. Preference was also given to colonial imports from England. Parliament did not, indeed, impose duties in the colonies on imports from foreign European countries until the nineteenth century, but the purpose of protecting English products from foreign competition in the colonial markets, which such duties would have served, was realized by the Staple Act, which, as we have seen, discouraged colonial importation of foreign goods.

The sugar and tobacco colonies—those in the West Indies and Virginia and Maryland—conformed to mercantilist ideals of empire and were highly prized, but the same was not true of New England and the middle colonies. During the seventeenth century and the first half of the eighteenth, by far the greater part of England's colonial trade was with the former. The value of her imports from the little island of Barbados in 1697-8 was nearly ten times that of her imports from all the New England colonies, and in the same year her exports to Barbados alone considerably exceeded in value her exports to New England, New York, and Pennsylvania combined.[40] Such figures speak eloquently. The English Government looked at colonies through mercantile eyes. It valued them for their trade, not as places of refuge for religious nonconformists or as the 'Seeds of Nations,' as William Penn called them. And at a time when England was generally believed to be underpopulated, colonies could not be valued as fields for English emigration, as they came to be in the nineteenth century. Widespread unemployment in the days of Elizabeth and the early seventeenth century had led to the belief that England was suffering from an excess of population and would therefore be benefited by emigration.[41] By the second half of the seventeenth century, however, opinion had changed, and thenceforward until the early nineteenth century precisely the opposite view prevailed. Emigration of Englishmen to the colonies was therefore generally regarded as an evil, to be justified only if it was likely to lead to counterbalancing advantages.[42] This attitude toward emigration reinforced commercial considerations in causing the government and mercantilists generally to prefer the West Indies to the northern colonies, since the development of the former by Negro slave labor did not involve any considerable emigration from England. Beer sums up the English attitude toward the New England colonies by saying that they did not fit into the colonial scheme.[43] Their surplus produce, generally speaking, was not wanted in England and found no market there, and they competed with England in fishing and shipping. To be sure, the picture changed very considerably as time went on. With the growth of population in the New England and the middle colonies, their consumption of British manufactured goods increased, and greater value came to be attached to them for this reason. In the year 1766-7 the value of British exports to New England, New York, and Pennsylvania was considerably greater than to all the British West Indies.[44] In Beer's opinion, the Treaty of Paris of 1763 marked a turning-point in British commercial policy, in that thenceforth 'greater stress was laid on colonies as markets for British produce than on colonies as sources of supply.' [45] England, however, offered the northern colonies no equivalent market, and they were forced to look elsewhere for the disposal of their surplus produce.

They turned to the West Indies. In most of the islands the planters found it profitable to concentrate on the production of sugar, which with its derivatives, molasses and rum, constituted the bulk of their exports, depending on imports for food, lumber, livestock, and necessary manufactures. Most of the sugar produced in the English islands was shipped to England, but large quantities of molasses and some rum were exported to the northern colonies, from which were imported fish, grain, flour, vegetables, dairy produce, live-stock, and lumber. This trade, which began in the seventeenth century, became of great importance. It was the basis of the flourishing New England industry of rum distilling, it contributed greatly to the growth of New England ship-building and fisheries, and it enabled the New England and middle colonies to meet their unfavorable trade balances with the mother country. To the West Indies it supplied the necessaries of life. In this trade, the balance was in favor of the northern colonies.

The West India islands were divided between England, Spain, France, Holland, and Denmark. In the seventeenth century, the northern colonies traded principally with the English islands, but the latter did not furnish a sufficient market for the increasing surpluses of the former in the eighteenth century. Other markets became necessary, and these were found chiefly in the French islands. In the early eighteenth century, sugar, molasses, and rum were produced more cheaply in the French than in the English West Indies. French sugar undersold English sugar in the markets of continental Europe, and increasing quantities of French molasses and rum were imported by the northern colonies. Threatened by this competition, the English sugar planters, who had an effective organization in London and much parliamentary influence, clamored for protection, and in 1733 Parliament passed the Molasses Act, which imposed very heavy duties on foreign sugar, molasses, and rum imported into the English colonies.[46] The purpose of the duties was to regulate trade, not to raise revenue. They were intended to be prohibitory, especially the sixpence-a-gallon tax on molasses, and would have been so had the law been enforced. The result would have been economic disaster for New England, and the act was naturally condemned by public opinion there. No real efforts were made to enforce it for twenty-five years, during which it remained virtually a dead letter.

During the Seven Years' War more serious attempts at enforcement were made as a means of checking wartime trade with enemy colonies, and soon after the war Parliament passed the Sugar Act of 1764 as part of a comprehensive plan of imperial reconstruction.[47] By this, the duty on foreign molasses imported into the British colonies was reduced from sixpence to threepence a gallon, the former duty on foreign raw sugar was retained, the importation of foreign rum was prohibited, and duties were laid on certain other foreign products. The act was intended both to regulate trade and to raise revenue, and as a revenue measure it marks a new departure in British colonial policy. It gave offense in the northern colonies, especially New England, to the commercial, shipping, and distilling interests and to the public generally, for it was understood that this law, unlike the earlier Molasses Act, was not to become a dead letter; it was modified in 1766 at the same time that the Stamp Act was repealed. A uniform duty of one penny a gallon was then levied on all molasses, British colonial and foreign colonial alike, imported into the British colonies.[48] This measure of appeasement, together with certain other changes made in the Sugar Act, was satisfactory to the northern colonial interests. With the repeal of the Stamp Act in the same year, the controversy between the colonies and the mother country subsided for the moment, to be renewed soon, however, with well-known consequences, by Charles Townshend's ill-judged attempt to obtain revenue from the colonies and reform the old colonial system.

*

*   *

That system, as we have seen, was basically commercial, but it had to take cognizance of other matters than trade, and notably of colonial defense. According to the accepted mercantile theory of colonization, England derived political strength and economic benefit from the trade of her colonies regulated primarily in her own interest, and in return for these advantages she assumed the obligation of defending the colonies by her navy against rival imperial powers. To have compelled or induced the colonists to contribute to the support of the navy would have been contrary to the principle of reciprocal service on which the colonial system was supposed to rest.[49]

As to military defense by land forces, it may be said that prior to the Seven Years' War the mother country recognized no obligation to protect the colonies from attacks by Indian tribes or to preserve law and order within them. The colonial charters authorized the grantees to provide for the defense of their settlements, and colonial militia systems quickly came into existence. Down to the middle of the eighteenth century, the British and French settlements in North America were separated by wide stretches of wilderness inhabited only by Indians, and the British Government relied upon friendly tribes, especially the Iroquois, for frontier defense in time of international peace. The good will of the savages was stimulated by distributions of presents, mainly at the expense of the British Treasury. In colonies peculiarly in danger of attack at the hands of hostile European powers, such as Nova Scotia, New York, South Carolina, and Jamaica, British garrisons were quartered, but their cost to the mother country was small. 'It was only under exceptional circumstances and under the stress of absolute necessity, that any English forces whatsoever were permanently maintained in America. This remained the practice until 1763.' [50] New York was singular among the colonies on the continent of North America in being garrisoned by British troops throughout the colonial period.

The same colonial particularism that hampered the British Government in its administration of the commercial system in the colonies also stood in the way of the establishment of an adequate system of colonial defense. An obvious remedy, from the point of view of English administrators, was the abolition of existing colonial governments and the union of the colonies in a single super-province, with a single executive head and military expenses defrayed from a common treasury. The Dominion of New England, formed during the reign of James II, was a long step in this direction, but this Stuart creation was swept away by the Glorious Revolution.

The bitter and prolonged imperial rivalry between France and Britain in the eighteenth century made the military defense of the British colonies a subject of prime importance and concern. The conflict with the French and their Indian allies partook of the character of both imperial and local warfare, but no general permanent principles defining the respective military responsibilities of colony and mother country were laid down. Prior to the Seven Years' War, there was, in Beer's words, 'no distinct theory nor any well-defined practice regarding the miltiary activities and duties of the colonies in time of war with a European power.' [51] The colonies were expected to repel invasion to the limit of their ability, and upon occasion colonial troops co-operated with British forces in offensive operations against the French. For example, Port Royal was captured in 1710 by a force of New England regiments and British marines, and Louisbourg was taken in 1745 by a New England force transported in colonial vessels and convoyed by a British squadron. During the period of the French wars, various schemes and combinations of schemes for colonial defense were tried, but intercolonial and sectional jealousies and animosities hampered, when they did not wholly prevent, intercolonial military co-operation, and British efforts to secure fixed quotas of men and money from the several colonies—the 'requisition system'— met with little success.[52] Early in the eighteenth century, parliamentary taxation of the colonies as a means of raising revenue to provide for their defense was considered, but nothing came of proposals that were made.

On the eve of the Seven Years' War, which was to settle the long struggle between Britain and France for predominance in North America, plans were proposed for increasing the military strength of the colonies and placing their defense on a more equitable and efficient basis, but it was impossible to put them into operation. One of these, the celebrated Albany Plan of 1754, of composite authorship but largely the work of Benjamin Franklin, provided for the establishment of a political federation of the continental British colonies, exclusive of the buffer colonies of Nova Scotia and Georgia.[53] The proposed powers of the new federal government included the raising of troops and building of forts and the levying of taxes to obtain the necessary revenue. The old spirit of particularism proved too strong, however, and none of the colonies approved the plan. Referring to the Albany Plan, Franklin wrote years later in his *Autobiography:* 'I am still of the opinion it would have been happy for both sides the water if it had been adopted. The colonies, so united, would have been sufficiently strong to have defended themselves; there would then have been no need of troops from England; of course, the subsequent pretence for taxing America, and the bloody contest it occasioned, would have been avoided.' [54] During the Seven Years' War, recourse was had again to the old requisition system, and again it proved far from satisfactory. In the military campaigns some of the colonies, generally those more immediately menaced, did well, while others displayed a lamentable lack of public spirit. From the military point of view, the requisition system was sadly deficient, and it was inequitable as well in that it penalized the more public-spirited colonies and rewarded the backsliders.

Experience gained during the Seven Years' War strengthened British opinion that reforms in colonial defense were necessary. Solution of the problem by means of a colonial union seemed to be ruled out, and the Grenville Ministry, which took office in 1763, determined to maintain a permanent standing army of some 10,000 men in the British possessions in America and to tax the colonists by parliamentary authority for the partial defrayal of the expenditure involved. Despite the fall of French power in North America, strong reasons could be given for keeping a permanent peace-time military establishment there. Great Britain had come into possession of a vast domain stretching from the Hudson's Bay Company's territories in the north to the Gulf of Mexico in the south, from the Alleghenies on the east to the Mississippi on the west, and she had acquired a number of West

Indian islands from France. Colonial defense was necessarily a major problem of British statesmanship. There were numerous frontier forts and trading posts to be garrisoned; there were restive Indian tribes to be dealt with; there was the menace of unfriendly Spanish power on the Mississippi; and in the background there was always the possibility of a war of revenge on the part of France.

The two measures of the Grenville Ministry for raising revenue in the colonies to meet the expenses of defending them were the Sugar Act of 1764 and the Stamp Act of 1765, which together were expected to produce somewhat less than one-half of the revenue necessary for the maintenance of the British troops stationed in the colonies. In addition, Parliament in 1765 passed a Quartering Act requiring the several colonies to provide barracks for the troops, as well as to furnish them with certain supplies and transportation. From the point of view of the British Empire this legislation was a tragic failure. Its most palpable result was to provoke the colonists to united opposition and a questioning of parliamentary authority over them. For the moment the British Government yielded. The Rockingham Ministry in 1766 repealed the Stamp Act and modified the Sugar Act; the most conspicuous result of the Quartering Act was an unseemly controversy between the British Government and the New York Assembly.

Then came Charles Townshend's disastrous Revenue Act of 1767. Its preamble was unmistakable. The new duties laid on articles imported into the colonies from Britain were intended not for the regulation of trade but for revenue, part of which was to go to 'defraying the expenses of defending, protecting, and securing' the colonies. Townshend merely taught the colonists to call still further in question all parliamentary authority over them. And meanwhile the expenses of the standing army were borne almost entirely by the tax-payers of Great Britain, resounding preambles to the contrary notwithstanding.

The office of Commander-in-Chief of the British forces in North America, which began with the appointment of the ill-fated General Braddock to that position in 1754, was continued after the Seven Years' War and served, indeed, as the principal unifying organ of British colonial administration in the years immediately preceding the outbreak of the Revolutionary War.[55] From time to time use was made of the British troops to assist the civil authorities in maintaining law and order in the colonies, and American patriots came to look upon the military establishment as an engine of British tyranny. The Continental Congress of 1774 complained of the authority of the Commander-in-Chief and of the existence of a standing army in America without the consent of the colonial assemblies, and in the Declaration of Independence George III was charged with having 'affected to render the Military independent of and superior to the Civil Power.'

Inquiring minds are invincibly interested in causation. All occurrences in human history, however, have had multitudinous antecedents, and since the historian is denied the use of experiment in the study of his data, it can never be ascertained which of these antecedents have exerted determining influence. Universal agreement concerning the causes of historical events and movements is therefore not to be expected. It is not surprising, then, that the American Revolution has been variously interpreted. One historical school, of which Edmund Burke was an early and conspicuous exponent, saw in parliamentary taxation of the colonies the chief cause of the discontent that resulted in the Revolution,

and we have noted that the principle of parliamentary taxation of the colonies was adopted by the British Government
in its attempt to solve the problem of colonial defense. On
the other hand, Josiah Tucker, a contemporary and a vigorous critic of Burke, ridiculed the latter's emphasis upon taxation as the basic cause of the quarrel between the colonies
and the mother country, attributing colonial discontent
rather to hostility to the commercial regulations of the old
colonial system.[56] The free-trade economists of the early nineteenth century also stressed the old commercial system as the
main cause of colonial discontent. Among modern scholars,
George Louis Beer was of the opinion that Burke's opinion
was essentially correct.[57] Louis Hacker, on the contrary,
comes much nearer to Tucker's interpretation, attributing
the Revolution primarily to what he regards as the conflict
between two rival capitalisms—British mercantile capitalism
and colonial mercantile and planter capitalism. Speaking of
events during the period immediately preceding the outbreak of the Revolution, he poses these questions: 'If in the
raising of a colonial revenue lay the heart of the difficulty,
how are we to account for the quick repeal of the Stamp Act
and the Townshend Acts and the lowering of the molasses
duty? And, on the other hand, how are we to account for the
tightening of enforcement of the Acts of Trade and Navigation at a dozen and one different points . . . ?'[58] Lawrence
A. Harper, to cite another present-day historian, rejects Professor Hacker's interpretation. He concludes from a consideration of the economic effects of the mercantile restrictions
of the old colonial system that there is no reason for supposing that they were the cause of the Revolution. The First
Continental Congress, Professor Harper remarks, was prepared to guarantee the British commercial system if the prin-

ciple of parliamentary taxation of the colonies were relinquished.[59] 'If there were any inexorable economic forces which were inevitably drawing the Colonies toward revolution,' he says, 'they are hard to detect and the colonists were unaware of them.' The sound conclusion seems to be that British taxation of the colonies and British measures for the more effective regulation of their trade should both be taken into account, together with various other factors, in any attempt to explain the colonial discontent that culminated in American independence. The American Revolution was many-sided, and, as in revolutions generally, separate grievances made common causes.

II

THE RISE OF ANTI-IMPERIALISM

So long as mercantile doctrines prevailed, colonies continued to be prized because of the advantages which Britain was supposed to derive from their trade. The time came, however, when doubts were cast upon the efficacy of the legal regulations and restrictions on which mercantilism relied for the attainments of its objects, when the right of the mother country to rule colonial dependencies was questioned and denied, and when, above all, the fundamental assumptions and conclusions of the mercantile system were challenged. It was then that British anti-imperialism had its origin. From the beginning of English colonization onward objections to particular aspects or predicted results of oversea expansion had occasionally been expressed, but they did not constitute anything that could correctly be called an anti-imperialist ideology.

In his classic attack on the mercantile system Adam Smith denounced the old colonial system root and branch and went so far as to assert that it would be beneficial to the people of Great Britain if the colonies were given up. He definitely associated anti-imperialism with *laissez-faire* economics, and the Manchester School looked back to him as the original Little-Englander.[1] But even before the publication of *The Wealth of Nations*, some of the French physiocrats had condemned the old French colonial system, which was essentially similar to the British; [2] and a British contemporary of Smith's, Josiah Tucker, wrote a number of pamphlets during the period of the American Revolution, the central idea of which, as stated by himself, was that 'the colonies in quarreling with the Mother Country are essentially hurting themselves; and are greatly, though not intentionally benefiting us, by obliging us to see and pursue our own true and lasting interests.' [3]

As a controversial pamphleteer, Tucker enjoyed a great vogue in his own day, and several of his pamphlets on economic and political subjects went through a number of editions. It is known that Adam Smith had a copy of Tucker's *Essay on Trade* in his library,[4] and his pamphlets were not unknown to later political economists. J. R. McCulloch in his *Literature of Political Economy,* published in 1845, gave the titles of some of them and remarked that Tucker displayed 'great sagacity,'[5] and Alfred Marshall has appraised his mind as one of 'finest quality.'[6] Tucker undoubtedly had some influence on the French physiocrats. Turgot had a high regard for his economic ideas and translated two of his pamphlets into French. He wrote in a private letter in 1770 that his own economic ideas were very similar to Tucker's and expressed astonishment that in a country where the press was free, Tucker was almost the only writer to express sound views on commerce.[7] It was unfortunate for the survivial of Tucker's reputation that most of his writings were occasional in character, inspired by current events and, though full of original and constructive ideas, bound to lose savor with the passing of the controversies that gave them birth—facts which should be taken into account in explaining why he exerted little influence on the subsequent course of English economic thought.[8] He planned an *opus magnum* on economics, but he never completed it, though an outline of it was appended to his *Elements of Commerce and Theory of Taxes,* which was privately printed in 1755.[9] He wrote extensively on the American colonies and their disadvantages to the mother country, but he never set forth his anti-imperial ideas in a comprehensive treatise.

Tucker's anti-imperialism is to be explained in large part by his economic ideas.[10] A clergyman of the Church of England, he resided at Bristol, as curate and rector, from 1737 to 1758, when he became Dean of the Cathedral at Gloucester. While at Bristol, which was then, next to London, the largest city and the most important center of commerce in Great Britain, he became deeply interested in economic questions and wrote a number of economic pamphlets. The most widely read was his *Brief Essay on the Advantages and Disadvantages which respectively attend France and Great Britain with regard to Trade* (1749), which went through several editions and won for him a reputation as a well-informed and thoughtful student of commerce. Tucker was one of the first to conceive of the whole range of economic life as a proper subject of inquiry, and he believed that it ought to be cultivated as such, especially by statesmen and legislators. This opinion he expressed as early as 1749, before anybody had produced a systematic treatise on economics.

Like the later classical economists, Tucker regarded self-interest as the psychological basis of economics; he recognized the existence of the sentiment of benevolence, but he believed it to be much weaker than the self-regarding instinct. Unlike the classical economists, however, he did not believe that private and public interests necessarily harmonize. They might, in his opinion, and often did, conflict, and he always maintained that it was the business of government to regulate the operation of self-interest so that it would conduce to the general welfare. He was not, therefore, an advocate of *laissez-faire*. On the contrary, he held that government ought to play an active part in moulding the economic life of the nation. But though he agreed with mercantilists in regard to the propriety of governmental action to promote national prosperity, he dissented vigorously from traditional mercantilist views on what constituted national prosperity. In a striking passage in his *Elements* he emphatically rejected what Adam Smith was later to refute as the basic economic doctrine of the mercantile system, namely, that wealth consists in the precious metals.[11] 'Suppose a country, separated from all the world, and yet abounding in . . . gold and silver,' he wrote, 'and the inhabitants of it [may be] much poorer than the poorest beggar in our strects . . . Suppose that the inhabitants are . . . industrious: . . . let us suppose that all the gold and silver was annihilated in one night, and what would be the consequences but plainly this, that the inhabitants would then devise some ticket or counter for the exchange of mutual industry.' It is evident from many passages in Tucker's writings that he, like Smith, regarded labor as the foundation of wealth. 'Industry and labor,' he said, 'are the only riches, money being merely the ticket or sign belonging to them.' His doctrine of self-interest helps to explain the opinion expressed in his colonial pamphlets that it was impossible to regulate effectively the trade of the colonies, and his dissent from the precious-metals theory of prosperity, a theory which was closely related to the colonial system, made it easy for him to question the economic value of colonies to the mother country.

In his earlier economic writings, however, Tucker did not take an anti-imperial position; he was not then opposed to the possession of colonies. He did, indeed, predict, as early as 1749, that the British colonies in America would revolt if the time should ever come when they felt themselves to be economically self-sufficient, but he did not as yet reject the mercantilist dogma that colonies were beneficial to their mother country as markets and as sources of supply. Before long, however, he became skeptical of the value of distant colonial possessions. It appears to have been the controversy over the Stamp Act that turned his thoughts seriously to the question of the political separation of the colonies from Great Britain.

In his opinions on nationalism, war, and international relations, Tucker was wholly at variance with mercantilism, and his views on these subjects undoubtedly had a good deal to do with his attitude toward the disputes that culminated in the revolt of the colonies. His economic studies led him to a consideration of the prevention of wars as a means of increasing population and convinced him that war was necessarily injurious economically to the victor as well as to the vanquished. During the Seven Years' War he was entirely out of sympathy with the patriotic fervor with which Pitt and victory inspired the English people. 'War, conquests and colonies are our present system,' he said in a private letter written during the war, 'and mine is just the opposite . . . I look upon the nation at present to be frantic with military glory and therefore no more to be argued with than a person in a raving fit of a high fever.' In 1763, shortly after the close of the war, he published, as a fragment of his contemplated comprehensive treatise, an anonymous tract, *The Case of Going to War for the Sake of Procuring, Enlarging, or Securing of Trade, Considered in a New Light,* in which he undertook to show that no country could gain from the destruction or impoverishment of its neighbors, that neither rulers nor peoples could be benefited by the most successful war, that trade would inevitably make its way to the country where goods were manufactured best and most cheaply, and that conquering nations could not manufacture cheaply. The pamphlet contains a striking analysis of the forces and classes in the community making for war. It attracted little attention at the time in England, which Tucker attributed to the bellicose disposition of 'the mob and the news-writers,' but it won some approval abroad, and Jeremy Bentham appears to have been acquainted with it, for in his *Principles of International Law* he referred to Tucker as an 'original writer,' whose object was 'to persuade the world of the inutility of war, but more particularly of the war then raging when he wrote.' In a later tract, *Cui Bono?*, published in 1781, when England and France were again at war, Tucker wrote: 'It is as much the real interest of Great Britain that France should be a rich country, and not a poor one, as I have already proved that the great riches of England are beneficial to France.' He did not underrate the tenacity with which men cling to cherished ideas, and he entertained no vain expectation that the fallacious arguments in favor of war would soon be discarded, but he hoped that the time would come when men would look upon going to war for the sake of trade and dominion in the same light in which they then regarded the madness of their ancestors 'in fighting under the banner of the peaceful Cross, to recover the Holy Land.' A contempt for 'the mob,' which is often expressed in his writings, was based, in part at least, upon its belligerent propensities and intemperate zeal for wars and colonial conquests.

Long before the revolt of the American colonies Tucker asserted that self-interest alone bound them to Britain. In the earliest of his American tracts he said that the British conquest of Canada, in freeing the colonies from the danger of French conquest, broke the tie of self-interest by releasing them from dependence upon the mother country for defense. This was the opinion of Turgot and other contemporaries, and it has generally been regarded by historians as sound. It was in the nature of colonies, according to Tucker, 'to aspire after independence, and to set up for themselves as soon as ever they find that they are able to subsist without being beholden to the Mother Country.' That the British colonies were the first to become independent he attributed to that 'bold free Constitution, which is the prerogative and boast of us all.' He ridiculed the idea that parliamentary taxation of the colonies was the original cause of their quarrel with the mother country, and referred to British statutes to show that from the seventeenth century there had been 'mutual discontents, mutual animosities and reproaches.' In a tract published in 1766 he ascribed colonial opposition to the Stamp Act not to that measure itself but rather to the colonists' hostility to the commercial regulations of the colonial system, which the British Government was trying to enforce. In this he anticipated the view taken by English free-trade political economists of the nineteenth century, who regarded commercial restrictions as the basic cause of the Revolution and believed that taxation merely hastened a crisis that was inevitable. In another pamphlet, written several years later, he predicted the eventual independence of Canada. 'Canada,' he said, addressing the Americans, 'when it has grown rich by our means, and our capitals, will assuredly set up for Independence, as you have done. And in a few years, we shall have the same scenes of malevolence and ingratitude displayed there, which you are pleased to exhibit in your provinces.'

As this quotation indicates, Tucker's anti-imperialism was

not due to any sympathy on his part for the cause of the colonists. His colonial pamphlets are full of contempt for those 'most ungrateful, ungovernable, and rebellious people,' and one of his most unfortunate predictions was that if they should gain their independence, they would remain a quarrelsome and disunited people to the end of time. Unlike his radical contemporaries in England, he accepted the doctrine that the American colonists were virtually represented in Parliament, and he never doubted its constitutional right to tax them. At the time of the dispute over the Stamp Act he argued in the strongest terms for the unlimited sovereignty of Parliament throughout the British Empire. His anti-imperialism was based wholly on British interests, not at all on American rights.

In contending that colonial trade could not be controlled effectively in the interest of the mother country, Tucker struck at the whole elaborate scheme of commercial regulation that went to make up the old British colonial system. His conclusions on this point followed from his doctrine of self-interest and were supported by his study of the history of colonial trade. In his *Treatise concerning Civil Government,* published in 1781, he declared that it was 'impossible to compel distant settlements to trade with the parent state to any great degree beyond what their own interest would prompt them to,' and in *Four Letters on Important National Subjects,* addressed to Lord Shelburne and published in 1783, he said that trade depended on interest alone.

Nor was it in our power, even when we were strongest, and they in the weakest stage of their existence . . . to compel them to trade with us to their own loss. Mutual interest was the only tie between America and Great Britain at all times and seasons . . . As to the planting of colonies for the sake of a monopolizing, or exclusive trade, it is the arrantest cheat, and self-deception, which poor, short-sighted mortals ever put upon themselves.

The doctrine of self-interest explains, moreover, Tucker's confident and happy prediction that the loss of the colonies would not result in a decline of British trade with them. The Americans, he said, could get better prices for most of their products in the British market than in any other, and could buy most of what they needed more cheaply there than elsewhere. 'The colonies, we know by experience,' he wrote in 1774, 'will trade with any people, even with their bitterest enemies . . . provided they shall find it their interest to do so.'

Like later anti-imperialists, Tucker called attention to the heavy burdens that the possession of colonies imposed upon the mother country. America, he said in 1783, 'ever was a millstone hanging about the neck of this country, to weigh it down; and as we ourselves had not the wisdom to cut the rope, and to let the burthen fall off, the Americans have kindly done it for us.' In the *Treatise concerning Civil Government* he voiced the hope that Jamaica and the Leeward Islands would become independent and declared that colonies were always an encumbrance to their mother countries, 'requiring perpetual and expensive nursing in their infancy, and becoming headstrong and ungovernable in proportion as they grow up, and never failing to revolt as soon as they shall find that they do not want our assistance.' Nor, in his opinion, were the bad results of imperialism solely economic. To it he attributed in large part the political evils of the day in England, especially the increasing influence of the Crown. Alluding to Burke's scheme for economical reform, he said that the abandonment of the colonies would be worth a thousand of the petty economies that reforming politicians were proposing.

On the eve of the American Revolution many Americans and some of their friends in England took the ground that Parliament had no lawful authority over the colonies. They claimed for the latter a status of constitutional equality with Great Britain and proposed that the Empire should be re-organized on this basis. Tucker discussed this 'Scheme of Independency respecting the Parliament, but not respecting the King' and pronounced it to be inadmissible from every point of view.

Tucker's proposal for solving the colonial problem was stated clearly and boldly in his pamphlet, *The True Interest of Great Britain set forth in regard to the Colonies,* published in 1774, at a time when scarcely anyone else, even in the colonies, had gone so far as to suggest secession from the Empire. It was 'to separate entirely from the North American colonies, by declaring them to be a free and independent people, over whom we lay no claim,' and then to offer 'to guarantee this freedom and independence against all foreign invaders whatever.' This proposal received respectful consideration in some of the English newspapers and reviews. In another of his American pamphlets, published in the following year, Tucker urged that all colonies in revolt at a certain date be cut off from the mother country by act of Parliament. When the War of Independence broke out, he was strongly opposed to the recovery of the rebellious colonies by military conquest, and he remained of this mind throughout the conflict. Toward the end of the hostilities he wrote in *Cui Bono?*: 'Were America this moment to lay herself at our feet, and to submit to a *Carte blanche,* provided we would take her again into favour,—it is evidently our interest not to ac-

cept of such a present.' Upon learning of Cornwallis's sur-
render at Yorktown, he said: 'To congratulate my country
on being defeated is contrary to that decency which is due to
the public. And yet, if this defeat should terminate in a total
Separation from America, it would be one of the happiest
events that hath ever happened to Great Britain.' After the
fall of Lord North's Ministry in 1782, when it was clear
that American independence was assured, Tucker thus
summed up his views on the American question in a letter
to his friend Lord Kames:

I look upon it to have been a very *imprudent* act to have
settled any distant colonies at all, whilst there remained an inch
of land in Great Britain capable of further cultivation; afterwards, to have been very *foolish and absurd* to have engaged in
their disputes either with the French or Spaniards, and to have
espoused their quarrels; and lastly, to have been the *height of
madness* to have endeavored to conquer them after they had
broken out in open rebellion. They were always, from first to
last, a heavy weight upon us, a weight which we ourselves ought
to have thrown off if they had not done it for us.

Tucker was not under the illusion that it would be easy to
persuade the English people or their government that separation from the colonies was desirable. 'Prejudices and pre-
possessions are stubborn things in all cases, but in none more
peculiarly obstinate than in relinquishing detached parts of
an unwieldy, extended Empire; there not being, I believe, a
single instance in all history of any nation surrendering a
distant province voluntarily and of free choice, notwithstanding it was greatly their interest to have done it.' This sentence occurs in Tucker's pamphlet *An Humble Address and
Earnest Appeal*, published in 1775. It is interesting to com-
pare with it the observation made by Adam Smith in his

Wealth of Nations, published in the following year: 'No
nation ever voluntarily gave up the dominion of any province, how troublesome soever it might be to govern it, and
how small soever the revenue which it afforded might be in
proportion to the expense which it occasioned.' [12]

The independence of the United States naturally confirmed Tucker in his opinion that oversea dependencies
could not be held permanently against their wishes. Shortly
after the defeat of Fox's India Bill in the House of Lords
and the consequent dismissal of the Fox-North Coalition
Ministry (December 1783), at a time when the East India
Company and its affairs were in the forefront of political
discussion, Tucker contributed an article to the *Bristol Journal,* in which he predicted the overthrow of British rule in
Bengal. If Britain had been unable to maintain her authority
over a couple of million people at a distance of only 3,000
miles, he was unable to understand how men could be so
'infatuated with party rage' or 'blinded with the hopes of
filthy lucre' as not to realize that a handful of proprietors
and directors of a trading company could not continue their
'detested usurpations over the lives, liberties and properties
of thirty millions at the distance of 10,000 miles.' He believed that the people of India, unlike the American colonists, had right on their side, and he felt confident that they
would recover their 'original and native independence.'

*
*   *

But Tucker, though a keen observer and an acute reasoner,
and ahead of his generation in many of his opinions, was
not the founder of a 'school,' and exercised no such influence

as did his illustrious contemporary, Adam Smith. Since *The Wealth of Nations,* in common with other classics, has paid the penalty of its fame in being talked about more often than it is read, it may not be superfluous to summarize the attack which its author made on the old colonial system.

In considering the benefits derived by the European countries from colonization, Adam Smith examined first those gained by Europe in general. These consisted, he held, in 'the increase of its enjoyments' and 'the augmentation of its industry.' The surplus produce of America furnished the people of Europe with many new commodities, thus increasing their enjoyments, and it stimulated their industry by enlarging the markets for their surplus products. Even countries that neither sent anything to America nor received anything from it had been benefited by the increased wealth of their neighbors. But he was careful to distinguish between the effects of colonial trade and the effects of those restrictions upon colonial trade which were the basis of the colonial systems of all colonizing states. The restrictions gave the mother country a virtual monopoly of the trade of its colonies, which tended to diminish both the enjoyments and the industry of the European nations in general, and of the American colonies in particular.

By rendering the colony produce dearer in all other countries, it lessens its consumption, and thereby cramps the industry of the colonies, and both the enjoyments and the industry of all other countries, which both enjoy less when they pay more for what they enjoy, and produce less when they get less for what they produce. By rendering the produce of all other countries dearer in the colonies, it cramps in the same manner the industry of all other countries, and both the enjoyments and the industry of the colonies.

His general conclusion in regard to the injurious effects on Europe at large of the colonial monopolies maintained by the mother countries was this: 'The surplus produce of the colonies . . . is the original source of all that increase of enjoyments and industry which Europe derives from the discovery and colonization of America, and the exclusive trade of the mother countries tends to render this source much less abundant than it would otherwise be.'

Adam Smith then turned to the particular advantages supposed to be derived by the various European countries from their respective colonies. The colonies had never furnished military forces for the defense of their mother countries, but, on the contrary, had been dependent upon them, to some extent at least, for their own defense in time of war. The Spanish and Portuguese colonies alone had contributed revenue toward the defense of their mother countries; the taxes levied upon others had never been sufficient to defray the expenses which they occasioned in time of war. From the military point of view the colonies were, therefore, a source of weakness rather than of strength. It followed that the benefit of colonies to a mother country consisted 'altogether in those peculiar advantages which are supposed to result from provinces of so very peculiar a nature as the European colonies of America; and the exclusive trade, it is acknowledged, is the sole source of all those peculiar advantages.' A good part of the rest of the long chapter in *The Wealth of Nations* on colonies is devoted to showing that the 'peculiar advantages' were illusory, special attention being paid to the British colonies.

The colonial trade, if unrestricted, would, according to Adam Smith, have opened a great though distant market for such parts of the produce of British industry as exceeded the demand of markets nearer home. It would have encouraged Great Britain to augment her surplus production and would have increased the quantity of her productive labor. Before the colonial monopoly had been established she had been a great trading nation, thanks to her commerce with the countries of Europe; and if the trade of her colonies had been left open to all nations, her own share of it would have been in addition to the trade which she had previously enjoyed. But as it was, the growth of her colonial trade had been at the expense of her foreign trade. 'The causes of decay in other branches of foreign trade . . . may all be found in the over-growth of the colony trade.' This overgrowth involved economic loss to Great Britain, since

whatever forces into a branch of trade of which the returns are slower and more distant than those of the greater part of other trades, a greater proportion of the capital of any country than what of its own accord would go to that branch, necessarily renders the whole quantity of productive labor annually maintained there, the whole annual produce of the land and labor of that country, less than they otherwise would be.

The colonial monopoly, moreover, by drawing British capital from other branches of trade had raised the rate of British profit and increased the competition of foreign capital in those branches, thereby subjecting Great Britain to a relative disadvantage in them. Furthermore, the colonial monopoly had rendered British industry more precarious than it would otherwise have been.

The industry of Great Britain, instead of being accommodated to a great number of small markets, has been principally suited to one great market . . . The expectation of a rupture with the Colonies, accordingly, has struck the people of Great Britain with more terror than they ever felt for a Spanish armada, or a

French invasion . . . In the total exclusion from the colony market, was it to last only for a few years, the greater part of our
merchants used to fancy that they foresaw an entire stop to their
trade; the greater part of our master manufacturers, the entire
ruin of their business; and the greater part of our workmen, an
end of their employment.

A moderate and gradual relaxation of the colonial monopoly was necessary, Adam Smith believed, in order to bring
about a withdrawal of capital from the overgrown colonial
trade.

His indictment of the old colonial system was most sweeping and severe. When he wrote, it was still the prevailing
opinion that the benefits reaped by Great Britain from the
regulation of her colonial trade were a fair compensation for
the burdens which the possession of the colonies entailed
upon her. The burdens were undeniable; Adam Smith
sought to show that the benefits were purely imaginary. The
colonial system was in essence a monopoly which, 'like all the
other mean and malignant expedients of the mercantile system, depresses the industry of all other countries, but chiefly
that of the colonies, without in the least increasing, but on
the contrary diminishing, that of the country in whose favor
it is established.' All the expense to which Great Britain had
been put by reason of her possession of colonies had been
incurred to support a monopoly from which she derived
nothing but loss. Merchants engaged in the colonial trade
had gained, but their gains had been at the expense of the
bulk of the British people.

Adam Smith believed that it would be to the economic
advantage of the British nation as a whole if the colonies
were given up. If this were done, Great Britain would not
only be saved heavy expense, but would be able to enter

into a commercial treaty with the former colonies which would secure to her a freedom of trade much more advantageous to her people than the previous monopoly. He foresaw the future greatness of America and envisaged such an alliance of the English-speaking peoples as many latter-day Anglo-Americans have dreamed of. But he was convinced that it was futile to argue in favor of giving up the colonies since 'no nation ever voluntarily gave up the dominion of any province, how troublesome soever it might be to govern it, and how small soever the revenue which it afforded might be in proportion to the expense which it occasioned.' This being the case, he proposed a plan of imperial reform, including colonial representation in the British Parliament, as a substitute for colonial independence.

In the concluding chapter of *The Wealth of Nations* Adam Smith returned to the subject of the colonies. The British Empire in America, he declared, had existed so far in imagination only. It was not an empire, but the project of an empire, 'a project which has cost, which continues to cost, and which, if pursued in the same way as it has been hitherto, is likely to cost, immense expense, without being likely to bring any profit; for the effects of the monopoly of the colony trade, it has been shown, are, to the body of the people, mere loss instead of profit.' His anti-imperial views were strengthened by the progress and outcome of the American Revolution, and he came to believe that the fallacy of imperialism was the subject on which it was most important to enlighten the public opinion of Europe. The fact that Adam Smith thought that the abandonment of colonies held under the old colonial system would be economically advantageous to Great Britain does not justify us, of course, in saying that he would have objected to such a relationship as has come to exist between Great Britain and the present self-governing British Dominions.

*

*　*

While Tucker and Adam Smith were arguing that the possession of colonies was detrimental to the interests of the mother country, others were denying her right to exercise political authority over them. The British radical movement of the eighteenth century is remembered chiefly in connection with parliamentary reform. Some of those most actively associated with it, however, took a deep interest in the cause of the American colonies and expressed views regarding the nature and proper organization of the British Empire that are worthy of examination in themselves and may assume a heightened significance by reason of modern constitutional developments in the Empire. It may be remarked in passing that the controversy between the colonies and the British Government over taxation was not without influence upon the agitation in England for parliamentary reform, since it hinged on the question of representation and inevitably threw into bold relief the unrepresentative character of the House of Commons.[18] The doctrine of virtual representation, used to justify parliamentary taxation of the colonies, turned out to be a two-edged sword, for it was impossible to show that the Americans had as much voice in the election of members of Parliament as the great majority of Englishmen at home, without admitting that the latter had none at all. If Sheffield and Manchester were not represented in Parliament, James Otis's answer was that 'they ought to be.' When the author of *The Regulations lately made concerning the Colonies, and the Taxes imposed upon Them, Considered* (London, 1765) insisted that the colonists were in the same condition as the majority of the inhabitants of Great Britain, that while neither could vote for members of Parliament both were nevertheless represented in it, Richard Bland of Virginia replied, in his *Enquiry into the Rights of the British Colonies* (1766), that neither were represented. Though Bland's purpose was to defend the rights of the colonists, not to champion the cause of the unenfranchised in Britain, he took occasion to remark that the reform of the British franchise would be 'a work worthy of the best patriotic spirits in the nation.' His tract and many of the other writings of the American Whig pamphleteers were reprinted in England, and it may well be that they had more effect on the movement for parliamentary reform than has commonly been supposed.

Of the early British radicals none rendered more valiant and sustained service to the cause of reform than Major John Cartwright.[14] His pamphlet *Take Your Choice,* a plea for universal male suffrage and annual parliaments, published in 1776, won for him the title 'The Father of Reform.' Two years before this, however, he entered the lists as a champion of American rights with a series of letters addressed to Parliament and printed in a newspaper in 1774. These appeared in pamphlet form later in the same year as *American Independence the Interest and Glory of Great Britain.* The publication was anonymous, because the writer foresaw that it would offend the Government and probably bar him from promotion in his profession. He caused a summary of his arguments, together with the tract itself, to be distributed to members of Parliament, and a second edition, containing some supplementary matter, was published in 1775, but British public opinion, aroused by the Boston tea episode, was then so strongly hostile to the colonies that his views seem to have made no great impression.

In his political philosophy Cartwright was a whole-hearted and uncompromising disciple of John Locke. The assumptions of the natural-rights school concerning the rights of man and the origin, nature, and purposes of government were for him not propositions to be proved, but axioms of politics to be accepted as self-evident. Since the Americans, in common with all mankind, had an inherent and absolute right to freedom, and since no people could be free who were not governed by their own consent, it followed that a Parliament in which the colonists were not represented could have no valid claim to authority over them. It was quite beside the mark to argue for such authority by appealing to charters or statutes or the original intention of the English Government in planting colonies or the former exercise of parliamentary authority over them, for inalienable human rights could not be affected thereby. It was not proper to quote British statutes to prove the sovereignty of Parliament over America, since it was these very statutes that were called in question, and therefore their testimony must be rejected. And as for charters, even if they had stipulated that the colonists should acknowledge the sovereignty of Parliament, still Parliament would have no right to such sovereignty, 'for freedom, notwithstanding all that sophistry may say to the contrary, cannot be alienated by any human creature; much less can he enslave his posterity.' Cartwright referred to the proposal that had been made several times for the admission of American representatives to the British Parliament only to dismiss it as thoroughly impracticable. The Americans would never consent to 'trust their property, their freedom, their dearest rights, their everything, in the hands of exiles, sent half-way to the Antipodes . . . and exposed to every temptation to betray them.'

Cartwright's ideas respecting the nature of the British Empire were substantially the same as those expressed by contemporary American radicals. For him as for them, the Empire was not a single state, consisting of a mother country and her dependencies, but a group of states, equal in constitutional status, with co-ordinate legislatures and a common king. According to this view the relations between the colonies and Great Britain were similar to those between Hanover and Great Britain, or to those between England and Scotland before the union of 1707. 'I would consider the American governments, like that of Ireland, as sister kingdoms,' wrote Cartwright, 'and I would cement a lasting union with them as between the separate branches of one great family.' To the argument that military necessity—the defense of the whole Empire—required that Parliament should have sovereign authority over all parts of it, he replied that

if an empire be too large, and its parts too widely separated by immense oceans, or other impediments, to admit of being governed on the principles essentially belonging to all free governments, it is an over-grown empire, and ought to be divided before it fall to pieces. The welfare and happiness of mankind supersede every other possible claim or pretension to govern.

Cartwright did not admit, however, that such an association of states as he envisaged would be deficient in defensive strength; and if uncertainty about securing the support of the American states for warlike projects should make British ministers cautious about embarking in continental wars, it would be a good thing. 'No ingenuous man will, however, entertain a serious doubt of the readiness of the Americans to contribute their share to every necessary expense of government, so long as they shall find themselves in possession of their freedom.'

What Cartwright proposed for the solution of the imperial problem was an act of Parliament declaring 'that it is inconsistent with the welfare of the people of the said colonies or states, and prejudicial to their natural inherent rights as men, to be governed by the parliament of Great Britain, or any other power foreign to themselves respectively,' and enacting that the colonies between the Gulf of St. Lawrence and the mouth of the Mississippi

are all held and declared to be free and independent states, each to be subject to such law and government only as now subsists, or shall hereafter be enacted and constituted within itself by its own proper legislature; and that of each and every of the said independent states, his Majesty is, and shall be held to be, the sovereign head, in like manner as he is of the legislature of Great Britain.

The act, he thought, ought to declare Parliament to be the protector of all the states, collectively and individually, against every foreign power, and the guarantor of the independence of each with respect to the others; and it should provide for a treaty to be made with them 'in order that a firm, brotherly, and perpetual league may be concluded between Great Britain and them for their mutual commercial benefit, and their joint security against all other kingdoms and states, as well as for the preservation of that warm affection and harmony which ought ever to subsist between a mother-country and her offspring.' By such a reorganization of the Empire, the king, Cartwright remarked, would be the gainer, since he would thereby 'receive fifteen independent kingdoms in exchange for as many dependent, and *hardly dependent* provinces, and become the father of three million of free and happy subjects, instead of reigning joint tyrant over so many discontented slaves, or losing by revolt so many of his people.' In a postscript to his tract, printed in the edition of 1775, he gave the text of his proposed emancipating act, and suggested as a suitable name for the association of free states that was his ideal, 'The Grand British League and Confederacy.'

Another pamphlet that appeared in 1774 was *A Declaration of the People's Natural Right to a Share in the Legislature*. The author was the philanthropist Granville Sharp, who is remembered principally for the very important part he played in the British anti-slavery movement.[15] His devotion to the cause of liberty made him a warm champion of the rights of Ireland and America, and it is with this subject that his tract is concerned. Sharp's conception of the Empire followed logically from the postulate expressed in his title. Since it was a natural right of man to participate in legislation, it was iniquitous and unlawful to legislate for the colonies without their consent. They were subject to no other legislature than their own, and the Empire was an association of equals.

And yet [he wrote], howsoever distinct these several parts or provinces may seem, in point of situation, as well as in the exercise of a separate legislative power for each, (which constitutional Right they have enjoyed beyond the memory of man,) they are nevertheless firmly united by the circle of the British Diadem, so as to form *one vast Empire*, which will never be divided, if the safe and honest policy may be adopted, of maintaining the *British Constitution*, inviolate, in all parts of the Empire.

The proposal that the colonies should be totally separated from Great Britain, which had just been made by Dean

Tucker, Sharp strongly condemned. Association of the colonies and Great Britain in a free commonwealth, not the disruption of the Empire, was his solution of the Britannic question.

> But how [he asked] will the trunk or stock of the vast British Vine appear, if we should entirely separate or lop off the branches? The American branches are already *detached,* indeed, (in point of distance,) and widely separated from the Trunk, by a vast Ocean; but the imperial Crown of Great-Britain is, nevertheless, a sufficient band of union or connexion between them. . . .

More widely read than either Cartwright's pamphlet or Sharp's was Dr. Richard Price's *Observations on the Nature of Civil Liberty, the Principles of Government, and the Justice and Policy of the War with America.*[16] This work was published in 1776 and more than 60,000 copies were sold during that year. Price was one of the foremost disciples of Locke and a leader in the radical movement. At the time his pamphlet was published he was already well known for his writings on ethics and finance and was on terms of intimacy with Lord Shelburne, Colonel Barré, and other members of Parliament. Believing that the public debt of Great Britain, then about £140,000,000, was an evil threatening the most serious consequences and that the attempt to coerce the colonies would, if persisted in, prove financially disastrous, and also thoroughly convinced of the justice of the American cause, Price sought to arouse British opinion in favor of a policy of pacification.

From the nature and principles of civil liberty as defined by himself, Price drew the 'immediate and necessary inference that no one community can have any power over the property or legislation of another community that is not

incorporated with it by a just and adequate representation.'
A country subject to the legislature of another, in which it
was not represented, was in 'a state of slavery.' The language
of the Declaratory Act of 1766 was the language of a master
to slaves. Englishmen were so accustomed to speaking of the
colonies as 'our colonies' that the meanest of them looked
upon himself as having a body of subjects in America, but
in reality 'the people of America are no more the subjects
of the people of Britain, than the people of Yorkshire are
the subjects of the people of Middlesex.' The only type of
empire consistent with Price's principles was that in which
all the component communities were free and mutually independent. His ideal was a voluntary, co-operative alliance
of self-governing states, co-ordinate with each other but
united through the crown. He believed that 'a common relation to one supreme executive head, an exchange of kind
offices, tyes of interest and affection, and compacts' would
afford a sufficient basis of imperial unity.

The similarity between the imperial ideas of Cartwright
and Sharp and Price and the actual relations which now exist
between Britain and the self-governing Dominions of the
British Commonwealth is obvious. This being the case, it
might seem incorrect to include their ideas in a discussion of
anti-imperialism. They did not advocate the total separation
of the colonies from the mother country. If, however, the
colonies had been recognized as being independent of Parliament, as they desired, the empire of the old colonial system
would have ceased to exist. Equality of status as between the
colonies and Britain was wholly inconsistent with eighteenth-
century mercantilist conceptions of empire.

Of the English radicals whose speculations on political and
social questions were influenced by the French Revolution,

the 'Jacobinical Radicals,' as they have been called, William Godwin was the arch-philosopher. In his *Enquiry concerning Political Justice,* published in 1793, he was not concerned to any great extent with the subject of imperialism, but colonies, however acquired and for whatever purpose retained, were wholly incompatible with his political ideals. 'Are these provinces held in a state of dependence for our own sake or for theirs?' he asked.

If for our own, we must recollect this is still an usurpation, and that justice requires we should yield to others what we demand for ourselves, the privilege of being governed by the dictates of their own reason. If for theirs, they must be told, that it is the business of associations of men to defend themselves, or, if that be impracticable, to look for support to the confederation of their neighbors . . . The principle which will not fail to lead us right upon this subject of foreign dependencies, as well as upon a thousand others is, that that attribute however splendid, is not really beneficial to a nation, that is not beneficial to the great mass of individuals of which the nation consists.

*

* *

The course of the War for Independence naturally stimulated speculation concerning the future of the British Empire. One product of this interest was a pamphlet published in 1782 entitled *The Interest of Great Britain with regard to her American Colonies Considered.* Its author was James Anderson, a man of some importance in his own day and a writer who is known to have influenced Jeremy Bentham in his ideas about colonies. Like Adam Smith, Anderson objected to the mercantilism of the old colonial system, and he looked upon Great Britain's colonies in the new world as a cause of war and a source of military weakness to her. It should be the aim of British policy, he urged, 'to preserve the vigour of the parent state independent of the colonies' and 'not for a moment to forget that sooner or later they must be separated from her, and that she must so act as to be prepared for the event.' All the European colonial powers ought to agree to abolish all their monopolistic commercial privileges in America and declare their colonial possessions neutral in time of war. The military events of the war then in progress explain Anderson's proposal that Great Britain should recognize the independence of the 'States of America' but should retain Georgia, the City of New York, and Long and Staten Islands.[17]

In 1783 Sir John Sinclair, a member of Parliament and later actively influential in establishing the Board of Agriculture, published a short tract, *La Crise de l'Europe,* in which he ventured to propose for serious consideration by the nations of Europe the question of a general emancipation of colonies.[18] In his *History of the Public Revenue of the British Empire,* a work which was for many years a standard treatise —the first volume appeared in 1785—he returned to this subject and urged that if his proposal were adopted Great Britain would be freed from a heavy burden of expenditure and would at the same time gain access to the markets of South America and the foreign West Indies. With a naïveté genuine or assumed, he remarked that France and Spain, having contributed so liberally to the British colonies in their revolt, could not consistently object to the independence of their own colonies! 'The same natural rights and privileges, which they supported in one part of America, every other district, and every other inhabitant of that continent, and of the islands in its neighbourhood, are equally entitled to.' In a later edition of his *History* he estimated the expenditure of Great Britain on account of the North American colonies, from 1714 to 1788, at £40,000,000, in addition to the cost of wars in which she had been involved mainly because of her colonies, which he reckoned at £240,000,000. Inquiries into expenditure for the colonies he deemed all the more necessary, since 'the rage for colonization' had not yet wholly subsided. 'We have lost New England; but a New Wales has since started up. How many millions it may cost, may be the subject of the calculations of succeeding financiers, a century hence, unless by the exertions of some able statesman, that source of future waste and extravagance is prevented.'[19]

According to mercantilist theory, the loss of the American colonies should have resulted in a marked decline of British exports and shipping, if not in the ruin of British industry. But as a matter of fact the United States, after their independence, consumed more British products than they had done when they were subject to the restrictions of the colonial system. For the years 1771-3, inclusive, the average annual exportation from Great Britain to the thirteen colonies amounted to £3,064,843; for 1790-92 it was £3,976,211, and for 1798-1800, £6,507,476.[20] During the six years ending with 1774 the average annual consumption of British products in the thirteen colonies was £2,216,824, and for a like period ending with 1792 it was £2,807,306. The figures for British shipping seemed to tell the same story. In 1772 British shipping, cleared outwards, amounted to 923,456 tons; in 1784 the figure was 932,219, and in 1785, for the first time, it passed the 1,000,000 mark.[21]

Arthur Young, who looked to agriculture as the source of England's wealth and was strongly opposed to mercantilist monopolies and the old colonial system, was one of those who invoked the *post hoc ergo propter hoc* argument, attributing the increasing prosperity of England immediately after the American Revolution to the loss of the American colonies, and drew the conclusion that all colonies were sources of weakness, not of strength, to a mother country. During his travels in France on the eve of the French Revolution he discussed with the Abbé Raynal the various evidences of British prosperity—the increase in population, consumption, and industry, the expansion of agriculture, manufactures, and commerce, and the increasing comfort of the people.

I mentioned the authentic documents and public registers which supported such a representation [he tells us] and I remarked that Abbé Raynal, who attended closely to what I said, had not seen or heard of these circumstances, in which he is not singular, for I have not met with a single person in France acquainted with them; yet they unquestionably form one of the most remarkable and singular experiments in the science of politics that the world has ever seen; for a people to lose an empire—thirteen provinces, and to GAIN by that *loss,* an increase of wealth, felicity, and power! When will the obvious conclusions to be drawn from that prodigious event, be adopted? that all transmarine, or distant dominions, are sources of weakness: and that to renounce them would be wisdom. Apply this in France to St. Domingo, in Spain to Peru, or in England to Bengal, and mark the ideas and replies that are excited. I have no doubt, however, of the fact.[22]

In attempting to appraise public opinion one should be careful, however, not to attribute too much weight to individual utterances and exaggerate their representative character. The great majority of Englishmen who acquiesced in the recognition of American independence did so not because they regarded it as desirable, but because they were convinced that it was inevitable. They were pessimists, not separatists. The tone that runs through the debates in Parliament on the peace treaties of 1782-3 is one of dejection; the speakers seem to have believed that the empire, the power, and the glory of Britain had passed forever.[23] Their words were not those of anti-imperialists, who viewed the independence of America with satisfaction; they were the words of disappointed imperialists. The American Revolution left a legacy of pessimism that colored all British thinking on the subject of colonies for a hundred years. It seemed to give historical validation to Turgot's celebrated botanical analogy—colonies are like fruit that falls from the tree when it ripens—and additional confirmation was seen in the Latin-American revolts of the early nineteenth century. The separation of mature colonies from their mother countries was elevated almost to the dignity of a law of nature.[24] The American Revolution did not, however, cause the British Government to abandon the commercial principles of the old colonial system or to adopt a more liberal policy of colonial government; much less did it cause it to favor the independence of Britain's remaining colonies.

Contemporaneous with the American Revolution were the beginnings of that transformation in English industry and society that goes by the name of the Industrial Revolution, and if it is easy to exaggerate the importance of the former as a factor in the change in Englishmen's attitude toward the Empire, it is scarcely possible to attribute too much influence, in the long run, to the latter. The mechanical inventions of the last half of the eighteenth century gave to the English manufacturers who adopted them such advantages over all foreign rivals that they came to rely more and more on their own competitive superiority and less and less on the legislative restrictions and monopolies of the mercantile system. They came, that is to say, to be economic liberals and advocates of *laissez-faire*. It was the spread of the new machine industry, whose beginnings synchronized with the publication of *The Wealth of Nations,* that prepared the soil for the growth of Adam Smith's ideas.

The early English free-trade movement of the last decades of the eighteenth century has generally been regarded as a product of economic theory rather than of economic interests, and as such different from the later Manchester School. Adam Smith represented the British manufacturers of his time as a class devoted to monopoly and mercantilism. It has been pointed out, however, that he failed to distinguish between manufacturers who adhered to old-fashioned methods of production and those who, even in his day, were adopting the new machinery.[25] In their desire for new foreign markets, increased supplies of raw material, cheap food, and improved international relations, the new manufacturers of the late eighteenth century clearly foreshadowed the great industrialists of the days of Cobden and Bright. New conditions were transforming them into champions of free trade. The cotton, pottery, and iron industries were the first to adopt the new inventions, and they took the lead in establishing a manufacturers' association that seems to have maintained an energetic 'lobby' in behalf of the Anglo-French commercial treaty of 1786, the first step taken by Great Britain in the direction of free trade.[26] The principal commodities in which France by this treaty made concessions to Great Britain were those in the production of which the latter enjoyed advantages resulting from the use of machinery; friends and foes of the treaty alike agreed that the cotton, hardware, and pottery industries would be its chief beneficiaries; and William Eden (after-

wards Lord Auckland), appointed by Pitt to negotiate the
treaty, was regarded as a champion of the new manufacturers.[27]

But the early free-trade movement did not have any serious effect on British colonial policy. Before the new economic liberalism had been put into operation to any great
extent, the war with Revolutionary France broke out. A re-
newal of the conflict with the old political and commercial
rival—the eternal enemy, as patriotic Englishmen thought—
as well as a crusade against revolution, it produced a re-
surgence of nationalist, mercantilist, and imperialist sentiment in England, and it stifled liberalism in all its phases
for more than a generation. Free trade suffered the same fate
as parliamentary reform. The struggle with Napoleon gave
heightened meaning to the old mercantilist slogan, 'ships,
colonies, commerce.' The British North American provinces
seemed more valuable as sources of supply for naval stores
when the countries of the Baltic were exposed to French influence and conquest; [28] and colonies were all the more prized
as markets when British manufacturers contemplated rue-
fully the effects on their fortunes of Napoleon's Continental
System and Jefferson's Embargo and Madison's War. The
Non-Intercourse Acts passed by Congress were cited to show
the loss that British trade might suffer if the remaining British colonies followed the example of the United States.[29]
When new colonial possessions—Malta, Ceylon, Trinidad,
the Cape of Good Hope—were the fruits of dearly won victory, British patriots were not disposed to question their
value.

*

*   *

But Waterloo closed an era, and during the period of international peace that followed, submerged radical movements revived. The rising school of Political Economy, whatever its exponents may have found to criticize in the specific teachings of Adam Smith, based their work on the foundations which he had laid. Ricardo's *Principles of Political Economy* appeared in 1817, and treatises on the same subject were published by Malthus in 1820, James Mill in 1821, and J. R. McCulloch in 1825. As sworn foes of mercantilism and all its works, the economists were of course opposed to the colonial system, and at a time when empire without commercial restriction seemed an anomaly, their teaching was naturally anti-imperialist in tone.

Closely related to the political economists were the Philosophical Radicals, who owned Bentham as their master, for between the new science of wealth and the new philosophy of utilitarianism there was a natural affinity. Bentham himself was a warm admirer of Adam Smith, and his foremost disciple, James Mill, was on terms of intimacy with Ricardo and other economists. In Mill, Ricardo, Malthus, and McCulloch utilitarian philosophy and *laissez-faire* economics were all but fused.[30] As free-traders these men condemned the commercial restrictions of the colonial system; as radicals in politics, they were opposed to the existing system of colonial administration, which they regarded as bureaucratic, oppressive, and unintelligent.

In their formal treatises the economists had little to say about colonies and colonial policy, but an article by McCulloch, published in the *Edinburgh Review* of August 1825, may fairly be taken as generally representative of their attitude.[31] The monopoly of the colonial trade, according to McCulloch, was either useless or pernicious—useless if the

mother country could sell in the colonies as cheaply as foreigners, for under such a condition the ties of language and
relation would give her the command of their markets without recourse to artificial restrictions; pernicious if she could
not sell as cheaply, because, though it might compel the colonies to buy from her what they could buy cheaper from foreigners, it created an artificial demand for her products and,
therefore, an artificial distribution of her capital and labor.
'It must divert a portion of them from some of the naturally
beneficial channels into which they would otherwise have
flowed, to force them into those where there is no real room
for them, and where they will be useless the moment the
monopoly ceases.' But even if the monopoly were beneficial,
it could never be strictly enforced. Spain was unable to enforce hers, and the British navy had found it impossible to
guard the American coasts from smugglers. Cheap goods
would make their way through every barrier. It had been
urged in support of the colonial system that it insured to the
mother country a regular supply of colonial produce, but
Germany, though possessing neither ships nor colonies, was
as well supplied with it as England. In return for the imaginary benefits—really detriments—derived from the monopoly
of the colonial trade the mother country imposed heavy
burdens on herself. In the interest of colonial producers, she
excluded foreign sugar and many other products from her
markets, to the great injury of British consumers; she incurred very heavy expenditure for the defense of the colonies, even in time of peace. The commercial relations between Great Britain and the United States proved the use-
lessness of the colonial monopoly, for the value of the commodities annually exported to the United States was more
than seven times as great as before the American Revolution;

and the present trade was natural, resting not on 'the miserable foundation of bounties and prohibitions, but on the gratification of real wants and desires.' The possession of the British North American provinces produced expense and nothing else for Britain, and it was difficult to see how any injury could result to her from the total and unconditional abandonment of them. Every man of sense knew that Canada must soon be annexed to the United States.

In considering Philosophical Radicalism in its anti-imperial aspect, the opinions of Bentham should first be examined. They can be found in a letter under the caption *Emancipate Your Colonies,* addressed to the French National Convention in 1793 but not published till 1830, in the essay on Peace in his *Principles of International Law,* and in his *Manual of Political Economy.*[32] Bentham, unlike the early Radicals, did not test political organization by its compatibility with natural law and abstract human rights. He and his followers applied to it, instead, the criterion of utility— the greatest happiness of the greatest number—and judged by this test, colonies were found sadly wanting.

From the point of view of the interests of the mother country, Bentham held that the colonies should be emancipated. Like Adam Smith, he reasoned that the commercial restrictions of the colonial system were economically detrimental to Great Britain. Even those placed upon the trade of the colonies, though supposedly in her interest, were really injurious to her; and they were accompanied by most burdensome counter-restrictions on her own trade, in the form of tariff discriminations against foreign imports, which forced her to buy at high prices from the colonies rather than at low prices from foreigners. Bentham laid great stress on the financial burdens of empire; to protect the colonies, keep them in dependence, and prevent them from smuggling, fleets and armies were necessary, and for these the people of Great Britain had to pay, for the colonies yielded no revenue. The possession of dependencies, moreover, increased the chances of war with foreign nations by arousing their jealousy and increasing the number of possible subjects of dispute with them. Bentham's plan for 'universal and perpetual peace' had for its twin bases the reduction of armaments and 'the emancipation of the distant dependencies of each state.' Colonies also bred political corruption in the mother country by putting at the disposal of the Government a multitude of civil and military offices.

From the point of view of the colonists, the effect of the colonial system was to sacrifice their real interests to the imaginary interests of the mother country. But even if all restrictions on their trade were abolished, distance and ignorance of colonial conditions would still make it impossible for Great Britain to rule them as well as they could rule themselves. Justice to the colonists, as well as the interests of the mother country, called for the emancipation of all adult colonies, though those that were unable to take care of themselves ought not to be turned adrift. The most important thing was to get rid of the false ideas that were used to justify the colonial system.

When we shall have ceased to consider colonies with the greedy eyes of fiscality, the greater number of these inconveniences will cease of themselves. Let governments lay aside all false mercantile notions, and all jealousy of their subjects, and everything which renders their yoke burthensome will fall at once: there will no longer be any reason to fear hostile dispositions and wars for independence. If wisdom alone were listened to, the ordinary object of contention would be reversed—the mother-country would desire to see her children powerful, that they might become free, and the colonies would fear the loss of that tutelary authority which gave them internal tranquility and security against external foes.[33]

Like many of Bentham's other works, those that have been referred to were not published for years after they had been written.[34] *Emancipate Your Colonies* was not published till 1830, the *Principles of International Law* and the *Manual of Political Economy* not till 1843, years after Bentham's death. But, as is well known, the spread of his ideas was not dependent on his own writings exclusively; his influence on British opinion owed much to the activities of his disciples. Of these the most important was James Mill, who was himself a radiating center of Utilitarianism.[35]

Mill prepared a series of articles for the supplement to the fourth, fifth, and sixth editions of the *Encyclopædia Britannica,* which expressed the orthodox Utilitarian creed on the subjects of which they treated. In the article 'Colony,' which appeared in 1824, he condemned the commercial restrictions of the colonial system, and laid it down that colonies were a source of vast expense and political corruption as well as a major cause of war. He was especially opposed to the use of them as convict settlements and strongly reprobated transportation as a punishment for crime.

In 1824 the *Westminster Review,* the leading organ of Utilitarianism, was founded, and, in the words of John Stuart Mill, it 'gave a recognized *status,* in the arena of opinion and discussion, to the Benthamic type of Radicalism.' [36] Whenever it had occasion to deal with the colonies, its anti-imperialism was manifest. It viewed them as 'impediments to commerce, drawbacks on prosperity, pumps for extracting the property of the many for the benefit of the few, the strong-

holds and asylums of despotism and misrule.' [37] It undertook
to prove that British dominion over Canada was bad, economically and politically, for both colony and mother country. If the voice of wisdom were heeded, Great Britain would
voluntarily relinquish all authority over the province, but
false notions respecting the value of colonies were still so
widely entertained that nothing but time and bitter experience would make the truth prevail.[38]

A subject that gave the Philosophical Radicals much concern was governmental waste and extravagance. From 1818
onwards Joseph Hume, who had acquired his Radicalism
from Francis Place, the tailor of Charing Cross and friend of
Bentham and James Mill, preached economy in the House
of Commons, where he appointed himself watch-dog of the
Treasury. The great expense to which Great Britain was put
by reason of her colonial possessions was one of his favorite
themes.[39] In a speech in the House of Commons in 1823, as
reported in *Hansard,* he said:

It was obvious, that the colonies, instead of being an addition
to the strength of the country, increased its weakness; and he
believed it would be better able to cope with any contingency
which might arise, if those colonies were freed from their allegiance, and became their own masters. The commercial advantages to England would be still the same; for we should continue
to be the principal suppliers. In the event of a war with America, we should have to defend Canada, and the distance to which
we should have to send supplies, would give fearful odds against
us in such a contest; while the expense would be five-fold more
than the colony was worth. Ought we not, then, to be relieved
from the drain which was caused by the colonies? [40]

Another Radical whose principal interest lay in public
finance, a subject on which he was recognized as an authority,

was Sir Henry Parnell, also a member of Parliament. In a work published in 1830, *On Financial Reform,* he argued that the number of British colonies should be greatly reduced, and that those which were retained should bear all the expenses of their own defense. Canada, he calculated, had already, in one way and another, cost the mother country fifty or sixty million pounds and was then an annual expense of at least six hundred thousand.[41]

During the decade of the 1830's the assumption that the colonies would inevitably separate from the mother country was almost a commonplace in Radical and Liberal circles. The Canadian Revolt of 1837 forced the Home Government to turn its attention to Canadian affairs, and in the course of debates in Parliament the separatist doctrine was frequently proclaimed.

Addressing the House of Lords on 18 January 1838, Lord Brougham declared that the Canadas were of no value to Great Britain and that the real question to be decided was not the suppression of the revolt but 'the mode in which a separation, sooner or later inevitable,' should take place. He hoped that when resentment and passion had cooled, the foundation would be laid for 'an amicable separation.' This, he was convinced, would be a positive gain, financially, commercially, and politically. His opinions, he said, had not been formed recently. 'They are the growth of many a long year, and the fruit of much attention given to the subject.' To devise means for rendering the inevitable separation 'kindly and gentle' he deemed to be 'the most sacred duty of every wise and virtuous statesman.' [42]

The Philosophical Radicals Grote, Roebuck, and Warburton expressed views similar to Brougham's. Grote thought that separation would be the best thing both for Great Britain and for Canada.[43] 'If we are wise,' said Roebuck, 'we shall see and arrange all matters in Canada, and in our other North American possession, so as to prepare them when a separation shall come, as come it must, to be an independent nation.' He thought it of the first importance that Canada should not be treated in such a manner as to drive it into the arms of the United States.[44] Warburton considered emancipation 'as natural an event in the history of the colonies as death to an individual' and concluded from his observation of all parties in the House of Commons that it was generally admitted that 'when a colony came to its strength and manhood, the inevitable consequence of our colonial system must be to have such a colony emancipated . . .' Like Roebuck he feared the aggrandizement of the United States. He hoped for the independence of the British North American colonies 'at no very distant period' and their union into 'an independent confederation.' [45]

The Prime Minister, Lord Melbourne, cannot be regarded as an anti-imperialist, but he evidently had his doubts about the permanence of the colonial connection. In introducing a bill for the reunion of the two Canadian provinces into the House of Lords (30 June 1840) he said: 'Whether it were decreed by the inscrutable will of Divine Providence that those great territories in North America should be severed from us, it is not for me to discuss.' [46] In the same debate Lord Ashburton, a Conservative peer, gave it as his opinion that the Canadians should have been told, before the revolt, that they could have independence as soon as popular sentiment was ripe for it.[47]

Thus by 1840 there was an aggressive and decidedly vocal body of anti-imperial opinion in England. It cannot be said that it had converted the whole British public, but it is not an exaggeration to say that it had put imperialism on the defensive. Those who still believed in the usefulness of colonies felt obliged to justify their faith.[48] The public as a whole took no interest in the colonies, and among statesmen and officials there was little enthusiasm for the Empire and little confidence that it would endure.[49] In a letter written to Lord Durham while he was in Canada, in 1838, Robert Baldwin, the Upper Canadian reformer, said that Durham was the first statesman 'to avow a belief in the possibility of a permanent connection between the Colonies & the Mother Country' and referred to 'the repeated references to the arrival of a time when these Colonies must cease to be a part of the British Empire which have not unfrequently proceeded from the very servants of the Crown.' [50]

The future was to be neither with the anti-imperialism nor with the imperialism of the early nineteenth century, but with the liberal imperialism that arose during the decade 1830-40, of which Lord Durham's *Report* is the most conspicuous product. The Empire was neither to be dissolved into formally independent fragments, though the time came when many observers believed that such an outcome was imminent, nor to be preserved unaltered. It was to be transformed. Yet anti-imperialism was not wholly a lost cause, for it made its contribution to the transformation. To the anti-imperialists the independence of the colonies was, after all, a means rather than an end. The end was the abolition of the old colonial system, with its burdensome restrictions on the trade of the colonies and the mother country, its subjection of the colonies to centralized bureaucratic control, its great expense to the taxpayers of Great Britain. The old colonial system has long since passed away, and the old anti-imperialism has disappeared. But if we consider working

constitutional practice rather than legal forms, it is difficult
to escape the conclusion that the British Empire of today,
so far at least as its self-governing parts are concerned, con-
forms more nearly to the ideals of the anti-imperialists of a
hundred years ago than to those of their opponents.[51]

MODIFICATIONS AND RELAXATIONS IN THE OLD COLONIAL SYSTEM

OF the mass of regulations comprised in the old colonial system, none was considered more fundamental than that which excluded foreign shipping from the trade of the British colonies. Legal exceptions to general rules were characteristic of the system, as of mercantilism in general, but to the rule in question only a slight exception was made before the American Revolution.

In days, however, when law enforcement was far less efficient than it is at present, commercial regulations were often honored in the breach rather than in the observance, and from early times contraband trade was carried on between English and foreign islands in the West Indies. In 1685 English colonial governors were instructed not to permit foreign vessels to trade with their colonies, but an exception was made in the case of Spanish ships coming to Jamaica or Barbados to obtain Negro slaves. Such ships were to be allowed to bring into those islands money or produce of the Spanish dominions in America.[1] English authorities connived at this illicit traffic, which was in violation of Spanish as well as of English law, as a means of gaining markets for English goods in Spanish America, especially for slaves brought from Africa to the English West Indies. It remained wholly illegal on the English side, however, till 1765, when Parliament passed the first of a series of free-port acts.[2] The preamble declared that the appointing of proper and convenient ports in some of the British colonies in America, for the more free importation and exportation of several goods and merchandizes, under certain restrictions and limitations, may be productive of considerable advantages to the manufactures of Great Britain, tend to the improvement of the revenue thereof, and be a means of increasing and extending the trade and navigation of all his Majesty's dominions.

By this statute, single-deck foreign vessels were permitted to import commodities of the growth or produce of any foreign colony in America into designated ports in Jamaica and Dominica, and to export therefrom to any foreign colony in America Negro slaves and commodities legally imported into those ports from Great Britain, Ireland, or any British colony in America. There were a few exceptions to the goods which might be so imported and exported, and the importation of manufactured articles from any foreign colony was expressly prohibited. Bryan Edwards, a Jamaica planter, in his *History of the West Indies,* said that 'the main argument which was originally adduced in defence of the establishment of free-ports in Jamaica, was founded on the idea, that these ports would become the great mart for supplying foreigners with negroes.' [3] The act of 1765 was to remain in force for only a few years, but it was continued by subsequent legislation, and in 1787 it was replaced by an act which added to the number of free ports in the British West Indies, limited the tonnage of foreign vessels permitted to enter them, and further restricted the commodities which such vessels were permitted to import and export.[4] This statute remained the basis of the free-port system until 1805, when it, in turn, was replaced by a new act.[5] Under this system the shipping of the United States was not admitted to the free ports. Importation in foreign vessels was limited to a list of commodities grown or produced in foreign European possessions in America, and the vessels (limited to ships of not more than one deck) had to be owned and navigated by inhabitants of those possessions. Speaking of the system in general, a recent writer remarks that its purpose was 'to foster and legitimize, as a matter of English law, trade between the British West Indian free ports and foreign plantations, a trade that was contraband in the eyes of every conscientious Spanish official.' [6] The free-port acts were a standing and attractive invitation to the Spanish colonists to break the laws of their colonial system by bringing their produce in their own vessels to the British islands in exchange for slaves and merchandize to be obtained there. It is evident that this trade assumed considerable proportions. The value of the imports of Jamaica alone, under the free-port system, has been estimated at £150,000 in 1791. [7] No free ports were established in any of the British colonies which became the United States, and none were established in any of the remaining British colonies on the continent of North America until 1808.

*

*   *

The loss of the Thirteen Colonies did not cause Great Britain to abandon her old colonial system. This is now well known to students of British imperial history, but it has not always been understood. Even as distinguished an authority on the history of British commerce as William Cunningham was misled into speaking of a 'revulsion' in British policy resulting from the American Revolution. [8] British prestige, to be sure, suffered the most serious blow it had ever sustained, and a spirit of pessimism and defeatism with regard to colonies was engendered—doubts about whether the colonial relationship could be a permanent one, whether the remaining British colonies would not inevitably, sooner or later, go the way of the Thirteen. In the realm of ideas, the acids of economic liberalism had begun to corrode the rationale of mercantilism; the opinions of David Hume, Josiah Tucker, and, above all, Adam Smith affected some members of the governing classes, and no doubt the outcome of the Revolution tended to give them greater influence. But Britain still possessed scattered fragments of empire in the West, and her East India Company had already embarked upon its career of political dominion in Southern Asia. Traditional theories of national power and prosperity were not suddenly thrown overboard. A navigation act of 1786 was based as clearly on the old mercantile ideas as those of the seventeenth century had been,[9] and well-informed writers, describing the commercial aspects of the colonial system as it existed in the years following the Revolution, pictured it as it had been before the Revolution. Bryan Edwards, for example, in the work referred to above, the first edition of which was published in 1793, in speaking of the acts of trade and navigation of the seventeenth century, said: 'These acts . . . form altogether the foundation of our colonial code; most of the subsequent acts now in force being framed in the same spirit, and intended to enforce and strengthen the system; with some few alterations and exceptions only, which however do not extend to any great and substantial change in the principle or ground work.' [10] Bryan Edwards had evidently heard of no 'revulsion' in British commercial policy. Yet for a brief season, immediately after the conclusion of the Revolutionary War, there seemed to be some prospect

that changed conditions would bring about a radical innovation in colonial policy, more specifically, that the merchant
ships of one foreign country, the United States, would be
permitted to trade with the British colonies. For the time
being, this effort of commercial liberalism failed, but the
episode is worthy of our attention. Powerful interests within
the Empire, in this case the West India planters, were beginning to invoke liberal principles.

Before the Revolution the trade of the British colonies in
the West Indies with those on the continent of North
America was limited by law, as we know, to British and
British colonial shipping. Almost the whole of it was with
the colonies that declared their independence in 1776. Nova
Scotia and Canada had practically no part in it. Ships owned
in Great Britain engaged in this trade, but they found it
difficult to compete with the smaller and more cheaply built
colonial (mainly New England) vessels, which were able to
make two and often three voyages a year to the West Indies.
The islands depended on this trade with the continental
colonies for necessities of life—lumber, livestock, fish, flour,
and most of their other provisions. Their principal exports
were sugar, molasses, rum, and coffee. The balance in this
trade was heavily in favor of the continental colonies, and
the specie and bills of exchange in which it was paid enabled
the latter to meet the unfavorable balance in their trade with
Great Britain. For example, the average annual importation
into the British islands from the continental colonies
amounted to about £720,000 for the years 1771-3, while the
average annual exportation from the former to the latter
was valued at only some £420,000.[11]

In 1775 Parliament passed acts prohibiting all commercial
intercourse between the loyal and the rebellious colonies,

and in the following year authorized the use of private vessels to seize ships engaged in this forbidden trade.[12] These Prohibitory Acts, as they were called, were not repealed till 1783, and during that period no trade could lawfully be carried on between the loyal British colonies in the West Indies and North America and the United States. The West Indies suffered severe economic distress, though restrictions on the exportation of grain from Great Britain were relaxed in their interest; the importation of provisions from Ireland was increased; lumber was imported from the Baltic countries; there was some trade with such parts of the revolted colonies as were under British military control; and, as would be expected, there was some violation of the Prohibitory Acts, especially by means of indirect trade through the neutral islands. No supplies to speak of were available for the West Indies from the loyal colonies of Nova Scotia and Canada.

During the peace negotiations of 1782, the question of commercial relations between the British Empire and the United States naturally received attention. In articles agreed to by the British and American commissioners it was provided that British merchants and merchant ships should enjoy in the United States the same privileges, and be liable to the same duties only, as the merchants and merchant ships of the United States, and that reciprocal privileges should be enjoyed by the merchants and merchant ships of the United States in all British territories.[13] These remarkably liberal provisions, however, were not included in the Provisional Treaty of Peace of November 1782, which was made definitive in 1783, and twelve years elapsed before any commercial treaty was made between Great Britain and the United States.

Lord Shelburne, who was head of the British Ministry

when the negotiations of 1782 were carried on, was a liberal in matters of commerce, an admirer of Adam Smith, and an advocate of reciprocity with the United States, and the same was true of his young Chancellor of the Exchequer, William Pitt. Shelburne, however, was defeated in the House of Commons by the Fox-North Coalition, and on 24 February 1783 he and his colleagues resigned. For nearly six weeks the king, who detested the Coalition, struggled to save himself from the humiliation of accepting its leaders as his ministers, and meanwhile the former ministers continued to hold office pending the appointment of their successors. It was during this strange interlude that Pitt, on 3 March, introduced into the Commons a bill 'for the provisional establishment and regulation of trade and intercourse between the subjects of Great Britain and those of the United States of North America.' [14] It was to apply until a treaty could be concluded for the permanent regulation of trade between the British Empire and the United States.

The bill provided for the repeal of the Prohibitory Acts, but this in itself would not permit American ships to trade with Great Britain or any part of the Empire, for the United States was now a foreign country, and under the Navigation Act, it will be recalled, products of foreign countries and colonies in Asia, Africa, and America could not be imported into Great Britain in foreign ships, and such ships were excluded from all trade with the British colonies. By further provisions of the bill, however, United States ships were to be admitted to the ports of Great Britain on the same terms as the ships of European countries, and the goods which they imported were to receive exceptionally favorable treatment: they were not to be subject to alien duties, as was the case with European products when imported in foreign ships.

As to the colonial trade, American ships were to be permitted to import into the British colonies in North America and the West Indies any products of the United States and to export thence to their own country any commodities whatsoever, and goods so imported and exported were to be liable only to the same duties as if they were the property of British subjects and carried in British ships.

These were extraordinarily liberal proposals, revolutionary from the standpoint of the old colonial system, and it is no wonder that they threw mercantile minds into a state bordering on panic.[15] The lead in opposing the bill in the House of Commons was taken by William Eden (afterwards Lord Auckland), an ambitious politician who was at this time strengthening his connection with Lord North by working for the establishment of a Fox-North Coalition Ministry. He had been a member of the Board of Trade, which was abolished in 1782, and enjoyed a considerable reputation as an authority on commercial matters. Eden pronounced Pitt's bill to be 'of the greatest importance of any that he had ever seen in parliament,' and declared that it 'would introduce a total revolution in our commercial system, which he was afraid would shake it to its very bases, and endanger the whole pile.' [16]

A Coalition Ministry was formed on 2 April, with the Duke of Portland as First Lord of the Treasury and formal head and the two Secretaries of State, Fox and North, as the real leaders. Pitt was in no position to push his bill, and it was dropped. The Prohibitory Acts were repealed, and an act was passed authorizing the making of temporary orders in council for regulating commerce between the United States and the British Empire.[17] On 14 May the first of a number of orders was issued. This related to trade between the United

States and Great Britain. It made an important exception to the rule previously governing importation into Great Britain from foreign territories in Asia, Africa, and America by providing that unmanufactured commodities produced in the United States might be imported in American as well as in British ships. The first Order in Council for the regulation of trade between British colonies and the United States was issued on 2 July. Lord North called upon William Knox for aid in framing the regulations, and the Order in Council was actually Knox's work.

William Knox, an Irish Protestant, had lived for several years before the Revolution in Georgia, where he held office in the royal government of that province and acquired an extensive landed estate, which was later confiscated.[18] Returning to England as Agent for Georgia in 1761, he soon acquired a reputation as a colonial expert. He attached himself to George Grenville, who was head of the Ministry from 1763 to 1765, and as a pamphleteer he supported Grenville's colonial policies and measures, notably the Stamp Act. In 1770 he became an undersecretary in the colonial office, or American Department as it was called, which had been created in 1768, and he retained this position until the department was abolished in 1782, when he returned to private life. Though he was subordinate to the Secretary of State at the head of the department, there is good reason for thinking that Knox had no little influence, from first to last, in determining policies. He himself afterwards asserted that he had been 'a principal actor in the executive government' during the Revolution, and the historian who has an unrivalled knowledge of his career believes that there is at least 'an element of truth in his claim.'[19] Lord George Germain, who was head of the American Department during the Revolutionary War, had great confidence in Knox, and he seems to have stood high in the esteem of Lord North, the then Prime Minister. Knox was a thorough-going mercantilist. In his *Extra Official State Papers,* published in 1789, he tells us that when he acceded to North's request for aid in drawing up regulations for trade with the United States, he made it clear that the principle which he would follow was that *'it was better to have no colonies at all, than not to have them subservient to the maritime strength and commercial interests of Great Britain.'* This principle, he adds, 'I make no secret of, for I have ever avowed it . . .' [20] He framed the regulations for trade between the British West Indies and the United States 'so as utterly to exclude the American shipping.' [21] In a letter written a few years after the Order in Council of 2 July 1783 had been issued, Knox said: 'I carried it thru' against the opposition of Mr. Fox and Mr. Burke, and thereby saved the navigation and maritime importance of this country and strangled in the birth that of the United States . . .' [22] There can be no doubt regarding Knox's authorship of the Order in Council.[23] He was so proud of it that he expressed the wish that it be engraved on his tombstone *'as having saved the Navigation of England.'* [24]

Knox would have been glad to see the wartime prohibition of all trade between the United States and the British West Indies continued if the needs of the latter had permitted it. In a memorandum he drew up on 'Intercourse between the British Colonies and the United States' he said:

If our North American Colonies were able to supply all the wants of our islands, as our islands can supply them with what they want of West India products, the line would be easy to draw; for it would only be necessary to confine their trade reciprocally to each other; but our North American Colonies in their present state cannot supply our islands, and therefore the United States must *for the present* be called in to their assistance, and the islands must be permitted to pay them in their products. But whatever permissions of this kind are given it should be remembered, that the object of this country is to *exclude the communication of foreigners with our Colonies,* and that whenever our North American Colonies shall be in a condition to supply our islands wholly, the interference of foreigners is to be prevented.[25]

Knox believed that the islands could be adequately supplied with salted fish from Newfoundland and Nova Scotia, with some assistance from the herring fisheries of Ireland and Scotland, and with salted meat from Ireland, and that therefore they should not be permitted to import these provisions from the United States.[26] As the Order in Council was finally drawn, it permitted, until further orders, the importation into any of the British West India islands of the following products of the United States: pitch, tar, turpentine, hemp, flax, all kinds of lumber, livestock, peas, beans, potatoes, all kinds of grain, flour, bread, and biscuits; it permitted, in return, the exportation from any of the British islands to the United States of rum, sugar, molasses, coffee, cocoanuts, ginger, and pimento.[27] In accordance with Knox's cardinal principle, this trade was strictly confined to British ships, and only British subjects could lawfully take part in it. It should be noted, too, that the list of American products permitted to be imported into the islands did not include fish, meat, or dairy produce.

Scarcely had the Order in Council been issued than there came from the press a tract which quickly went through several editions and won for its author a high reputation as an authority on matters of trade. This was Lord Sheffield's

Observations on the Commerce of the American States with Europe and the West Indies . . . and on the Tendency of a Bill now depending in Parliament. The bill in question was the one that Pitt had introduced in March, and the author argued that it was of most dangerous tendency. By permitting trade between the British West Indies and the United States in the latter's shipping, he declared, the bill relinquished 'the only use and advantage of colonies or West Indian islands, and for which alone it would be worth while to incur the vast expence of their maintenance and protection, *viz.* The monopoly of their consumption; and of the carriage of their produce.' Sheffield was not afraid of retaliation by the United States; he doubted whether, under their existing weak central government, they could be brought to act as a nation, and even if they did adopt concerted measures, they would not be able to prevent smuggling. He made himself the spokesman of all the interests that were opposed to any relaxation of the old restrictive system. The influence of his pamphlet may have been exaggerated. Edward Gibbon, a friend of Sheffield's, wrote in his autobiography: 'The sale of his "Observations on the American States" was diffusive, their effect beneficial; the Navigation Act, the palladium of Britain, was defended, and perhaps saved, by his pen; and he proves, by the weight of fact and argument, that the mother-country may survive and flourish after the loss of America.' [28] Sheffield fired the opening gun in a lively war of pamphlets which reflected a significant conflict of interests within the Empire. His *Observations* did not appear, however, till after the July Order in Council, of which Sheffield heartily approved,[29] and it seems doubtful whether the Government would afterwards have followed any different course of policy as regards trade with the United States if

Sheffield had not written. His arguments for maintaining the British shipping monopoly in the trade of the colonies made him the idol of the shipping interests and of all others who, for whatever reason, wished to confine the trade of the colonies exclusively to British ships.

The question of policy, however, was not yet settled. What was done in 1783 as regards West India trade was avowedly temporary, and a new ministry, formed by Pitt in December of that year, after the king had rid himself of the Fox-North Coalition, decided that a thorough investigation of the whole subject was called for. It was accordingly referred, in March 1784, to a newly appointed committee of the privy council for trade and plantations.[30] The inquiry included the taking of testimony from many witnesses and extended over nearly three months. The committee made its report on May 31.[31]

Meanwhile, petitions and remonstrances poured in from the West Indies protesting against the restrictions on their trade with the United States and, in the words of Bryan Edwards, anticipating 'the most dreadful consequences, if the system of restriction should be much longer persisted in.'[32] The powerful West India Interest, which maintained an effective and influential organization in London, was thoroughly aroused,[33] and the West India arguments were set forth in a number of pamphlets that were published at this juncture. On the other hand, representatives of the British shipping interests and American Loyalist refugees, anxious to promote the prosperity of Nova Scotia and Canada, whither thousands of Loyalists had fled during and immediately after the Revolutionary War, made common cause against any departure from the principle of the Navigation Act in favor of United States shipping in West India trade. There was a more or less well-organized group of Loyalists in London, some of whom had considerable influence in governing circles and were regarded as experts on colonial questions, and they foresaw a great increase in the trade of the loyal North American colonies with the West Indies if United States shipping continued to be excluded from the West India trade. With unwarranted optimism they anticipated that Nova Scotia, Newfoundland, and Canada would soon be able to supply the West Indies with almost all the products which they had previously obtained from the Thirteen Colonies. Bryan Edwards attributed to the Loyalist partisans in this controversy 'a lurking taint of resentment and malignity . . . and at least as ardent a desire to wound the new republic through the sides of the West Indians, as to benefit Nova Scotia at their expense.' [34] Edwards, himself a West India partisan and a pamphleteer on that side,[35] may not have been altogether fair to the Loyalists, but what he said was true, without much doubt, of some of them—of George Chalmers for one, whose *Opinions on Interesting Subjects of Public Law and Commercial Policy arising from American Independence* appeared at this time.

A Scot by birth, Chalmers had emigrated to Maryland as a young man, practiced law in Baltimore during the years immediately preceding the outbreak of the Revolution, and, according to his own later testimony, laid the foundations of a personal fortune there.[36] He detested the Revolutionists and all their works, and in 1775, his hopes of fame and prosperity in America having been blasted, he returned to England in bitter and vindictive mood. He was a prominent member of the Loyalist group in London. In his *Opinions* he predicted dire disaster to Britain if American shipping should be permitted to trade with the British West Indies and saw nothing to be alarmed at even if the United States should retaliate against British shipping. He was confident that Great Britain and Ireland, together with the remaining British North American colonies, could supply the West Indies with all they needed, except perhaps lumber, which could be obtained from the Baltic countries, and even as to lumber, Canadian and Nova Scotian production would undoubtedly increase greatly.[37]

To what extent the Committee for Trade and Plantations was influenced by the arguments of the pamphleteers or by the voluminous testimony given by witnesses it is impossible to determine. Representatives of all interests and points of view were given a patient hearing, but a good deal of weight should be given to the remark of a modern historian, that 'a Committee made up largely of successful politicians, several of whom were hostile to America, could scarcely have been expected to upset long established traditions.' [38] Charles Jenkinson (afterwards First Earl of Liverpool) was the most active and influential member of the Committee and had more to do with framing the report than any of the others. Bryan Edwards believed, whatever his opinion may be worth, that Loyalists had an undue influence on the Committee,[39] but, quite apart from this, the survival of mercantile-mindedness, together with wishful thinking, would seem to go far toward explaining its attitude. The West Indians failed to convince its members that the islands would suffer disaster unless American shipping were admitted to their ports, the Loyalists seem to have satisfied them that the remaining British North American colonies would very soon be able to supply the West Indies with the North American products they needed, and the shipping interests made a powerful appeal to British patriotism. At a time when many British merchant ships were idle and many thousands of demobilized British seamen were unemployed, the arguments of the shipowners were probably the most influential of all. The Committee recommended regulations for West India trade substantially the same as those already in operation. 'A fuller vindication of the policy of the Coalition or a clearer statement of some of the old commercial principles could scarcely have been offered.' [40]

Orders in council relating to the West India trade continued to be issued from time to time during the next few years, but they made no change in the principles of the order of July 1783, and its essential provisions were incorporated in an act of Parliament, intended to be permanent, which was passed in 1788.[41] Article xii of Jay's Treaty, which was negotiated in 1794, would have permitted small American vessels (of not more than 70 tons burthen) to carry to the British West Indies any products of the United States which British vessels could lawfully carry. A proviso was added, however, that American vessels should not carry any molasses, sugar, coffee, cocoa, or cotton either from the British West India islands or from the United States to any part of the world except the United States.[42] This article was not approved by the Senate, and its operation was suspended by an additional article of the treaty as finally ratified.

American shipping was similarly barred from sea-borne trade with the British colonies in North America during the years following the Revolution. The earliest regulations for trade between those colonies and the United States were contained in an order in council of 8 April 1785, which permitted the importation of certain products of the United States into Nova Scotia and New Brunswick, but only in British ships and only for such time as the governors of those colonies should declare it to be necessary. The importation by sea of American products into Canada (the Province of Quebec) was totally prohibited.[43] The act of Parliament of 1788 referred to above, which dealt with the trade of the North American as well as of the West India colonies, prohibited all importation from the United States, even though carried in British vessels, into the maritime provinces of Nova Scotia, New Brunswick, Cape Breton Island, St. John's (Prince Edward Island), and Newfoundland, but provided that in case of emergency the governors might authorize, for limited periods, the importation of various kinds of lumber, livestock, grain, flour, bread, beans, and potatoes, but only in British shipping. No goods were permitted to enter Canada from the United States by sea.[44]

From what has been said it should be evident that the loss of the old colonies left mercantilism still dominant in British colonial policy. The old Empire had been wrecked, but the old colonial system was still afloat and substantially intact. This statement, it should be understood, is made with reference to the British colonies in the western hemisphere. A new British Empire, very different in character from the old, was coming into existence in the East. With the growth of British rule in India it became clear that commercial rules framed for American colonies were not suitable for Asiatic dependencies. Article XIII of Jay's Treaty permitted American ships to trade between the United States and British territories in the East Indies, and in 1797 Parliament allowed the ships of all friendly foreign countries to trade with those territories subject to regulations to be made by the directors of the East India Company.[45]

During the long period of war with France (1793-1815) many modifications were made in the old system to meet special and local conditions and temporary emergencies.

West India governors, for example, often found it necessary to allow American ships to import provisions and lumber in violation of the law, and acts of Parliament were passed to indemnify them. During most of these years American vessels were actually trading with the British West Indies. The many departures from what was regarded as normal were not intended to be permanent, however, and it would be unprofitable and confusing to attempt a description of them.

*

* *

The return of peace after the Napoleonic War and an economic depression of unprecedented range, intensity, and duration which followed were distinctly favorable to a revival of agitation for commercial reform. No parliament, not even the Tory Parliament of the day, could long remain unaffected by the flood of petitions for relief from all interests and classes. Acute economic distress led to serious unrest and disturbances, but it was evident to the more enlightened members of the governing classes that measures of repression, resorted to in the name of law and order, solved no problems, since they dealt only with symptoms of the economic malady and did nothing to remove its causes. Nor did the economic dislocations incident to the transition from war to peace seem sufficient to account for the extent and continuance of distress.

Henry Brougham, the most brilliant of the Whig opponents of Lord Liverpool's Tory Ministry, was one of those who believed that the root of the evils from which the country was suffering was to be found not in temporary circumstances which time would alter but in the survivals of mercantilism. On 17 March 1817, he introduced resolutions in the House of Commons calling for an immediate revision of the existing system of commercial regulations. In the course of a long speech Brougham paid his respects to 'a class of men, who, blending with what is termed true mercantile knowledge much narrow-minded, violent, national prejudice, or, as they call it, genuine British feeling, assume to themselves the style and title of the "sound statesmen," and certainly do in good earnest exert a real and practical influence over the affairs of the nation.' [46] These persons, he said, were clinging to the remnants of an exploded theory, the practical results of which were embodied in every volume of the statutes down to the latest. In the debate which ensued, Frederick Robinson (afterwards Viscount Goderich and Earl of Ripon), who then held the office of Vice President of the Board of Trade, professed agreement with much of what Brougham had said and admitted that the restrictive system was largely responsible for the existing distress, though he was acutely conscious of 'the infinite difficulty . . . in extricating ourselves from that system.' For the time being, nothing came of Brougham's resolutions. The Government regarded them as a virtual censure, and they were easily defeated.

For alterations in the old colonial system that involved changes in policy and were intended to be permanent, we need not go back of 1820. Five years of peace had brought no signs of economic recovery. The commercial, manufacturing, and agricultural interests were still complaining of their sorry plight, and requests for relief continued to pour in at Westminster and Whitehall. Various proposals for reform had been advanced and discussed, but a thoroughgoing application of free-trade principles to British commerce and industry had not yet been seriously considered by the Government or Parliament. On 8 May 1820, however, an important and impressive petition from London merchants, protesting against 'every restrictive regulation of trade, not essential to the revenue,' was laid before the House of Commons by Alexander Baring (afterwards Lord Ashburton), head of the great banking house of Baring Brothers.[47] It can fairly be claimed for this document that it started the movement in political circles for commercial reform along free-trade lines. Several years later, after far-reaching reforms had been effected, William Huskisson declared that this petition embraced 'all the great principles of commercial policy upon which Parliament has since legislated.'[48] Its author was Thomas Tooke, a free-trader and follower of David Ricardo. He was not as yet very widely known but was later to achieve a reputation as an economist in his own right. In the last volume of his *History of Prices,* published in 1857, Tooke gave what was probably a fairly accurate account of the origin of the petition and of the events leading up to its presentation.[49] From this it appears that Tooke was discouraged by his failure to secure signatures to the petition he had drafted, but that when Samuel Thornton, a merchant and financier of great influence in the City of London, a former governor of the Bank of England, a member of Parliament, and a supporter of the existing Tory Government, finally decided to sign, his example was promptly followed by half of the directors of the Bank, who considered his signature as a guarantee that the petition contained nothing inconsistent with sound Tory principles. A small deputation of the signers waited on Lord Liverpool, who expressed his entire concurrence with the petition in principle, but stated that considerations of expediency and justice to vested interests prevented the Government from holding out the prospect of any great or immediate change in commercial policy. 'A great point had been gained,' Tooke wrote, 'in eliciting . . . from the head of the Government an explicit and unequivocal expression of opinion in favour of the doctrines and principles of Free Trade,' and in his opinion the members of the Ministry were 'far more sincere and resolute Free Traders than the Merchants of London.' Tooke arranged for Baring to present the petition in the House of Commons.

It was declared in the petition that freedom from restraint was calculated to enlarge the foreign trade of the country and give the most beneficial direction to its capital and industry; that the maxim of buying in the cheapest market and selling in the dearest, acted upon by every merchant in his individual dealings, was strictly applicable to the trade of the nation; that a policy based on these principles would 'render the commerce of the world an interchange of mutual advantages, and diffuse an increase of wealth and enjoyments among the inhabitants of each state'; and that existing prejudices in favor of the restrictive system sprang from 'the erroneous supposition that every importation of foreign commodities occasions a diminution or discouragement of our own productions to the same extent.' The petitioners called for an immediate investigation of the effects of the existing system, believing that it would probably indicate that relief could be obtained by the removal of restrictions, and expressed the opinion that the adoption of a liberal policy by Britain would lessen commercial hostility toward her in foreign countries and have a salutary influence on their policies.

In presenting the petition Mr. Baring referred to the prevalent distress, proposed a number of changes in the existing commercial system that he thought practicable, and emphasized the importance of a careful and minute inquiry into all possible means of improving trade. His speech was greeted with 'loud cheers from all sides of the House.' In the debate that followed, Robinson said he had always thought that the restrictive system was 'founded in error, and calculated to defeat the object for which it was adopted,' yet it was 'so deeply rooted, that it was difficult to induce any gentleman to oppose it.' [50]

On motion of Lord Lansdowne a select committee of the House of Lords was appointed on 26 May 1820, to inquire into the means of extending and securing the foreign trade of the country, and a similar committee was appointed by the House of Commons, on motion of Baring, on 5 June. In the debate on Lansdowne's motion Lord Liverpool, who had been Prime Minister since 1813 and was to remain so until 1827, said that he did not doubt the soundness of the general principles of free trade, but that Britain could not then act unreservedly on those principles. 'The commercial regulations of the European world have been long established, and cannot suddenly be departed from.' [51] Lord Liverpool has usually been thought of as a representative of reaction and repression. He was strongly opposed to Catholic Emancipation and Parliamentary Reform, but there is no reason to doubt his commercial liberalism, cautious though he was in its application. It was clear that he would not move hastily or in doctrinaire spirit along the path of commercial reform, but it was no small thing that the head of the Government publicly endorsed the theory of free trade. In 1820 he went further in the support of free-trade principles than any of his predecessors except Pitt had done.[52]

Lord Lansdowne's committee confined its first report, which was presented on 3 July, to a single item of commerce, the timber trade with the northern countries of Europe and the North American colonies, on which there had been much discussion in commercial and shipping circles.[53] The report of the Commons' committee, presented on 18 July, was of wider scope, though admittedly far from complete.[54] The committee included in its membership Thomas Wallace (afterwards Lord Wallace), its chairman and most active member and at the time Vice President of the Board of Trade, Frederick Robinson, President of the Board, and William Huskisson, who then held the minor office of Commissioner of Woods and Forests. It was mainly due to these men that effect was given to the policies advocated in the report. What Wallace accomplished for commercial reform was gratefully recognized by London merchants and financiers. Baring later told the House of Commons that there was 'but one opinion amongst them, and that was that, since the first establishment of the Board of Trade, all the exertions of all its former Presidents were not, when united, equal to those which had been made by the right honourable gentleman alone'; and David Ricardo paid tribute in the House to 'the extraordinary merits' of Wallace.[55] In the reconstruction of the Ministry following the suicide of Lord Castlereagh in 1822, Wallace's legitimate claims to advancement were disregarded, and he resigned from the Board of Trade. His reputation was eclipsed by the fame of Huskisson, who became President of the Board in 1823, and historians were tardy in giving him his deserts.[56]

Like the petition of the London merchants, the report of the Commons' committee was an unequivocal confession of faith in free-trade principles.

Your Committee are satisfied that the skill, enterprize, and capital of British merchants and manufacturers require only an

open and equal field for exertion; and that the most valuable
boon that can be conferred on them, is, as unlimited a freedom
from all interference, as may be compatible with what is due to
private vested interests that have grown up under the existing
system, and those more important considerations with which the
safety and political power of the country are intimately connected . . . They are convinced, that every restriction on the
freedom of commerce is in itself an evil, to be justified only by
some adequate political expediency . . . The time when monopolies could be successfully supported, or would be patiently
endured, either in respect to subjects against subjects, or particular countries against the rest of the world, seems to have
passed away. Commerce, to continue undisturbed and secure,
must be, as it was intended to be, a source of reciprocal amity
between nations, and an interchange of productions, to promote
the industry, the wealth, and the happiness of mankind.

At the same time the committee was emphatic in opposing
any sudden overthrow of the existing system. Statesmanship
and equity called for moderation in reform. The state of the
law relating to British trade in general was complicated and
baffling in the extreme, and the regulations of the colonial
system were necessarily involved in this confusion. The committee was impressed by 'the excessive accumulation' and
'complexity' of the laws regulating commerce, which, according to a compilation that had recently been made, numbered
upwards of two thousand. This welter of confusion was detrimental to commercial enterprise, and in the committee's
opinion 'an accurate revision of this vast and confused mass
of legislation' would be a very valuable service to trade.

In the years that followed, it seemed to ardent free-traders
that the old system, like Charles II, was an unconscionable
time a-dying, yet there was good ground for Wallace's estimate of this report as the 'most material step of this country
to a departure from the course of restrictive policy which its

legislature had hitherto pursued, and to the establishment of a more enlarged and liberal policy towards foreign states than any which had yet prevailed.' [57]

The parliamentary committees on trade, which were re-appointed in the session of 1821, made further reports, but their only specific recommendation that directly touched the colonial system was one relating to the timber trade. This involved the question of colonial preference.

As early as the reign of Queen Anne, Parliament encouraged the importation of naval stores from the colonies. On the ground that it was desirable to lessen England's dependence on Norway and the Baltic countries for her supply of these materials, so essential to the navy and the mercantile marine, an act was passed in 1704, during the War of the Spanish Succession, granting bounties on the importation into England from her American colonies of tar, pitch, turpentine, hemp, masts, yards, and bowsprits, all of which were placed on the list of enumerated articles that the colonies were forbidden to export to foreign countries.[58] The policy of encouraging the importation of colonial timber by laying heavy duties on timber imported from the Baltic began during the Napoleonic War, when the Continental System shut off supplies from northern Europe and immediately threatened British sea power. In order to attract needed capital to lumbering in Canada and the maritime provinces, some assurance had to be given that Baltic timber, which cost only about one-third as much to transport to British ports as North American timber, would not be able to recover its former place in the British market after the war. British colonial wood of all descriptions was accordingly given highly preferential treatment in the customs act of 1809. In the following year the duties were doubled, and

later acts imposed additional duties.[59] Timber from the
British North American colonies suitable for naval purposes
was admitted duty free.[60] An immense impetus was given to
lumbering in the colonies, especially in Upper Canada and
New Brunswick. The colonial timber trade suddenly became,
and for some years remained, the principal factor in the development of British North America. For a time ships engaged in it represented nearly one-fourth of the tonnage
cleared outwards from Great Britain and exceeded the tonnage employed in the West India trade by nearly one-half.[61]
The Commons' committee on trade devoted its first report
of 1821 exclusively to the timber trade and made definite
recommendations for alterations in the duties. Before 1809,
it reported, British supplies of timber had come mainly
from northern Europe, since then an increasing proportion
had come from the North American colonies, and in 1820
the use of European wood was pretty much confined to expensive buildings. The basic duty on foreign timber was 65s.
per load, and the committee proposed to reduce this by 10s.
and at the same time place a new duty of 10s. on colonial
timber. Taking into account the higher freight paid by the
latter, they calculated that it would enjoy an effective preference of 30s., which they considered a reasonable and adequate degree of protection.[62]

As soon as proposals to lower the duties on foreign timber
came under discussion, the shipping interests, British and
colonial, at once took fright, fearing that the changes recommended would result in the ruin of the North American
timber trade, which, it was stated in the House of Commons,
gave employment to 1520 vessels and 17,600 seamen.[63] The
most active champion of the shipping interests in Parliament
was Joseph Marryat, who foretold general disaster if colonial

timber were deprived of its existing protection in the British market. He estimated that commerce with the Baltic countries, because of the comparative shortness of the voyages, would give employment to less than half the number of ships and seamen required for an equal volume of trade with the British colonies in North America, and on the basis of British trade with Norway and Sweden in 1819 he predicted that four-fifths of the timber trade with northern Europe would be carried in foreign shipping.[64] If the timber trade with the colonies should be destroyed by Baltic competition, the British shipping interests would sustain a calamity of the first order, British manufacturers would suffer severely from the decline of British exports to the colonies, British landholders would lose the protection which their timber enjoyed against Baltic timber, emigration to the British North American colonies would be discouraged, and if the free-traders should have their way about timber, they would next attack the corn laws. Marryat's speech was a good example of the reaction of mercantile-mindedness to the challenge of free trade. It was of such arguments as these that Wallace was no doubt thinking when he said that 'in the course of his official experience, he had found that on every occasion when the shipowners had come forward to oppose a public measure originating with the government, they were universally in the wrong.' [65]

By an act passed in 1821 the timber duties were revised in accordance with the committee's recommendations. The measure encountered considerable opposition, but the changes made seem to have had little effect upon the relative position of colonial and Baltic timber in the British market. The preference that the former enjoyed under the new duties amounted in practice, it has been estimated, to a protection of about 275 per cent.[66] The act of 1821, nevertheless, was significant. Wallace described it as 'the first step in receding from a system detrimental to our commercial relations and towards conciliating those foreign powers without whose good will the relations of mercantile intercourse could never be securely established.' [67]

*

* *

On 25 June 1821, Wallace, on behalf of the Government, laid before the House of Commons a comprehensive plan for the revision of the navigation system.[68] The objects in view were to simplify and consolidate the law by freeing it from 'a great part of that immense mass of legislation which successive centuries had heaped on it' and removing 'those contrarieties and contradictions' which made it 'obscure and difficult of application,' and to extend British commerce. He believed that the only ground on which restrictions on trade ought to be continued was the maintenance of maritime power. That fundamental object of the navigation laws had his full approval.

In 1822 Wallace and Robinson introduced five bills to give effect to the Government's program of commercial reform. They aroused considerable apprehension in shipping circles but little opposition in Parliament; they were all passed during the session without substantial amendments and received the royal assent on 24 June. The first of these acts swept away an immense amount of dust that had accumulated on the statute-book through the centuries, repealing a vast number of enactments relating to England's trade with foreign countries, inconsistent with subsequent legislation or rendered unnecessary by it, which had been passed from

the reign of Edward III to 1660.[69] The second repealed various enactments made since the Restoration relative to importation into the United Kingdom, in order that other
regulations might be embodied in a single new act.[70] The
third was a new navigation act regulating the importation of
goods into the United Kingdom 'so far as relates to the
Countries or Places from whence, and the Ships in which,
such Importation shall be made.' [71] This introduced a number of modifications in the old navigation system, though it
did not deal with the trade of the colonies. Under the law
as it now stood, British ships were permitted, in the interest
of British commerce, to import into the United Kingdom
from Europe, for re-exportation, the products of foreign
countries or colonies in Asia, Africa, and America. Changed
conditions in Spanish America resulting from the Wars of
Liberation were recognized by permitting importation into
the United Kingdom of the products of 'any Country or
Place in America or the West Indies, being or having been
a Part of the Dominions of the King of Spain,' in ships of the
producing country or of the port of usual first shipment.
In 1783, as we have seen, the importation of products of the
United States in the ships of that country had been permitted, and a similar permission was given in 1808 with regard to imports from Portuguese possessions in South
America.[72] As to imports from continental Europe, the restriction of the importation of specified commodities to
British ships and ships of the producing country was relaxed
by legalizing it from any European port in vessels belonging
to that port; and certain discriminations made by earlier acts
against imports from Russia, Turkey, the Netherlands, and
Germany now disappeared.

The last two of the five acts made important modifications

in the colonial system. The first of these related to trade between the British colonial possessions in America and the West Indies and other places in America and the West Indies. Robinson, who introduced the bills, pointed out that the old restrictions on the imports and exports of the colonies, which made England the emporium for their commerce and confined their trade strictly to English ships, had not been adhered to in the case of the eastern colonies or of India.

The trade of Ceylon, of the Mauritius, of the Cape of Good Hope, is at this moment comparatively free: the trade of the East India Company's territories has never been shackled by the peculiar restrictions of the Navigation Laws . . . we have not deemed it prudent, or even practicable, to apply to possessions of such vast extent, such a dense population, such abundant resources, such facilities for active commerce, and such means of circulating and promoting wealth, a principle of systematic restraint.—And who will say that the interests either of commerce or of navigation have suffered . . . ?

And even in the western hemisphere, he said, 'the rigid application of our ancient colonial policy is no longer in existence. The relaxation may have been the result of accident and circumstances, rather than of design; but it is sufficient for my argument to show that the change has actually taken place.' [73] He was alluding to the institution of free ports, which he regarded as an important departure from the old colonial system. The ships of the United States had not been admitted to the free ports in the West Indies, but free ports had been established in Nova Scotia and New Brunswick, to which they were permitted to bring specified products of their own country.[74] Robinson proposed to repeal the many laws regulating the trade of the colonies, which had been

passed at different times and with different objects—'intricate and confused,' he called them, and 'in no small degree
contradictory'—and incorporate the whole system of colonial
trade in two statutes.

The first of these was 'an act to regulate the Trade between
His Majesty's Possessions in America and the West Indies
and other Places in America and the West Indies.' [75] This
act was the result, at least in large part, of measures which
the United States had taken in retaliation for the continued
exclusion of American ships from the British West Indies.
After the return of peace in 1815 the British Government
made it clear that the exclusion of American vessels from the
West Indies was to be more strictly enforced than it had been
during most of the period of the Anglo-French wars (1793-
1815). West India governors were no longer to be permitted
to open the ports of their colonies to American vessels for
reasons of emergency, and American diplomatic efforts to
put trade between the United States and the British West
Indies on a new basis failed. In 1818 the United States resorted to full-blooded retaliation. Congress passed a navigation act closing the ports of the United States to British
vessels arriving from a colony that was closed to American
vessels, and British vessels sailing with cargoes from American ports were put under bond not to land them in any
colony closed to American ships. 'A non-intercourse in
British vessels was thus established with ports closed by
British laws against American ships.' [76] In 1820 Congress
passed a still more drastic navigation act. Indirect trade
between the United States and the British West Indies was
carried on by way of the Dutch, Danish, and Swedish islands,
but it involved a great rise in the price of imports in the
British islands and a fall in the price of their exports. It is

not surprising that the British West India planters protested against the British restrictions which had led to the American retaliation, nor that the West India assemblies called loudly for relief. The British Government decided that the time had come to relax the navigation laws in the interest of the West Indies.[77]

Robinson's act permitted the importation into designated free ports in the British colonies in America and the West Indies of specified articles (including grain, flour, vegetables, livestock, lumber, and naval stores) produced in foreign countries or colonies in America and the West Indies in ships of the producing country or colony as well as in British ships, and the exportation from those ports in such foreign ships, directly to the country or colony to which the ship belonged, of any articles produced in any of the dominions of the British crown or of any other articles which had been legally imported into those ports. The shipping of the United States was thus given an exceptional position in trade with the British colonies in the western hemisphere, since the privilege of importation into those colonies in ships of the producing country had not yet been extended to the products of foreign countries outside the western hemisphere, and though it was nominally conceded to all foreign countries in America, the United States was the only one of them which possessed any considerable merchant shipping. It was foreseen that trade between the British North American colonies, especially the Maritime Provinces, and the British West Indies would be affected by the admission of United States shipping to the West India ports, and it seemed only fair that Nova Scotia, New Brunswick, and the Canadas should be given a moderate degree of protection against competition from the United States. The act, accordingly, imposed duties on foreign commodities imported at the free ports, whether imported in British or foreign vessels. The free ports in the Maritime Provinces, however, lost the position they had held as entrepôts in indirect trade between the United States and the British West Indies.[78] It was not intended to allow privileges to the shipping of foreign countries which were not prepared to respond reciprocally, and the act therefore authorized the making of orders in council to prohibit trade with any foreign country or colony in America or the West Indies in which British ships did not enjoy reciprocal privileges.

Unfortunately, new friction arose between Great Britain and the United States over the West India trade. Robinson's act, as has just been said, laid duties upon foreign goods imported into the British colonies in America and the West Indies, but it provided that no discriminating duties should be imposed on foreign ships or the goods imported in them. In the United States, however, there were discriminating duties on foreign vessels and their cargoes, and these duties were not removed. On the contrary, Congress passed an act in 1823 which provided, in effect, that they should be maintained unless and until products of the United States carried in vessels of the United States were admitted to the colonial ports on the same terms as the like products of the United Kingdom or other parts of the British Empire. Huskisson declared this to be 'a pretension unheard of in the commercial relations of independent states,' as unreasonable, he said, as it would be on Britain's part 'to require that sugar or rum from our West India Islands should be admitted at New York upon the same terms and duties as the like articles, the growth and production of Louisiana . . .'[79] The British Government did not go to the length of prohibiting trade between the British colonies and the United States, as it was authorized to do, but a retaliatory tonnage duty was levied by order in council on American ships entering the colonial ports.[80] American and British vessels could now trade between the United States and the British colonies, but they were subject to mutual discriminations. Diplomatic negotiations failed to achieve a happier solution, and by an order in council of 27 July 1826, American ships were excluded from the British West Indies. Retaliation followed, and the ports of the United States were closed to British vessels coming from any of the British colonies in America or the West Indies. Direct trade between the United States and the British West Indies was thus totally prohibited. There was considerable indirect trade, however, by way of the foreign West India islands, and the value of American exports to the West Indies in general fell off only slightly following the British order in council of 1826, but there was a decided decline in the American tonnage engaged in the West India trade. This question played a part in the American election of 1828, which brought Andrew Jackson to the presidency, and it was during his administration that the issue was finally resolved. British ships and their cargoes coming from the British colonies were admitted to the United States without payment of discriminating duties, and American ships were permitted to import almost all products of the United States into the free ports in the British colonies on the same terms and to export British colonial produce to any country outside the British Empire. Foreign goods imported into the British colonies continued to be subject to duties, irrespective of the nationality of the ship in which they were carried, as was the case with foreign goods imported into the United States. In the negotiations leading up to what Americans called the 'Reciprocity of 1830' both sides receded from positions which they had previously taken, and the result was a compromise. 'Broad-minded common sense on each side of the Atlantic had at length prevailed to remove a disagreement which had been an irritating source of suspicion and jealousy between the two countries for almost a half-century.' [81]

To return to the five acts of 1822, the last of them regulated trade 'between His Majesty's Possessions in America and the West Indies and other Parts of the World.' [82] Here the principle of confining the trade of the colonies to British shipping was adhered to; the privilege of importing foreign goods into the British colonies in the western hemisphere in ships of the producing country was not extended to the products of foreign countries outside the western hemisphere. Other restrictions on colonial exports and imports, however, were abolished or drastically altered. The rule that 'enumerated articles' produced in the colonies must not be exported directly to places outside the Empire, a basic principle of the old colonial system ever since the Navigation Act of 1660, was now abandoned. Henceforth all products of the British colonies in America and the West Indies and all commodities that had been legally imported into them could be exported directly to any foreign port in Europe or Africa. Significant also as a departure from long-established policy was another provision of this act, which permitted British ships to export from foreign ports in Europe or Africa directly to any British colony in America or the West Indies a considerable number of specified commodities. The list, however, did not include any of the more important manufactured goods produced in Great Britain, and duties were imposed upon foreign goods when imported at the colonial ports.

The significance of the commercial reforms of 1822 was not lost on contemporaries. Their importance was said to be 'vast beyond all question, not only from the direct effect of their enactments, but from the nature of the system, of which they mark the commencement; this being the first instance in which practical statesmen have professed to act under the more liberal principles of political economy.' [83] Government and Parliament were actuated by various motives, of which the desire to relieve commercial distress by extending British trade and enlarging the markets for British industry was the most immediate. But the innovations of 1822 were not thought of as temporary palliatives to meet a transient emergency. They were looked upon as the beginnings of a new commercial system.

*

*   *

In the reshuffling of ministerial portfolios by Lord Liverpool in 1822-3, Robinson became Chancellor of the Exchequer, and Huskisson succeeded him as President of the Board of Trade, in which office he served from March 1823 to August 1827. A member of Parliament for more than twenty-five years, Huskisson had held various offices, though none of Cabinet rank, and had long been recognized as an authority on finance, currency, and trade. Canning, of whom he was a political follower, called him 'the best practical man of business in England.' Huskisson was distrustful of doctrinaire projects of reform and believed that it was the part of statesmanship to exercise caution in the application of

general theories; and like Adam Smith and all patriotic
Britons, he would never sacrifice defense to opulence. In
cases where the interests of trade and of navigation could
not be reconciled, he believed that the latter should be paramount. At the same time he was convinced that restrictions
and prohibitions alone could not maintain a large mercantile
marine. Its only durable foundation lay in an extensive commerce, and the history of commerce, as he read it, demonstrated the wisdom of economic liberalism:

whenever you give a free scope to capital, to industry, to the
stirring intelligence and active spirit of adventure, which so
strongly mark the present times, you are in fact opening new
roads to enterprise, and affording new* facilities to the interchange of the productions of the different regions of the earth
. . . an open trade, especially to a rich and thriving country, is
infinitely more valuable than any monopoly, however exclusive,
which the public power of the State may be able, either to enforce against its own Colonial dominions, or to establish in its
intercourse with other parts of the world.[84]

Huskisson often used the term 'free trade,' but like others
of his day he did not mean by it the absence of all protecting
duties. On the contrary, his name is associated with the system of imperial preference, which is incompatible with thorough-going free trade. He meant the absence of prohibitions
and prohibitory duties, which, he once said, 'are a premium
to mediocrity . . . destroy the best incentive to excellence,
the best stimulus to invention and improvement . . . con-
demn the community to suffer, both in price and quality,
all the evils of monopoly, except in as far as a remedy can
be found in the baneful arts of the smuggler.' [85] He looked
to Spain as the best illustration of the effects of the prohibitory system—

the most perfect model of fallen greatness and of internal misery, of which modern civilization affords an example—an example to be traced not only in the annihilation of her commerce and maritime power, but in her scanty revenue, in her bankrupt resources, in the wretchedness of her population, and in her utter insignificance among the great powers of the world. The commercial policy of Spain is simply this—to admit nothing from other countries—except what the smuggler brings in.[86]

At the Board of Trade Huskisson continued and enlarged upon the work of Wallace and Robinson, to whom he gave full credit, and the measures which he carried through won for him a high place among the reforming British ministers of the nineteenth century.[87] Years after his death he was referred to as an oracle of economic wisdom second only to Adam Smith and an incarnation of far-sighted statesmanship. Huskisson himself spoke of the reforms of the 1820's as a return to the commercial liberalism of Pitt in the years before the French Revolution. In commercial reform Huskisson's name is associated particularly with three general policies—the abolition of the prohibitory system, the establishment of international reciprocity, and imperial preference. His reforms in colonial commerce, which embodied these principles, came in 1825, but he had already applied two of them to the foreign trade of the United Kingdom.

The earliest of his measures of reciprocity was an important reform in the old navigation system, though it did not directly affect the colonial system. This was the Reciprocity of Duties Act, which became law in 1823.[88] The use of alien duties as a means of encouraging English shipping goes back to the sixteenth century. These were additional duties imposed on goods when imported into England in foreign vessels. Similarly, in many cases, smaller drawbacks were allowed on goods when re-exported in foreign vessels. It goes without saying that foreign countries which were building up mercantile marines of their own would resent these discriminations against their shipping. The United States was the first to retaliate effectively, imposing alien duties and discriminating tonnage duties on foreign ships as well. A reciprocity treaty was finally negotiated in 1815 whereby, in the direct trade between the United States and the United Kingdom, alien duties on imports in each other's ships and discriminating tonnage duties on the vessels were reciprocally removed. A similar treaty was later made between Great Britain and Portugal. In 1821 the Netherlands gave Britain a blunt warning by granting a premium of 10 per cent on all goods imported in Netherlands vessels, which was equivalent to imposing alien duties on imports in foreign ships; and Prussia took retaliatory action. In such a situation, Huskisson declared, Britain must either embark on commercial warfare or else adopt the policy of reciprocal equality of shipping duties. Resolutions which he introduced, and which were agreed to by the House of Commons without a division, were the basis of an act authorizing the making of orders in council permitting the importation and exportation of goods in foreign vessels on the same terms as in British vessels, provided the country to which the vessel belonged gave reciprocal treatment to goods imported and exported in British vessels. By the same authority additonal duties might be levied on imports in the ships of any foreign country that discriminated against British shipping. In order to secure the object in view, reciprocity treaties had to be concluded with foreign countries, and such treaties were entered into with all the important European countries and with several of the new republics of Spanish America.[89] It is not to be supposed that Huskisson was motivated in this or in any of his other commercial reforms primarily by a spirit of abstract altruism or devotion to the theory of free trade. He was first and foremost an Englishman, and enlightened national self-interest was the mainspring of his policy. In common with Ricardo and other economists, he believed that his own country would gain even more than others from the adoption of more liberal commercial principles, for 'those who had the largest trade must necessarily derive the greatest advantage from a better international regulation.' [90] In defending the Reciprocity of Duties Act a few years later, Huskisson made it clear that his commercial liberalism had been inspired in great part by the fear of foreign retaliation.

If the system of discriminating Duties for the encouragement of Shipping were a secret known to this country alone; if a similar system were not, or could not be, put in force in every other country, I should not be standing here to vindicate the measure to which I have just referred, and the present policy of his Majesty's Government. So long as, in fact, no independent trading community existed out of Europe, and so long as the old Governments of Europe looked upon these matters,—if they looked to them at all,—as little deserving their attention and were content, either from ignorance or indifference, not to thwart our System, it would have been wrong to disturb any part of it.[91]

In 1824 Huskisson struck what he intended as a body blow at the prohibitory system by carrying the repeal of existing prohibitions on the importation of silk manufactures, substituting therefor *ad valorem* duties, and reducing the duty on raw silk.[92] The silk industry in England had long been a special object of governmental solicitude and favor, and foreign competition in the British market had been totally prohibited by law, though smuggling on a great scale flourished notoriously. Huskisson believed that this evil was directly attributable to the prohibition and would disappear with it. Here, however, events did not justify his hope. An official of the Board of Trade later testified that nearly one-half of the French silk goods imported during the year after Huskisson's reform was smuggled.[93] But it seems probable that improvements in the English silk industry were largely due to the manufacturers' anticipations of foreign competition. Other measures passed in the same year removed other prohibitions, notably the repeal of the laws prohibiting combinations among workmen and forbidding their emigration.[94]

The most comprehensive of the commercial reforms with which Huskisson was associated were effected by a series of laws passed in 1825. In that year a fresh start was made in commercial legislation. All existing laws relating to the customs and navigation—six or seven hundred acts of Parliament, Huskisson said—were swept from the statute book,[95] a new navigation act was passed,[96] and what amounted to a new customs code was created by acts levying new duties in lieu of those previously in force and providing for the management and regulation of the customs, for the prevention of smuggling, for the registration of British vessels, for the warehousing of goods, for the granting of bounties on the exportation of certain goods from the United Kingdom, and for regulating the trade of the British possessions.[97] The task involved in revising, simplifying, and consolidating the laws relating to the customs was one of great magnitude and difficulty. Huskisson later stated that 'there were no fewer than five hundred statutes, relative to the Customs alone, to wade through.' The immense amount of necessary laborious detail fell mainly to customs officials, notably James Deacon Hume,

Comptroller of Customs in London, who prepared a convenient compilation of all the new laws relating to the customs, navigation, smuggling, warehousing, and colonial trade. Since customs duties affected trade and were levied for purposes of protection as well as of revenue, the Board of Trade, as well as the Treasury, was directly concerned in customs reform, and Huskisson collaborated effectively with his colleague the Chancellor of the Exchequer, 'Prosperity' Robinson as he was nicknamed. 'Robinson's task was to safeguard a sufficient revenue; Huskisson's, to rejuvenate industry.' [98] The President of the Board of Trade did not spare himself. 'No individual, he believed, who had filled his situation had ever become engaged in a more extensive correspondence than himself, or had received more numerous deputations, or had been a party at more conferences than he had met at the Board of Trade since these alterations [in customs duties] were first announced in Parliament.' [99]

That announcement was made by Huskisson in a perspicacious and luminous speech in the House of Commons on 25 March 1825,[100] in which he proposed to abolish prohibitions and reduce excessive protective duties on the importation of manufactured articles and to lower duties on raw materials used in manufacturing. From these changes he anticipated many beneficial results: increase of revenue, decrease of smuggling, benefit to consumers, improvement in Britain's relations with foreign countries, which would eventually follow her example of commercial liberalism, and invigoration of British industry no longer deprived by an artificial monopoly of the vitalizing stimulus of competition. He adopted it as a general rule that duties imposed to protect British manufactures ought never to exceed 30 per cent. Existing colonial preferences, in general, were continued in the tariff of 1825, the principal colonial products that received favored treatment being chocolate and cocoa, cinnamon, cloves, cochineal, cocoanuts, coffee, ginger, hemp, hides, bar and pig iron, molasses, pepper, pitch, rice, rum, sugar, tar, timber, and wool. Duties on imported grain were imposed by the corn laws and were not included in the general tariff. In some cases preferences were not uniform for all parts of the Empire. Sugar grown in British possessions in the East, for example, was charged with a duty of 10s. a hundredweight above that paid by British West India sugar. An exception, however, was made by a special act of 1825 in favor of Mauritius; this provided that all produce of that island should be admitted to the United Kingdom on the same terms as the like produce of the British West Indies.[101]

In another parliamentary speech, also delivered in March 1825, Huskisson outlined his policy with regard to the trade of the colonies.[102] He spoke of the 'almost general revolution' in the world's colonial commerce which had taken place as a result of the independence of the United States and the Latin-American countries and referred to what had already been done in the way of relaxing old restrictions in the British colonial system. This work he proposed to carry further. In 1822 the United States had been permitted to carry on a limited trade in its own ships with the British colonies in the western hemisphere, and he saw no reason for withholding this privilege from foreign countries in general. He would go even further and allow, on a basis of reciprocity, the ships of any foreign country to import any products of the country to which the ship belonged (with a very few exceptions) into any British colonial possessions and to export therefrom any articles of their growth or production to any part of the world except the United Kingdom and its dependencies. Trade within the British Empire would continue to be reserved to British shipping. 'Are we,' he asked, 'more jealous of the navigation of Denmark, Sweden, Prussia, Holland, or the Hanse Towns, than that of the United States? . . . Is it fair or politic to grant to the one what we withhold from the other?' He believed that the prosperity of the colonies was cramped by the existing restrictions on their trade and declared that 'whatever tends to increase the prosperity of the Colonies cannot fail, in the long run, to advance, in an equal degree, the general interests of the Parent State.' The West India planters, he thought, would be materially benefited by the admission of foreign shipping, both in supplying the needs of their plantations on reasonable terms and in disposing of their produce; and he hoped that under a more liberal commercial system the British colonies on the continent of North America would feel no desire to part company with their mother country. At a time when pessimism regarding the Empire was rife in England and the doctrine of separatism was openly proclaimed, Huskisson took his stand as a liberal imperialist.

At any rate [he said], let us, as the parent state, fulfil our duties with all proper kindness and liberality. This is true wisdom; affording us, on the one hand, the best chance of perpetuating a solid and useful connexion, and on the other, the best hope if (which God avert!) in the progress of human events, that connexion is ever to be dissolved, that the separation may not be embittered by acrimony and bloodshed; and the certain consolation that, however brought about, it will not have been hastened or provoked by vexatious interference or oppressive pretensions on our part.

Huskisson's advocacy of commercial liberalism in colonial policy was no doubt strengthened by his interpretation of the American Revolution. He took issue with those who attributed the Revolution primarily to British taxation and saw in commercial restriction its principal cause. In a later speech he said:

It is generally believed, that the attempt to tax our American colonies, without their consent, was the sole cause of the separation of those Colonies from the mother country. But, if the whole history of the period between the year 1763 and the year 1773 be attentively examined, it will, I think, be abundantly evident, that, however the attempt at taxation may have contributed somewhat to hasten the explosion, the train had been long laid, in the severe and exasperating efforts of this country to enforce, with inopportune and increasing vigour, the strictest and most annoying regulations of our Commercial and Navigation Code. Every petty adventure in which the colonists embarked was viewed, by the merchants of this country, and the Board of Trade of that day, as an encroachment on the commercial monopoly of Great Britain.[103]

Huskisson's interpretation of the Revolution was shared by political economists and became that of the free-trade school in general.

The changes in the regulation of colonial trade which Huskisson proposed were embodied in acts passed in 1825—a navigation act and possessions acts to regulate the trade of the British colonial possessions.[104] Under these new laws the ships of foreign countries in general were allowed to import into any of the British possessions in Asia, Africa, or America the products of their respective countries, directly from those countries, and to export goods from those posssessions to any non-British country. This privilege, however, was limited to the ships of countries that granted reciprocal privileges to British ships, or, in the case of countries that had no colonial possessions, placed British commerce and navigation on the footing of the most favored nation, unless it should seem expedient to grant the privilege without a *quid pro quo,* in which event this could be done by order in council. Under this legislation reciprocity treaties were concluded during the ensuing years with most of the important shipping countries, and the vessels of those countries were duly admitted to trade with the colonies by orders in council.[105] In the case of the British colonial possessions in America and the West Indies, trade with foreign countries (both in British and in foreign ships) was confined to designated free ports, but the free-port system was not extended to Britain's possessions outside the western hemisphere. A tariff of duties on foreign goods imported into the British colonies in America and the West Indies and the island of Mauritius was set up, but it did not apply to other British possessions.[106] Duties were specified on a considerable list of goods, and there were a few express prohibitions and exceptional restrictions on importation. All goods not enumerated were charged with duties of 15 per cent *ad valorem.* In accord with the principle laid down in the Renunciation Act of 1778, namely, that Parliament would not in the future levy taxes on the colonies for revenue, the object of these duties was protective, not fiscal, and the revenue arising from them was controlled by the colonial legislatures. The object in view, as explained by Huskisson, was to give British products, especially manufactured articles, moderate protection in the colonial markets.

There was now a bilateral imperial preferential system. From the beginnings of the colonial system in the seventeenth century, Parliament, as we have seen, had given tariff preferences to various colonial products imported into the mother country. It now gave tariff preferences on a wider scale to British goods imported into the British colonies in the western hemisphere and the island of Mauritius. The new imperial duties were in addition to the low duties imposed on imports by the colonial legislatures for local revenue purposes. These latter did not discriminate between goods imported from the United Kingdom and other parts of the Empire and goods imported from foreign countries, and they were not supposed to serve any protective purpose, though in some cases, they may have given a measure of encouragement to local colonial production.

Unfortunately for Britain, and for Huskisson's peace of mind, the commercial reforms of 1825 were quickly followed by a financial crash. By 1823 the long post-war depression had drawn to a close. At the end of the parliamentary session of that year attention was called to 'the flourishing condition of all branches of our commerce and manufactures,' and at the opening of the session of 1824 the King's Speech contained these hopeful statements: 'Trade and commerce are extending themselves both at home and abroad. An increasing activity pervades almost every branch of manufacture. Agriculture is recovering from the depression under which it laboured.' [107] The country entered upon a short period of extraordinary, and unhealthy, boom. Commodity prices rose, the interest rate was low, credit was obtained on inadequate security, many new commercial companies were formed, stocks advanced to astonishing heights, and a mania of speculation swept over the land. The stage was set for a crash, and it came in the closing months of 1825. The failure of country banks led to a financial panic, which reached its height in December, when great London banking houses were forced to close. Charles Greville noted in his Diary: 'The state of the City, and the terror of all the Bankers and Merchants, as well as of all owners of property, is not to be conceived but by those who witnessed it.' [108] The Government correctly attributed the economic malady to the preceding frenzy of speculation, and for this the existing banking and currency system had been in large part responsible.[109] Many people, however, and especially the champions of those interests which conceived themselves to have been injured by the recent commercial changes, professed to see in the new-fangled 'free trade' policies which Parliament had adopted, the cause of the general suffering.

Huskisson, who was the main target of attack and abuse, ably defended the measures for which he had been responsible, notably in speeches on the silk industry, on navigation, and on shipping.[110] On the basis of official accounts of shipping and tonnage he had no difficulty in disposing of the assumption of the shipping interest that there was an alarming decrease in British shipping and a corresponding increase in foreign shipping in the trade of the United Kingdom. For example, in a petition from workmen connected with the Port of London the existing distress was contrasted with full employment and prosperity in 1825 and was attributed to a great influx of foreign shipping alleged to have taken place in 1826. Huskisson showed that the foreign tonnage entering London amounted to 302,122 tons in 1825 and only 215,254 in 1826.[111] His opinion was that 'there would have been a much greater . . . degree of distress among Ship-owners, if those alterations had not been made in our commercial policy, of which they short-sightedly complain; and it would have been better for their relief, if they had been adopted at an earlier period after the restoration of peace.' [112] The shipping interests failed to make a convincing case for measures of relief, and their parliamentary spokesmen were unable to secure the appointment of a committee to inquire into their alleged distress. The shipowners' predictions of ruin were not borne out by events. During the next twenty years British tonnage not only increased greatly, but the percentage of its increase was greater in trade with foreign countries, in which it was exposed to competition with foreign shipping, than in intra-imperial trade, where it still possessed a monopoly. Other factors than changes in legislation played their part, no doubt, in bringing about this increase, but it can at least be said that these changes did not prevent it.

*

*   *

Huskisson thought of the reforms we have been considering as drastic, though not revolutionary. Commenting upon the modifications he had proposed in colonial trade in 1825, he said: 'It is not to be dissembled, that this is a great change in our Colonial System.' [113] Opponents accused him of being a doctrinaire innovator, pursuing abstract theories without regard to consequences. To his more thorough-going free-trade contemporaries, on the other hand, his reforms seemed extremely moderate, and in the light of experience they soon came to be regarded by them as inadequate and ineffectual.

This was the view taken by Sir Henry Parnell, a free-trade member of Parliament. In a book, *On Financial Reform*, published in 1830, Parnell said: 'If free trade . . . is the right policy, the work of introducing it still remains to be done.' [114] He concluded from trade statistics that the tariff changes of 1825 had had very little effect in increasing the importation of foreign manufactures into the United Kingdom, and he asserted that the measures of 1822 and 1825 regarding colonial trade had completely failed in their purpose —'in point of fact, they have had no kind of effect in making the trade of the colonies more free than it was before.' [115] He stated that the imperial duties on foreign manufactures imported into the colonies were virtually prohibitory, and that the attempt to free colonial trade and at the same time give the British manufacturer protection in the colonial market must inevitably fail. He favored the total removal of protection and with it, of course, the abolition of the entire bilateral preferential system. So long as the colonists were compelled to obtain their manufactured goods from Britain, they were entitled to demand preference for their products in her market, 'but when we shall relieve them from all vexatious restraints, and allow them to resort to all the markets of the world, they will have no longer any claim to the monopoly of the British market.' [116] In predicting that British manufacturers, because they were able to produce more cheaply than foreigners, would continue to supply the colonists with most of the manufactured goods they needed, even though the protecting duties in the colonies were removed, Parnell expressed a belief that was in the minds of all British free-traders who were interested in colonial commerce. What he neglected to point out was that the colonial producers would not find themselves in a like happy state in the British market if they were deprived of their preferences. Continental European manufactures, generally speaking, could not compete in the colonial markets with British manufactures, but Cuban and Brazilian sugar could compete —and all too successfully—with Jamaica sugar in the British market.

Fifteen years after Huskisson's reforms a committee of the House of Commons was appointed to conduct an inquiry into the British tariff. It was predominantly a free-trade committee, the radical free-trader Joseph Hume was its chairman, and the most influential evidence was given by free-trade witnesses. The committee reported that the tariff exhibited a lack of consistency and aimed in many instances at incompatible objects, that as a whole it was highly protective, and that some of the duties were in fact prohibitory.[117] They declared emphatically that the success of British manufactures was not to be attributed to the exclusion of foreign competition, remarked that the existence of protection in Britain was always used by foreign countries as justification for protective legislation of their own against British manufactures, and voiced the hopeful belief, held by all British free traders, that other countries would follow Britain's example if she adopted a more liberal tariff policy. The committee recommended that the whole protective system be reconsidered and changes made in such manner that existing interests might suffer as little as possible in 'the transition to a more liberal and equitable state of things.'

The testimony of witnesses indicated the existence of considerable discontent in the colonies with the working of Huskisson's colonial system. Mr. MacGregor, a secretary of the Board of Trade, told the committee that the limitation of imports from foreign countries to the free ports in the colonies often worked great economic hardship; in some cases the expenses involved in landing cargoes at the free ports and relading for transportation to other ports nearly doubled freight charges. The imperial duties, according to this witness, were another cause of colonial discontent since they increased the cost of living, especially in the West Indies. A case in point was the duty on salted beef and pork, which was intended to give protection in the West Indies to producers in the United Kingdom and the British North American colonies. In Hamburg and Bremen the prices of these provisions were only about one-half of the British prices, and large quantities were imported from those cities. Other witnesses before the committee were G. R. Porter, head of the statistical department of the Board of Trade, who looked upon all protective duties as wrong in principle, and James Deacon Hume, who was in favor of abolishing the whole protective system without regard to what other countries might do and 'without even asking them.' [118]

The report of this Committee on Import Duties seems to have had little immediate effect. But another era of commercial change was approaching, and in this the radical reforms advocated by the committee were carried out.

IV

THE FALL OF THE PREFERENTIAL SYSTEM

THE old colonial system on its commercial side was modified, as we have seen, during the third decade of the nineteenth century, but it did not come to an end until the triumph of free trade a generation later. 'The Colonial System,' Richard Cobden said in 1842, 'with all its dazzling appeals to the passions of the people, can never be got rid of except by the indirect process of free trade, which will gradually and imperceptibly loosen the bonds which unite our colonies to us by a mistaken notion of self-interest.' [1] In the present chapter we shall see how the process of free trade swept away the preferential system.

There were, as has been pointed out in the preceding chapter, two sides of imperial preference as it existed in the early nineteenth century: there was discrimination in favor of colonial as against foreign products in the mother country, and there was discrimination in favor of British (and British colonial) as against foreign products in the colonies. These were regarded as two parts of a single system which must stand or fall together.[2] In the British tariff, preference to colonial products had originally been given to the 'enumerated articles,' those colonial products whose exportation from the colonies to foreign countries was prohibited, the preference being intended partly as compensation to colonial producers for the prohibition; but it was applied to other colonial products, and it was retained and extended after the principle of enumeration was abandoned in 1822. In 1840 there were more than eighty articles in the British tariff schedules upon which differential duties were levied in favor of the produce of the colonies.[3] These duties, of course, had the effect of increasing the prices to British consumers of the commodities on which they were imposed.[4]

The duties the British Parliament levied on foreign goods imported into the colonies applied to the colonies in America and the West Indies and to Mauritius. In the case of the British colonies in the Mediterranean, Africa, and the East (except Mauritius), authority to levy import duties was given to the king in council. In the Australasian colonies there were no imperial duties, but the legislative authorities of New South Wales and Van Dieman's Land were authorized to lay duties of not more than 15 per cent on foreign goods.[5] In 1850 the Australian colonies were given power to impose such duties as they might see fit on imports, British and foreign alike, but they were not permitted to levy differential duties till 1873. The colonies, generally speaking, had local customs duties of their own, and in most cases these formed the largest item of their revenue.[6] The theory was that the colonial duties were for revenue only, and the imperial duties for the regulation of commerce, but in fact the former did not always aim exclusively at revenue. In some cases, colonial tariffs discriminated against foreign countries, and even between different parts of the Empire.[7]

*

* . *

Sir Robert Peel never fully accepted the views of some of his free-trade contemporaries on imperial questions. Though he came to be deeply influenced by the free-trade doctrines of the Manchester School, he was not prepared to carry them out literally at the expense of the integrity of the British Empire. He was never a 'Little Englander' in the sense in which the term may be applied to Cobden or Bright. He was a reformer on the instalment plan, disinclined to push theories to their logical limit. Nevertheless some of his commercial measures did strike directly at the foundations of the British imperial system, and in the ranks of those who supported him in the great battle of the corn laws were not a few who actually looked forward to the dissolution of the Empire as one of the beneficent results of free trade.

Peel's tariff of 1842 reduced the duties upon many imports, and it has generally been spoken of as a free-trade measure. Yet it not only retained but extended colonial preference.[8] In arguing against that feature of it, Lord Howick (afterwards Earl Grey), a free-trade Whig, asserted that the Government was proposing to carry preference 'to an extent never yet contemplated.'[9] It was agreed by most of those who took part in the parliamentary debates on this tariff that the preferential system was essential to the preservation of the Empire. In opposing a resolution against its extension Peel gave expression to this view. He asked:

What is the principle for which the noble Lord contends? The principle is this: that you shall treat your colonies without discrimination, as foreign countries in this respect . . . If that principle be correct there is an end of your colonial system . . . If you sanction this proposition, then you ought also to say, let the colonies assert their own independence, and provide for their own maintenance.[10]

Preference was upheld by a vote of 281 to 108.[11] The tariff of 1842 embraced some 825 items, and upon no fewer than 375 of them differential duties were levied in favor of the colonies.[12] Thus it is clear that at the beginning of Peel's Ministry the principle of colonial preference was still unshaken in Great Britain. A member of the House of Commons who supported preference said of the act of 1842, 'I approve of all the principles upon which this tariff has been framed: Prohibition repealed, moderate duties substituted, the differential principle extended, and the degrees of protection revised and modified.' [13]

In 1842 important changes were made in the colonial customs. Gladstone, then President of the Board of Trade in Peel's Ministry, in explaining the alterations proposed by the Government, informed the House of Commons that the parliamentary duties then levied upon goods imported into the British colonies in America could not be justified 'either with regard to the interests of the revenues of the colonies themselves, or with regard to the principles laid down by Parliament with respect to its colonial legislation.' He pointed out that in the Asiatic dependencies the protective duties in favor of British manufactures were low, while in the American colonies they were so high as often to be prohibitory. Speaking for the Government, he proposed to abolish all existing parliamentary duties levied on British goods imported into the colonies, chief of which were those on spirits, not because it was undesirable to tax spirits, but on the ground that such taxes were unnecessary, and scarcely compatible with the principle of the Renunciation Act of 1778. As the law then stood, taxes were laid, moreover, upon many foreign products imported into the colonies which did not compete with those of the mother country, and which could not, therefore, be called taxes for the regulation of trade. Gladstone proposed to select those articles which it seemed desirable to tax for the regulation of trade, and to permit the free importation of all others.[14]

The 'possessions act' of 1842 substituted new duties for those previously in force in the colonies and added to the list of exemptions. Upon foreign imports not specifically enumerated or exempted, it lowered the rate of duty to 4 per cent. Colonial legislatures were permitted to lay duties for revenue up to 5 per cent upon British products and upon such foreign goods as were not taxed by the Imperial Parliament. The act provided, however, that if any colony imposed a higher duty upon a British product than was charged upon the foreign product, the imperial duty upon the latter should be increased by the amount of the difference.[15] It thus made important alterations in the colonial customs, but it retained the principle of imperial preference.[16] It is clear, therefore, that at the beginning of Peel's Ministry the preferential system was intact in the colonies as well as in the mother country.

The budget of 1844 involved no such conspicuous changes in taxation as its predecessor of 1842. It is, however, of significance in the subject with which this chapter deals, for it shows a willingness on the part of the Minister who had come to power in 1841 as a protectionist, to relax the preferential system. In the financial statement of 1844 the Chancellor of the Exchequer proposed to remove entirely the duty on foreign wool. The tariff of 1842, while admitting colonial wool duty-free, had imposed a duty of a penny a pound on foreign wool worth one shilling or more, and of a half-penny on foreign wool of less value. Despite warnings from the protectionist benches that Peel and his colleagues were taking a dangerous step in the direction of free trade, the abolition of the tax encountered no formidable resistance in Parliament. Many British wool growers accepted the Government's assurance that it would not prove injurious to them.[17] The interests of the Australian wool-growers, however, were not entirely overlooked in Parliament. Mr. Miles, one of the leading protectionists in the House of Commons, called attention to the extraordinary increase in recent years in the growth of wool in Australia and its importation into the United Kingdom. The quantity imported had increased from 2,493,337 pounds in 1831 to 17,483,783 in 1843—and this, said Mr. Miles, under the slight degree of protection afforded by the low duty on foreign wool. The remission which the Government proposed was small in amount, he admitted, 'but it showed which way the wind blew.' [18] In the House of Lords, the Duke of Richmond, one of England's greatest landlords and flock-masters, predicted serious injury to Australian as well as to British wool, if the Government carried its proposal. Gladstone admitted that the abolition of the duty might have 'a depreciating effect on the price of Australian wool.' But, while conceding the claims of colonies to consideration in the British customs, he held that in this case 'they were trivial as compared with the great value of the change to the manufacturers of wool.' [19] The fact is that the abolition of this duty, like the repeal of the corn laws two years later, was a measure in the interest of British manufacturers and consumers which disregarded immediate colonial interests. It did not, however, have the depressing effect upon Australian wool that had been predicted. John Bright asserted in the House of Commons in 1845 that it was 'unanimously allowed' that the repeal of the duty had injured neither British nor Australian wool growers, and his statement was not challenged.[20]

The preference previously enjoyed by colonial coffee,

while not abolished, was materially reduced in 1844. Under the tariff of 1842 colonial coffee paid 4*d.* a pound upon importation into the United Kingdom, as against 8*d.* paid by foreign coffee. The Government now proposed to lower the latter duty to 6*d.*, leaving a differential duty of only 2*d.* in favor of the colonial product. A free-trade member of the House of Commons, Mr. Ewart, moved to equalize the foreign and colonial duties at 4*d.*, frankly avowing that he was aiming a blow at the entire preferential system. 'He was the enemy of such duties,' he said, 'for they were unsound in principle, and he was satisfied they could not long continue.' He even denied that in the long run preference was of benefit to the colonial planter. It created a temporary prosperity for him, it was true, but it rested upon an insecure foundation that must eventually give way.[21] He found a special reason for advocating cheap coffee in the pleasing expectation he had formed that it would reduce the consumption of spirits and promote sobriety among the working classes. The Chancellor of the Exchequer defended the Government's proposal, on the ground that it would benefit the British consumer and at the same time preserve to the colonial coffee grower a fair degree of protection.[22] Under the operation of the act of 1844, however, the quantity of colonial coffee consumed in the United Kingdom was not diminished, nor was the amount of foreign coffee materially increased.[23]

Substantial modifications were made in 1844 and 1845 in the preference enjoyed by sugar, the most important colonial product. The sugar duties were not included in the general tariff, but were levied annually by separate acts. Until 1844 foreign sugar had been virtually excluded from the British market by prohibitive duties. Prior to the emancipation of the slaves, which took effect in 1834, the West India colonies had been able to do more than supply the British demand. But the effect of emancipation was to reduce the production of sugar in the islands, and, in order to insure an adequate supply for British consumption, Parliament presently lowered the duties on British East India sugar, with the result that large quantities of it were brought into the British market.[24]

Anticipating an increased demand for sugar in the United Kingdom, Peel concluded that a larger supply ought to be made available for home consumption. He was unwilling, however, to permit the importation of foreign sugar cultivated by slave labor, or to leave the British West India planters, who had suffered severely in consequence of emancipation, without a fair degree of protection. He proposed, accordingly, to retain the duty of 24s. per hundredweight on British colonial sugar, and the prohibitive tax of 63s. on foreign slave-grown sugar, but to lower the duty on foreign sugar produced by free labor from 63s. to 34s. He expected that by virtue of this reduction considerable quantities of free-labor sugar would be imported from Java, Manila, and China, whereas the slave-grown sugar of Brazil and Cuba would still be excluded. The Chancellor of the Exchequer, who was in charge of the bill, did not deny that its effect would be to check a rise in the price of sugar in England, but he warned the sugar interests that in the long run the worst evil that could befall them would be a marked advance in the cost of sugar to the English consumer. From the language he used, the West India planters were justified in assuming that the amount of protection which the Government proposed to leave them would not be reduced in the near future.[25]

The proposed alterations in the sugar duties were opposed in the House of Commons for different reasons by free-trade Liberals and protectionist Conservatives. The Liberal leader, Lord John Russell, was in favor of admitting all foreign sugar, whether the produce of free or of slave labor, at 34s. and objected to a differential duty based upon what he called a new principle, the principle of morality in international trade.[26] Mr. Ewart, opposed to differential duties on general principle, desired to see the distinction between colonial and foreign sugar entirely done away with. Mr. Miles, speaking as a staunch protectionist and in behalf of the colonial sugar interests, insisted that the reduced degree of protection contemplated by the Government was insufficient. When the House went into committee on the sugar-duties bill, the opposition that developed was strong enough to defeat the provision lowering the duty on foreign sugar produced by free labor by a vote of 241 to 221. Peel, however, refused to accept amendment, and by what amounted to a threat of resignation he compelled the House to reverse its vote and pass the bill.[27]

Further changes were made in the sugar duties in 1845. The tax on colonial sugar was reduced from 24s. to 14s., and that on foreign free-labor sugar from 34s. to 23s., while the prohibitive tax of 63s. was retained on foreign slave-grown sugar.[28] A resolution to abolish the colonial preference by equalizing the duties on foreign and colonial sugar was supported by some of the free traders, but was decisively beaten by a vote of 217 to 84. The acts of 1844 and 1845 did not greatly increase the consumption of foreign free-labor sugar, and the colonial product still retained a virtual monopoly of the British market.[29]

The preferential system received its first severe shock at

the hands of Peel in his commercial legislation of 1846, especially in the alterations then made in the corn laws and the
timber duties.[30] In the case of the corn laws colonial preference had never been an object of primary importance. Their
main purpose had been the protection of British agriculture
from external competition. When Peel took office in 1841
this policy was still adhered to. The importation of grain
was then regulated by an act passed in 1828, whereby the
duties on foreign cereals were arranged on a sliding scale,
varying inversely with their prices in the British market.
In the case of foreign wheat the act imposed a duty of one
shilling per quarter when the price stood at 73s. or above,
a duty which rose as the price fell, reaching 25s. 8d. when
it was between 61s. and 62s. For every shilling or fraction
thereof by which the price fell below 61s. the duty was increased by one shilling.[31] The average duty on foreign wheat
for the ten years ending in 1841 was 30s. 8d., high enough
virtually to exclude it from the British market.[32]

Though the act of 1828 was a Tory measure, the Whigs
permitted it to stand unaltered during their almost un-
broken tenure of office from 1830 to 1841. Its principal beneficiaries were the landlords, and the Whig party, as has been
said, was a landlord party only one degree less than the Tory.
The conviction was rapidly gaining ground, however, especially among the middle and lower classes, that the social
misery then prevalent, the 'condition-of-England-question,'
as Carlyle called it, was in large measure attributable to the
corn laws; and the propaganda of the Anti-Corn Law League
kept the question of reform constantly in the public mind.

Peel's corn law of 1842 revised the grain duties downward,
but preserved the protective principle and the sliding scale.[33]
Under it the duty on foreign wheat rose from 1s. to 19s. as

the price fell from 73s. to 51s. and remained constant at 20s. for all prices below 51s. For the year 1843 the average price of wheat was 50s. 1d., so that the average duty was 20s. Under the act of 1828 it would have been 36s. 8d.

The legislation that has been described gave preference to colonial grain. Under the act of 1828 colonial wheat paid 5s. when the price was below 67s., and was admitted at a nominal duty of 6d. when it rose above that figure. For the ten-year period ending in 1840 the average duty on colonial wheat was only 5s. Despite this seemingly great preference, however, very little of it was actually imported, and British agriculture enjoyed a substantial monopoly of the home market. How little the preference really benefited the Canadian farmer is shown in a petition adopted by the Assembly of Upper Canada in 1840:

Your Majesty's faithful Commons are aware that the products of these colonies are admitted into the ports of the mother country at a duty of 5s. per quarter, when wheat is below an average of 67s. per quarter, but from the expense of transportation from the interior to the sea, and thence to the United Kingdom, experience proves that they derive very little advantage from this protection.[34]

Under the corn law of 1842 colonial wheat was admitted at uniform duties of 1s. for prices at or above 58s., and 5s. for prices below 55s., while for intermediate prices duties were arranged on a sliding scale. For the year 1843, therefore, the average duty on colonial wheat was 5s., as against 20s. paid by the foreign product.

In that year, however, an extraordinary preference was granted to Canadian wheat and flour. Since 1831 wheat grown in the United States had been admitted into Canada duty-free. Considerable quantities of it had been imported into the province and there manufactured into flour, which was exported to the United Kingdom, where it was admitted at the preferential duty payable on colonial flour.[35] British agricultural interests objected to this indirect importation of foreign wheat in the form of colonial flour, and the 'possessions bill' of 1842, as originally introduced, placed a duty of 3s. on foreign wheat entering Canada. But in Canada the opposition to this provision was so strong that it was dropped from the bill. The Parliament of Canada, however, was anxious to secure the free entry of Canadian wheat and flour into the United Kingdom, and in order to gain this favor it levied a duty of 3s. on foreign wheat entering the province,[36] whereupon the Imperial Parliament admitted Canadian wheat into the United Kingdom at a nominal duty of 1s., irrespective of price, and wheat flour at the duty payable upon the quantity of wheat used in its manufacture.[37] This Canada Corn Law, as it was called, was opposed by a number of agrarian protectionists among Peel's followers, whose fear of Canadian competition was by no means allayed when the Prime Minister assured them that what was intended as a boon to the agriculture of Canada would not prove injurious to that of Great Britain. It was also opposed by some Whig free-traders, who objected to building up new protected interests in the colonies. Lord Howick spoke for this group when he said:

When the act [the corn law of 1842] should be swept away and gathered into that lumber of old, absurd, repealed measures, what would be the position of the Canadian merchant who, by the measure the House was called upon to sanction, had been induced to invest his capital in extensive mills for grinding corn, and in making arrangements for forwarding flour to this country? In his opinion the Canadian would have a very good claim upon the Government of this country for compensation.[38]

Lord Howick's party forgot about compensation to colonial interests when it abolished the preferential system!

The law of 1843 was followed by an increase in the production and exportation of Canadian wheat, in the investment of capital in flour mills, and in the construction of new canals to improve the St. Lawrence waterway, for which an expanding volume of trade was anticipated. From October 1843, when it took effect, to January 1846, 1,462,-260 hundredweight of wheat flour manufactured in Canada was imported into the United Kingdom, more than was admitted from foreign countries and the other British colonies combined from 1842 to the same date.[39] The capital invested in mills and improved transport facilities suffered severely when presently Canadian flour lost its protection in England.[40] No doubt other factors than the Canada Corn Law ought to be taken into account in explaining the developments that followed it,[41] but Canadians generally attributed them to it.

The farmers of Australia, whose only important products were grain and wool, saw no reason why their wheat should not be admitted to the British market on the same terms as that of Canada. Petitions were received from legislatures and governors in Australia asking that the tax on Australian grain be lowered. On 8 May 1845, Mr. Hutt introduced a resolution in the House of Commons for equalizing the duties on Australian and Canadian grain and flour. He called attention to the excellent quality of Australian wheat, and asserted that the great distance of the Australian colonies would not prevent their exporting considerable quantities of grain to England if the duty were reduced. He told the House that Australia viewed the 5s. tax on its wheat as unjust and indefensible, and warned the Government that it was unwise to arouse a sense of injustice in distant colonies. He said:

Up to last year Australian wool had a protection in the British market of 1d. per pound as against foreign wool. You took that protection off last year, in accordance with the principle of sound policy and scientific legislation. The Australians lost their monopoly. They never complained of it. But they do complain, loudly and indignantly complain, that whatever turn you take they are always sacrificed to your policy. You remove the duty from European wool, and tell the Australian farmer that the proceeding is required by the principles of free trade; and then you insist on charging a duty of twenty per cent upon his corn, and justify your conduct on the principle of protection and monopoly. What are the people of our colonies to think of the justice and consistency of the British Government? . . . The right Hon. Baronet [Peel] may probably observe, by and by, a 'cloud' rising in the southern horizon. Do not complain if it be so. You have taught the people of Australia how to ensure attention to their demands; you may some day reap the harvest of your act.[42]

Notwithstanding the evident justice of the Australian demand, the motion was negatived by a vote of 147 to 93.[43]

The disastrous failure of the Irish potato crop in 1845 greatly strengthened, as is well known, the movement for the repeal of the corn laws. In November the Whig leader, Lord John Russell, came out in favor of repeal, and in January 1846 Peel began one of the greatest of all parliamentary battles. The majority of his party looked upon his conversion to free-trade principles as a betrayal and a breach of honor, but he could count on Whig and Radical support. Peel proposed to admit all foreign grain at the nominal duty of 1s. per quarter after 1 February 1849, until which date temporary duties were to be arranged on a new sliding scale. Colonial grain was to be admitted at once at the one-shilling duty.[44] His plan, therefore, contemplated the abolition of the colonial preference in grain at the end of three years.[45]

The preferential feature of the corn laws, as has been said, had been merely incidental; the taxes on grain had not been designed, like the sugar duties, primarily to protect colonial interests. It is not strange, therefore, that in the debates on Peel's great measure comparatively little was said about the colonies or the preferential system. A few members, however, chiefly among the opponents of the bill, did dwell upon its imperial aspects.

The argument that free trade would destroy the colonial system and lead to the dissolution of the Empire was presented most effectively by Lord Stanley (afterwards Lord Derby). He had held the office of Colonial Secretary in Peel's Ministry, but had resigned because he could not agree with his chief on the repeal of the corn laws. 'Destroy this principle of protection,' he said, 'and I tell you in this place that you destroy the whole basis upon which your colonial system rests.' [46] Dissentient peers protested that the corn bill would tend to 'sap the foundations of that colonial system, to which, commercially and politically, this country owes much of its present greatness.' [47]

It was suggested that if the experiment of free trade was to be made, it should have been tried first with the colonies, by extending to all of them the principles of the Canada Corn Law, and preserving colonial preference. Sir Howard Douglas, formerly a colonial governor, and one of the members of Parliament most conversant with colonial questions,

enlarged upon the advantages of complete free trade between the United Kingdom and the colonies, with protection
against foreign countries. He would have been glad to see
the commercial organization of the Empire take the form of
an imperial zollverein.[48]

It was asserted with much force by opponents of the bill
that it broke faith with Canada, that it would injure that
colony severely, and very likely drive it to annexation with
the United States. 'You are going to break the promises held
out to Canada,' said Lord Stanley, referring to the act of
1843. 'I will say nothing of the shock you will give to the
loyalty of the people . . . You are doing your utmost to irri-
tate them by the breach of your engagement . . . political
independence may follow closely upon commercial independence.' [49] In the debate on the third reading of the bill
in the House of Commons, Lord George Bentinck, the
leader of the protectionist Conservatives, referred to dis-
quieting news from Canada and urged that further action
be postponed till full information respecting conditions
there had been received. The Assembly of the province, it
was known, had gone on record as opposed to the new commercial policy of the British Government.[50]

Peel did not propose to alter the preference enjoyed by
British goods in the colonies, but it was not difficult to show
that justice required that this should be done. To quote
Lord Stanley again:

I presume that if you deprive the Colonies of all the protection
they now enjoy, you intend to repeal that Act of Parliament
which compels the Colonies to impose a differential duty in favour of your produce. I can conceive no grosser injustice than
your refusal to do that . . . Protection is mutual—free trade
must be mutual also.[51]

Soon after Peel's resignation, as we shall see, an act was passed empowering the Queen to assent to acts of colonial legislatures to abolish the differential duties in the colonies in favor of Great Britain.

The members of Parliament who supported Peel touched but lightly upon the imperial aspects of his bill. No doubt those of them who privately hailed it as the first step toward the dissolution of the Empire deemed it prudent not to make public their opinions and hopes. Others, however, undertook to refute the charge that it was based upon anti-imperial principles. The Prime Minister himself tried to show that it did not involve the abandonment of preference and would not result in the loss of the colonies. He insisted that discriminating duties would still be left in favor of many articles of colonial production. 'Your colonial relations,' he said, 'are perfectly compatible with the just and cautious application of a liberal policy in the commercial intercourse between the mother country and its dependencies.' [52] Lord John Russell remarked that differential duties did not create the only tie between colony and mother country, and said there was no reason to anticipate the dissolution of the Empire.[53] Earl Grey (formerly Lord Howick) went so far as to assert that free trade would actually strengthen the imperial tie. His conception of empire, however, was radically different from that associated with the old colonial system.[54] What he looked forward to was a co-operative alliance between self-governing colonies and the mother country. He anticipated those later free-trade imperialists who have insisted that free trade was essential to the preservation of the Empire.[55]

Peel's corn bill became law on 26 June 1846, and the preference to colonial grain was thereby put in process of speedy extinction.[56] On the same day a tariff bill received the royal assent.[57] By exempting from duty a large number of imports, including vegetables, meats, and domestic animals, it abolished many differential duties in favor of the colonies. Practically speaking, however, it affected the preferential system principally with respect to timber. In 1821, as explained in the preceding chapter, the duty on foreign timber was reduced to 55s., and a tax of 10s. was levied upon colonial timber.[58] In 1841 the Whig Government proposed to reduce the colonial preference by lowering the foreign and raising the colonial duty, but it did not survive to carry the measure. In his financial statement of 1842, Peel proposed to reduce duties on foreign lumber for the benefit of British consumers, but insisted that it must be done in such a way as not to injure the lumber industry of the British North American colonies.[59] He proposed, accordingly, to reduce the foreign duty from 55s. to 25s. and at the same time virtually to abolish the tax on colonial timber. Despite the opposition of the Canadian lumber interests he persisted in his policy, expressing the conviction that they could continue to compete successfully in the British market with Baltic timber.[60] The tariff of 1842 lowered the duty on foreign timber immediately to 30s., and after 1843 to 25s., while on colonial timber it retained a mere nominal tax of 1s.[61] Thus 24s. became the amount of the differential duty in favor of the colonial product.

The tariff of 1846 materially reduced this preference, providing for the reduction of the tax on foreign timber to 15s. after 1847. The Canadian lumber interests at once took alarm, and their case was pleaded, though unsuccessfully, in Parliament. One member said that if this measure was carried, Canada might as well be presented to the United

States. 'It would appear,' he added, 'that Ministers were actuated almost by hostile feelings towards our colonies.' [62] Lord George Bentinck warned the House not to tamper with Canada's attachment to the mother country.[63] Several protectionists, pointing out the importance of the North American lumber trade to British shipping, predicted serious injury to the latter from the Government's measure.

The gloomy forebodings of men like Lord Stanley and Lord George Bentinck were by no means fantastic. The Canadian press teemed with protests against the repeal of the corn laws and the reduction of the timber duties; local boards of trade remonstrated; threats of separation from the Empire and annexation to the United States were freely and openly made.[64] Lord Elgin, who arrived in Canada at this crisis as Governor General, wrote that among the commercial classes in the colony the conviction was almost universal that it had better be annexed to the United States.[65] In his opinion, however, the proper solution of the Canadian problem was not a restoration of the old system, but a further development of free trade by the repeal of the navigation laws and the extension of commercial intercourse with the United States. But even free-traders admitted that the commercial legislation that has been described entailed grievous wrong upon Canada.

When Peel left office in 1846, many colonial products were still favored by discriminating duties in the British tariff, among the more important being sugar, molasses, spirits, rice, and lumber; and many British products, especially manufactured articles, continued to receive preferential treatment in the colonies by act of Parliament.[66] Nevertheless, the commercial principles upon which Peel acted were ultimately fatal to the whole system of protection, of

which preference was a part; and one after another the remaining protective duties were removed until presently the
triumph of free trade was complete.

Sugar was by far the most important commercial product
of the British colonies, and the English sugar duties, affording the colonies, as they did, a virtual monopoly of the English market, may be said to have formed the keystone in the
arch of imperial preference.[67] When Lord John Russell, the
leader of the Liberal party, succeeded Peel as prime minister, in July 1846, colonial sugar was admitted to the United
Kingdom at a duty of 14s. per hundredweight, and foreign
sugar produced by free labor at 23s., while slave-grown sugar
was excluded by the prohibitory tax of 63s.[68] This exclusion
was defended not only on the score of protecting colonial
interests, but on grounds of justice and humanitarianism
as well. Since Parliament had abolished slavery throughout
the Empire to the grave discomfiture of the West India sugar
planters, it seemed but a measure of justice that it should
assure them protection in the British market from the competition of sugar produced by slave labor. Moreover, it was
contended with much plausibility that the admission of the
slave-grown product would increase the demand for slaves
in foreign sugar-growing countries, and thus give a renewed
impetus to the slave trade, which Great Britain had done so
much to put down. Peel, anxious as he had been to abolish
prohibitory duties and to cheapen food in England, had
never contemplated the admission of slave-grown sugar.[69]

Within a month of his accession to power Lord John Russell, to the dismay of the sugar interests and to the moral
indignation of anti-slavery philanthropists, announced a
plan for the readjustment of the sugar duties upon a new
and permanent basis. He proposed to retain the 14s. duty

on colonial sugar, but to admit all foreign sugar, whether the produce of free or of slave labor, at 21s., and to reduce this latter tax annually until it reached 14s., when the differential in favor of the colonies would disappear.[70] The sugar interests had not stood by the agrarians in the recent contest over the corn laws, and now in their own hour of peril had no claim to the gratitude of the landed interests. The latter, however, had not yet given up hope that the free-trade movement would be checked, and protection restored to British agriculture. Accordingly when the Prime Minister set forth his plan for the settlement of the sugar duties, their leader in the House of Commons, Lord George Bentinck, announced that they would stand by the sugar planters. 'My Friends around me,' he said, 'are determined to support the East and West India interests. They are resolved to support British capital wherever they find it invested.'[71] The protectionists believed that in urging the admission of slave-grown sugar, free trade was exposing its most vulnerable spot, for upon that issue it would antagonize the anti-slavery philanthropists, many of whom on commercial grounds were free-traders. Throughout the debates on the sugar duties they were able to buttress their cause with the moral sanction of humanitarianism.[72] On the other hand, the Government, which depended for its parliamentary majority upon the free-trade conservatives, was supported by most of that group. Peel himself, though still opposed on principle to the admission of slave-grown sugar, voted with the ministers because he was unwilling to drive them from power by combining with the protectionists.[73]

Bentinck opened the attack upon the Government by offering a resolution against the proposed alteration of the sugar duties on the ground that it would 'tend to check the advance of production by British free labor, and to give a great additional stimulus to the slave trade.' [74] A debate extending over two evenings resulted in a victory for ministerialists and Peelites over protectionists and humanitarians by a vote of 265 to 135.[75] The arguments, so far as they related to preference and the imperial system, may be summarized briefly.

The protectionists insisted that the measure was unnecessary because a supply of sugar adequate to the needs of British consumption could be secured without admitting the slave-grown product or abandoning the colonial preference. They ridiculed predictions of a sugar famine. Any deficiency in the West India supply, they asserted, could be more than made good from the East Indies and Mauritius, and production in the West Indies would revive if the planters were assured a sufficient supply of labor.[76] Russell's plan, they reiterated, would ruin the British West Indies, for wage-paid labor could not compete on even terms with slave labor in the production of sugar.[77] One champion of West India interests assured the House that half the plantations in Jamaica would be thrown out of cultivation if the Government's measure were carried.[78] It was freely predicted, moreover, that it would destroy the imperial system and lead to the dissolution of the Empire.[79] According to Lord Ashburton, whose words well expressed the rationale of the old colonial system:

The principle advocated . . . would involve the loss of the colonies. What was the object of colonies at all? There might be parts of the globe, like Malta and Gibraltar, which were kept as points for armaments, or as places of refuge for our naval forces, but all other colonies were preserved for benefit of trading with them, and for the advantage of having a privileged trade with them. The system of reciprocal protection was the system of colonies; and they would cease to be of any value the moment we deprived them entirely of the system of protection.[80]

Dissentient peers gave as one of their reasons for opposing the bill that it 'might occasion such distress and discontent as would ultimately lead to the separation of those very important Colonies, which, when deprived of the protection that is justly due to them, might also lose their allegiance.' [81] Lord Stanley, the leader of the protectionists in the House of Lords, pointed out that the charge of monopoly hurled by the free-traders at the sugar planters could be justified only by a very loose use of that term, since the protection they sought to retain was compatible with the freest competition between the sugar-growing colonies of the West and East Indies and Mauritius.[82] He also remarked that a measure which retained a tax on sugar of 14s., or about 50 per cent *ad valorem,* was far from complete free trade.[83]

The ministers and their supporters, on the other hand, insisted that the admission of slave-grown sugar was necessary in order to lower the price of sugar for the benefit of the working classes at home.[84] Protection as a system of commerce, they triumphantly proclaimed, was doomed. They admitted that the abolition of differential duties struck at the foundations of the old colonial system, but the time had come, they urged, for a new and better colonial system. In words that now sound prophetic, Russell voiced this opinion:

You must adopt an altered, and, as I think, an improved policy. It was the habit of this country . . . to provide that they should have a monopoly of the commerce and productions of the colonists; and that the colonists should be obliged to take, exclusively, the produce and the manufactures of the mother country . . . The colonists, I think, derive great advantage from being connected with this country . . . and this Empire has an immense advantage also in the loyalty, the strength, and the assistance of the colonists. But these colonists must not hereafter exist on the limited and restricted system of former days; that must be acknowledged to be erroneous, and other principles must prevail. I believe that both the mother country and the colonists will flourish all the more for the abolition of useless restrictions, and that after some period of murmuring, perhaps some passing cloud of discontent, we shall acknowledge both in this country and in the magnificent possessions belonging to us, that we have been heretofore mistaken in following the former policy of restriction, and that the affection felt reciprocally will be all the stronger when neither party is subject to any restrictions imposed by the other.[85]

The manufacturers' argument that the admission of slave-grown sugar would enlarge their foreign markets was, of course, not overlooked in a Parliament in which they were so largely represented.[86] Russell's bill became law in August 1846. It gave the British sugar planters five years in which to prepare for the eventual equalization of duties and the abolition of the preference which they had enjoyed ever since the seventeenth century.[87]

Acute distress in the sugar colonies, especially in the West Indies, forced the Government to consider measures for their relief. Free-traders were inclined to ascribe their condition, to some extent at least, to the great commercial and financial crisis of 1847, while protectionists insisted that it was to be explained solely by the recent changes in the sugar duties.[88] Whatever its precise causes, there could be no doubt of its extent and severity, which was revealed by the failures of the great sugar houses in England, and by numerous petitions from the West India interests praying Parliament for relief. In February 1848, upon motion of Lord George Bentinck, a select committee of the House of Commons was appointed to inquire into conditions affecting the sugar and coffee interests, and to consider what measures could be adopted for their relief.[89] Bentinck, who had been laboriously acquiring all available information respecting the effects of the act of 1846 upon British commerce and industry, as well as upon the West Indies, was appointed its chairman, in which capacity he displayed great zeal and energy. He personally expressed the hope that Parliament would be induced to restore protection to colonial sugar, but the majority of the members of the committee were reckoned as free-traders.[90] The committee came to the conclusion that the sugar colonies should be afforded immediate relief, but that the existing distress could not be attributed solely to recent events. One of its principal causes was the lack of an adequate supply of free labor in the West Indies, for which no provision had been made when the slaves were emancipated. The ultimate prosperity of the sugar colonies, so the committee reported, depended upon their means of successful competition with foreign producers, and not upon permanent protection against them. It recommended a differential duty of 10s. in favor of colonial sugar, to last for a period of six years, 'being of opinion that the temporary encouragement would have the effect of preventing the immediate and otherwise inevitable abandonment of the majority of the estates, and secure time for bringing into operation the intended measures of relief.' [91]

The committee presented its report on 29 May 1848, and on 16 June the Prime Minister announced his plan for West India relief. He refused to abandon the principle of the act of 1846, but was prepared to modify its provisions so as to postpone for a few years the date for the equalization of duties.[92] A new act, deferring it to 1854, was accordingly passed. It provided for the annual reduction of the duty on colonial sugar until 1851, when it would reach 10s., where it was to remain fixed. Upon foreign sugar the tax was to be lowered annually until 1854, when it, too, would reach 10s., and the colonial preference would be extinguished.[93] As the day for the termination of their protection drew near, the West India interests petitioned for its continuance, but in his budget speech as Chancellor of the Exchequer in April 1853, Gladstone bluntly served notice on them that it was 'entirely impossible for the Government to hold out the smallest hope that their recommendation can be adopted.' [94] After 1854 no discrimination was made in the British customs between foreign and colonial sugar. The bulwark of colonial preference had fallen before the assaults of free trade.

In 1851 another colonial preference of some importance was abolished. Prior to that year there had been a differential of 2d. a pound in favor of colonial coffee, with the duties at 4d. and 6d. on colonial and foreign coffee respectively. With that degree of protection the quantity of colonial coffee entered for home consumption in the United Kingdom had risen from 23,720,000 pounds in 1846 to 28,832,-000 in 1850, while, during the same period, the importation of foreign coffee had fallen by more than 10,000,000 pounds. In fact, during the year 1850, the gross importation of colonial coffee exceeded the total quantity of coffee, foreign and colonial combined, that was entered for home consumption.[95] This fact was regarded by the Government as affording convincing proof that the differential duty was operating to restrict unduly the importation of foreign coffee to the disadvantage of the British consumer, and that it was no longer needed to protect the colonial planter. Ceylon was the only British possession deeply affected by the proposal to abolish this preference, since coffee planting had almost come to an end in the British West Indies. It was asserted in the House of Commons that Ceylon could not compete in the British market on even terms with the slave-grown coffee of Brazil, but the Government's measure was carried, and a uniform duty of 3*d*. was levied upon colonial and foreign coffee alike.[96]

*

*   *

The British Government could not equitably insist upon maintaining the British preferences in the colonies when it was abolishing colonial preferences in Britain, and when Lord John Russell explained his plan for the readjustment of the sugar duties in 1846, he announced that he intended to bring in a bill to permit the colonies to abolish the existing protective duties in favor of British produce to which they were subject. It was unfair, he said, not to permit the colonists, as well as the people of England, to buy in the cheapest market.[97] Since these duties in the colonies had been imposed by the Imperial Parliament, they could, of course, be removed only by virtue of the same authority. Accordingly, late in the session of 1846, and in a thinly attended House of Commons, a bill was introduced, which applied to the British colonies in America and to Mauritius —and these were the only colonies to which the parliamentary duties extended—empowering the queen by order in council to give her assent to acts of colonial legislatures reducing or repealing protective duties imposed upon their imports from foreign countries by the Imperial Parliament; it provided that such colonial acts should go into operation when the royal assent thereto had been proclaimed in the colony, precisely as if the change had been made directly by the Imperial Parliament. This very important bill passed the House of Commons by a vote of 47 to 8.[98] Its opponents, though negligible in number, did not fail to attack it with vigor, and to show that it involved the repudiation of an essential principle of the imperial system. Bentinck said:

The effect of this bill would be to take away the monopoly that, up to the present time, the manufactures and produce of Great Britain had enjoyed in the British Colonies. It would also altogether overturn the colonial system of this country, which has consisted in defraying colonial expenses by the monopoly of trade which her subjects had enjoyed with the colonies. If the present Bill passed, the first act of the British colonial legislatures would be to do away with all differential duties.[99]

Sir Howard Douglas, formerly governor of New Brunswick, and one of the members of the House most interested in imperial questions, declared that the bill was

a more immediate and portentous confirmation of his apprehensions of the gradual subversion of the colonial system, than he could have expected . . . He had observed on a former occasion, that having converted the Colonies into commercial independence by allowing them to regulate their own commercial affairs . . . it would be a question of time, and of money, how long political connexion would survive commercial independence.[100]

Even among those members who were in favor of abolishing British preference in the colonies there was a disposition to find fault with the bill on the ground that it would lead to commercial confusion within the Empire. Changes in the colonial customs, some of them thought, ought to be made directly and uniformly by the Imperial Parliament, not separately by the several colonial legislatures. They argued that to confer upon the latter the power to tamper with imperial statutes might prove a dangerous precedent.[101] The Government and its followers expressed the hope that all the colonies would seize the opportunity offered them to sweep away protective duties and adopt the new commercial principle of free trade. But the colonies were not compelled to do this, and it could not be denied that the bill might result in disunity in the commercial policy of the Empire.

The intent of the law was not to confer full commercial autonomy upon the colonies. It enabled them to repeal or reduce existing imperial duties, but it gave them no authority to impose protective duties upon British goods, or even new protective duties upon foreign goods. The Prime Minister explicitly stated that 'the whole power which they gave the colonies was to repeal duties already existing; they did not give them any power of enacting differential duties, or of imposing duties on British goods, which they did not at present possess.'[102] The Colonial Secretary, Earl Grey, was equally emphatic on this point. He 'hoped it would not be supposed that, by passing this Bill, they abandoned the right and authority which Parliament always possessed, of regulating the general trade of the colonies and the mother country, in the manner most conducive to the welfare and prosperity of the Empire.'[103] And many years later, in his old age, the veteran free-trader wrote:

When the system of Free Trade was adopted no question had ever been raised as to its being right to maintain this authority of Parliament (though on some occasions the wisdom with which it was exercised was disputed), nor was it imagined by any one

that it was to be relinquished because the new policy of reliev-
ing trade from injurious restrictions was to be adopted. It was,
on the contrary, assumed by all parties as a matter of course
that the commercial policy of the Empire would continue to
regulate as heretofore all measures relating to the trade of the
Colonies.[104]

For several years after 1846, the governors of those colonies
which possessed representative legislatures were instructed to
withhold their assent to bills imposing differential duties.[105]
By the Australian Colonies Constitution Act of 1850 the
colonies of Australia, though authorized to levy duties upon
imports, both foreign and British, were expressly forbidden
to impose differential duties.[106] It was not until 1873 that
they were finally permitted to do so, and then only in order
that they might remit duties upon each other's products.[107]

The colonies to which the act of 1846 applied were not
slow to avail themselves of the permission it gave them. Late
in 1846 Earl Grey wrote to Lord Elgin, recently appointed
Governor General of Canada:

. . . it is of the utmost importance that the Provincial Legislatures should strenuously co-operate with the Imperial Parliament. So far as the repeal of the differential duties hitherto imposed upon Imports into the Colonies from Foreign Countries,
for the purpose of favoring the British producer, I can have no
doubt that the Colonial Legislatures will gladly avail themselves
of the power conferred upon them, by at once putting an end
to these duties.[108]

In the following June, Elgin brought the subject to the
attention of the Canadian legislature,[109] which proceeded to
pass a new provincial tariff. This repealed all imperial duties
in Canada and abolished the distinction in taxation between
British and foreign goods.[110] Similar action was taken by the

legislatures of other colonies,[111] and within a few years British preference in the colonies was a thing of the past.

*

*   *

In 1853 Disraeli, who had succeeded to the leadership of the Conservative party in the House of Commons left vacant by the death of Lord George Bentinck, described all that then remained of the protective system as its 'rags and tatters,' and urged that the principles of free trade be carried out to their full extent.[112] The 'rags and tatters' were disposed of by the tariff acts of 1853 and 1860, and with them disappeared the last vestiges of the preferential system.

In his first budget speech as Chancellor of the Exchequer, in 1853, Gladstone laid down as one of the general rules for tariff revision the abolition of colonial preference wherever possible. He said:

We propose in many instances, where there are at present differential duties in favor of British possessions, to merge those differential duties altogether by lowering the foreign articles to the level of the colonial; but where we are not able to lower the foreign articles to the level of the colonial we have not thought it would be considerate in any case to raise the duty on the colonial article.[113]

The tariff of 1853 abolished differential duties in favor of the colonies on rice, soap, starch, hams, and manufactures of fur, skin, wool, and cotton. It left them upon the following articles only: timber, tallow, butter, cheese, eggs, apples, ginger, licorice, caraway seed, wine, spirits, and manufactures of silk.[114] On other goods the colonies enjoyed no preference.

It was the famous tariff of 1860, the last great reform of the British customs effected by free trade, that finally extinguished colonial preference.[115] Though it grew out of the Cobden Treaty, which had been negotiated with France earlier in the same year, this tariff granted no exclusive commercial privileges to that country; the changes it made in the customs applied to all nations.[116] Nor were they confined to the articles involved in the French treaty.

Of the few remaining differential duties which this act abolished, the most important without doubt were those on timber.[117] Ever since 1842 colonial timber had been admitted at a nominal tax of 1s. per load of 50 cubic feet. The duty on foreign timber had been lowered by successive tariffs to 7s. 6d., where it stood in 1860. The Government now determined to abolish the colonial preference by reducing the foreign duty to one shilling. As on earlier occasions, the British North American timber interests protested vociferously, though in vain.

The funeral oration of imperial preference was pronounced in Parliament by Judge Haliburton, a Nova Scotian by birth, and a vigorous opponent of those forces that were relaxing the bonds of empire.[118] In opposing the equalization of the timber duties, he said:

In former days it was the policy of this country to nurture its colonies . . . the toast drunk on all occasions was 'Ships, colonies, and commerce' . . . now it was 'cotton twist and cotton yarn' . . . In those good old days it was thought necessary to cultivate the Colonies, and, on this principle, that those who begot children were bound to protect and support them . . . every encouragement was given to that forest country to furnish supplies of timber to England at a period when the North of Europe, the only other place that England could get timber from, was . . . closed to this country . . . The matter was one of great injustice, not with respect to the few shillings a ton, but on the tenure of our Colonies . . . He could tell them, from his knowledge of the people of North America, that this measure was cutting the first strand of the cable which connected these provinces with this country.[119]

But to those who predicted irretrievable disaster to the Empire from the abolition of the timber preference, Gladstone was adamant. He said:

I have so often received the most solemn warnings that in consequence of the reduction of the differential duties on foreign timber total and absolute ruin was about to fall on the Colonies of British North America, which are now more flourishing than ever, that it is natural I should have become utterly impervious, and that these threats should not find entrance into my mind.[120]

Free trade could not fail to destroy the old British imperial system, based as it had been upon mercantilist and protectionist principles. Its triumph involved not only the abolition of commercial preference within the Empire, and the repeal of the navigation laws, which took place in 1849 and will be dealt with in the following chapter, but also the withdrawal from the colonies of military forces previously maintained at the expense of the mother country for their defense and police, and the concession to them of wider powers of self-government. Writing in 1853, Earl Grey suggested the relation of free trade to colonial administration and defense:

While it was our policy to maintain a monopoly of the trade of the Colonies, it was necessary for the Home Government to exercise a considerable control over their internal administration, because otherwise this monopoly would certainly have been evaded; . . . the abandonment of that system has removed the necessity for this interference . . . I think it will follow, that when this country no longer attempts either to levy a commercial tribute from the Colonies by a system of restriction, nor to interfere needlessly in their internal affairs, it has a right to expect that they should take upon themselves a larger proportion than heretofore of the expenses incurred for their advantage.[121]

Many of the apostles of the new commercial dispensation, accustomed as they were to identify the Empire with the old imperial system, held, and not unnaturally, that the repudiation of the latter involved ultimately the dissolution of the former. Why, they asked, should Great Britain continue to bear the burdens incident to the possession of colonies, when she derived from them no countervailing benefits? Nor could those who believed that the old system had been sound take much interest in colonies, now that the principles underlying the system had been discarded. In the colonies, too, men began to calculate what benefits they enjoyed by remaining in the Empire and whether these were worth the price of continued political subordination to the mother country. So widespread was the anti-imperial sentiment of the day that Earl Grey, in his book on colonial policy, felt it necessary to explain the grounds for his 'dissent from the views of those who wish to dismember the British Empire by abandoning the Colonies.'

Free trade, it must be admitted, came near to dissolving the British Empire. But it also made possible in time the conception of a new type of empire, in which colonies were to be viewed rather as allies and partners, free to regulate their own affairs to suit themselves, than as dependencies.

THE END OF THE OLD NAVIGATION SYSTEM

THE 'logic' of free trade called for the abolition of protection all around, protection of shipping as well as of agriculture and manufactures. 'I am glad to see y^r bold measure on the Navigation Laws . . . You cannot halt between two opinions. Free trade in all things or general Protection.' So Lord Elgin wrote to Lord Grey,[1] but reform does not necessarily follow a logical pattern, and down to the end of the Peel Ministry the foes of protection in Britain, while enlarging upon the iniquities of the corn laws, had little to say in criticism of the navigation laws.[2] There was good historical precedent for this. The British free-trade movement had from the outset made an exception in favor of British shipping and conceded to it a privileged position. The defense of the island realm depended upon sea power, sea power depended upon a national mercantile marine, British-built, British-owned, and British-manned, and the mercantile marine depended—so it was generally taken for granted—upon the protection given to British shipping by the navigation laws. The great increase in British tonnage since the middle of the seventeenth century was popularly attributed to those laws,[3] and if this was an instance of *post hoc ergo propter hoc* reasoning, as some of the nineteenth-century opponents of the old system argued, their criticism made no wide appeal. 'The Father of Free Trade' himself had spoken words that quickly became classic in eulogy of the Navigation Act of 1660, which in his day had long been venerated as the palladium of British security and cherished as almost a fortieth article of the national faith:

The defence of Great Britain . . . depends very much upon the number of its sailors and shipping. The act of navigation, therefore, very properly endeavours to give the sailors and shipping of Great Britain the monopoly of the trade of their own country, in some cases by absolute prohibitions and in others by heavy burdens upon the shipping of foreign countries . . . The act of navigation is not favourable to foreign commerce, or to the growth of that opulence which can arise from it . . . As defence, however, is of much more importance than opulence, the act of navigation is, perhaps, the wisest of all the commercial regulations of England.[4]

It is true, as we have seen, that the old British navigation system was modified in important respects by legislation passed by Parliament in the 1820's and ensuing reciprocity treaties, but when Peel left office in 1846 British shipping still possessed a legal monopoly of very important branches of British trade and a virtual monopoly of others. The navigation system, if such it can be called, was a product of history, distinctly not a work of art. In this it resembled other historical complexes to which the name of 'system' has been given, the feudal system, for example. The mass of regulations of which it consisted became exceedingly intricate, they were never codified, and by no means all of them could be found in the statutes known as navigation acts. These latter were supplemented and qualified by provisions of other acts (acts relating to the registration of British vessels and British seamen, to the regulation of the customs, to tonnage duties, to the trade of the British colonial possessions, etc.), orders in council, and treaties, and the whole unwieldy jumble exemplified the maxim that there is no rule without an exception. A witness who gave evidence before a parliamentary committee in 1848 admitted that he did not understand the navigation laws and added that there were very few persons who did understand them.[5] In the last days of the old system a critic asserted that it was comprehended only by 'a few official persons and a few inquirers in political economy,' and a modern scholar has questioned whether officials deserved this compliment: 'Foreign secretaries, diplomatic agents, presidents and secretaries of the board of trade, even queen's advocates, were very fallible when the tangled mass of law and treaty had to be interpreted.'[6] Any brief discussion of the old system that aspires to be intelligible can scarcely avoid erring historically on the side of over-simplification.

In 1845 Parliament passed a navigation act,[7] the last, as it turned out, in the long series of statutes for the encouragement of English shipping that began in the fourteenth century. It was a consolidating act and introduced no new principles of policy. It went through both houses of Parliament without debate; no free-trade voices were raised in opposition. An attempt will be made to state the principal provisions of the act in the following paragraphs:

1. Various European products, specifically enumerated, shall not be imported into the United Kingdom, for home consumption, except in British ships, or in 'ships of the country of which the goods are the produce, or in ships of the country from which the goods are imported.' The list includes lumber, hemp, flax, dried fruits, olive oil, grain, wine, and brandy. The restriction on shipping did not apply to European products not enumerated nor to the enumerated products if they were to be warehoused for re-exportation. These could be imported in any ships, and there were

no restrictions on shipping in the case of exports from the United Kingdom to the Continent of Europe.[8]

2. Products of Asia, Africa, or America shall not, with certain exceptions, be imported into the United Kingdom, for home consumption, from the Continent of Europe in any ships, British or foreign. The object of this rule was to secure the long voyages from Asia, Africa, and America for British ships. The most important exceptions had to do with Asiatic and African products imported into Mediterranean ports of Europe; these, provided they had not been brought into the Mediterranean by way of the Atlantic, could be imported into the United Kingdom from such Mediterranean ports. Since manufactured goods were deemed to be products of the country in which they had been manufactured, goods manufactured in Europe could be imported into the United Kingdom even though the raw materials of which they were made were Asiatic, African, or American— refined sugar and cigars, for example.

3. Products of Asia, Africa, or America shall not, with certain exceptions, be imported into the United Kingdom, for home consumption, except in British ships or in ships of the country 'of which the goods are the produce and from which they are imported.' [9]

4. No goods shall be exported from the United Kingdom to any British possession in Asia, Africa, or America, except in British ships.

5. No goods shall be exported from any British possession in Asia, Africa, or America to any other of such possessions, nor from one part of any such possession to another part of the same, except in British ships.

6. No goods shall be imported into any British possession in Asia, Africa, or America in any foreign ships except ships

of the country of which the goods are the produce and from which they are imported. This rule was qualified by the Possessions Act of 1845, which confined the foreign trade of the British possessions in America to certain designated 'free ports,' and also limited the privilege of trading with British possessions granted to foreign ships to

the ships of those countries which, having colonial possessions, shall grant the like privileges of trading with those possessions to British ships, or which, not having colonial possessions, shall place the commerce and navigation of this country, and its possessions abroad, upon the footing of the most favored nation, unless Her Majesty, by Her Order in Council, shall in any case deem it expedient to grant the whole or any of such privileges to the ships of any foreign country, although the conditions aforesaid shall not in all respects be fulfilled by such foreign country.

No foreign country should be deemed to have fulfilled these conditions unless it had been declared by order in council to have done so.

7. No goods shall be carried coastwise from one part of the United Kingdom to another, or from any British possession in Asia, Africa, or America to any other of such possessions, or from one part of any of such possessions to another part of the same, except in British ships.

8. No ship shall be deemed to be a British ship unless duly registered as such, and every registered British ship shall be navigated by a master who is a British subject and a crew of which at least three-fourths are British seamen; in the case of ships employed in coasting voyages from one part of the United Kingdom to another, or in voyages between the United Kingdom and any of the Channel Islands or the Isle of Man, or from one of those islands to another, or from one part of any of them to another part of the same, or in

fishing on the coasts of the United Kingdom, or of any of the said islands, the entire crew shall be British seamen. The proportion of British seamen necessary for the legal navigation of British ships may be reduced by royal proclamation. Under an act for the registering of British vessels passed in the same year,[10] no ship could be registered as a British ship unless it had been built in the United Kingdom, the Channel Islands, the Isle of Man, some British possession in Asia, Africa, or America, Malta, Gibraltar, or Heligoland, and unless it was wholly of British ownership.

9. If any goods be imported, exported, or carried coastwise in violation of the law, such goods shall be forfeited, and the master of the ship shall forfeit one hundred pounds.

It should be noted that by virtue of (3), (4), (5), and (7) above, British (including British colonial) shipping possessed a legal monopoly of trade within the Empire. It also possessed, under (3), a virtual monopoly of importing into the United Kingdom, for home consumption, the products of non-British countries and possessions in Asia, Africa, and America, other than the products of the United States, since such countries, the United States excepted, had little or no shipping available for long oceanic voyages. Thus in 1843 there were 118 recorded entries of vessels into the United Kingdom from foreign possessions in Asia, of which 117 were British. From the United States, on the other hand, there were 1067 entries, of which approximately two-thirds were American.[11]

Viewing the Navigation Act of 1845 in retrospect, we can see, more clearly than contemporaries, that it came toward the end of an era in the history of British shipping. The use of the steamship was growing rapidly in British navigation, and the age of iron in shipbuilding was at hand. It is important to realize, however, that by far the greater part of the world's sea-borne commerce was still carried in wooden sailing vessels. 'The bulk of trade,' Lord Ellenborough confidently asserted in 1849, 'must always be carried on, not by steamers, but by sailing ships.' [12] In a shipping return laid before the House of Commons in 1844 steamers appear first for the year 1822.[13] The registered tonnage of the British Isles as of 31 December 1848 was recorded as 3,249,380 for sailing vessels and 151,029 for steamers.[14] During the 1840's there was a severe depression in British shipping, as in other areas of British industry. This was no doubt in large part a phase of a wider depression, but the shipping interests called attention to what they regarded as especially unfavorable conditions in their field, emphasizing the modifications and relaxations of the navigation system that had taken place in the 1820's. Some of the witnesses who gave evidence before a House of Commons committee of inquiry on shipping in 1844 referred to the increase of steam navigation as a cause of the depression, on the ground that it had diminished the demand for sailing vessels. The witnesses, however, were not in agreement on this point, and most of them do not seem to have considered the development of the steamship as an important cause of the depression.[15] Steamships were used primarily for the conveyance of passengers and mail, not as yet to any considerable extent for the transportation of cargoes. In their construction, moreover, Britain had the lead over other countries.[16]

In view of the approaching era of iron shipbuilding, in which the British were to enjoy a decisive competitive superiority over all rivals, some statements of Brodie M'Ghie Willcox, Managing Director of the Peninsular and Oriental

Steam Navigation Company, may seem more significant to us than they did to his contemporaries. Mr. Willcox was testifying before the committee referred to above:

Do you employ any iron-built vessels?—We have one, and we are now about to build another.

Do you contemplate making any extension of property of that kind?—In my opinion I think that eventually almost all steam vessels will be built of iron. We, of course, do not feel ourselves authorized to rush into experiments, being a joint-stock company, but still we are bound to go a little with the march of the time, and therefore we built that one as a trial.

In what respect are the iron steam vessels superior to others?—Increased speed, from drawing less water; another thing is, that there is no dry rot.

Would not those reasons apply to sailing vessels as well if built of iron. If steam vessels can be built of iron advantageously, why should not sailing vessels?—I do not know why they should not . . .

What is the relative difference in expense between vessels built of iron and vessels built of wood?—I should say that the iron vessels are 10 to 15 per cent. less in cost . . .

And this country can beat the rest of the world, so far as iron is concerned?—Decidedly.

So that that would be an advantage to this country over every other?—A very great one.[17]

Buried in the evidence presented to a later committee of inquiry are the following equally interesting statements in a paper handed in by one of the witnesses:

Supposing the abolition of all protection, England must always possess a superiority in shipbuilding, owing to the greater cheapness with which she can build iron vessels . . . if the iron system should be found on a fair trial to succeed (and to steamers the point has not been denied), Great Britain must ever possess the power of underselling the foreigner . . . The chief objection urged against them [iron ships] is the difficulty of repairing them, but this difficulty decreases with the increase of civilization; and although iron sailing vessels are not just now on the increase, yet their superior qualities so far exceed their disadvantages, that little doubt has been expressed of their ultimate success.[18]

It does not appear, however, that such prophetic statements as the foregoing made any great impression. In the 1840's the typical merchant ship was still a wooden-built sailing vessel, and it was of such that both the friends and the foes of the navigation laws were principally thinking. Early experiments with iron ships as cargo-carriers do not seem to have been very successful, and it was not until the 1850's that they began to be used extensively for this purpose.[19] In 1847 iron ships were still so rare that no rules for their classification had been laid down at Lloyd's.[20]

The British mercantile marine was the largest in the world. According to evidence given before a House of Lords committee in 1848 the total gross tonnage of the British Empire in 1846 was 3,817,112, and that of the next largest mercantile marine, the American, was 2,562,084. Of the British total, 3,199,785 belonged to the United Kingdom and 617,327 to the colonies.[21] In the days of wooden-built merchantmen, however, Britain did not possess the decisive superiority over all other countries that was to be hers when iron supplanted wood in her shipyards. As regards money costs, ships were built more cheaply in some foreign countries, notably in Norway, Sweden, and Prussia.[22] In the United States the cost of shipbuilding was higher than in those countries, though perhaps not higher than in Britain; but the thirties and forties of the nineteenth century were the golden age of the American merchant marine, and the

sailing packets built in the United States for the trans-
Atlantic trade possessed the great advantage of being
speedier than their British rivals. Nearly all the trade between the Scandinavian countries and the United Kingdom
was carried in ships of those countries, and in the trade between the United States and the United Kingdom the American tonnage employed was considerably more than twice
the amount of the British.[23] According to testimony given
by a Liverpool shipowner in 1844, all that enabled British
shipping to keep up at all in the trade between Liverpool
and the United States was the use of ships built in the
British North American colonies.[24] Detailed evidence was
presented to the committee on shipping to show the greater
cost of British navigation, both in regard to wages of seamen
and provisioning, in comparison with foreign navigation.[25]
One witness suggested a connection between import duties
and the navigation laws:

We should not be able to compete with the foreigner till we
made our people able to live as cheaply on shore as the foreigner
does. So long as you have high duties on tea, sugar, and the
articles that the sailor or the working man lays out the greatest
portion of his earnings upon, you will not be able to compete
with the foreigner . . . Take off the duties, and let our people
live as cheaply as the foreigner; then I think we could compete
[in shipping] with the foreigner.[26]

There were differences of opinion, however, regarding the
real as distinguished from the money cost of shipbuilding in
Britain and in foreign countries. George Richardson Porter,
in the course of testimony given before a parliamentary committee on the navigation laws in 1848, said: 'But with regard
to the Cost of building Ships, I believe there is no Country
in the World where Ships are built cheaper than they are

in England, taking the Quality and Duration of the Ships into account, the Goodness of the Materials, and the Manner in which they are put together.' [27] Similar opinions were frequently expressed during the debates in Parliament on the navigation laws in 1848 and 1849.

It was, however, the preponderant opinion in shipping and naval circles that the withdrawal of protection from British shipping would be disastrous to the mercantile marine and therefore to Britain's naval strength. Duncan Dunbar, chairman of the General Shipowners' Society, testifying in 1847, gave it as the opinion of British shipowners in general that the welfare of the mercantile marine depended upon the continuance of the navigation laws,[28] and there seems to be no reason to question that he was representing fairly the view prevalent in shipping circles.

*

*   *

In the case of the preferential system, public opinion in the colonies was, generally speaking, on the side of protectionism. It was otherwise with respect to the navigation system. Here colonial opinion, especially Canadian opinion, was an important factor in bringing about the victory of free trade, or, at any rate, was used effectively by opponents of the navigation laws in Britain as an argument in favor of abolishing the old system. Sir Robert Peel, who, though out of office, took an active part in the parliamentary battle for the repeal of the navigation laws, placed first among the reasons for drastic reform of the old system the situation in which the colonies found themselves as a result of recent changes affecting their trade:

If I look to the position of our colonies, in consequence of the application of the principles of free trade to many articles of their produce—if I look to the fact that many European countries have found out that they have a fair claim to insist on those privileges in navigation which we insist on for ourselves— if I look to our reciprocity treaties, and to the various complicated claims arising under them—if I look to the mutilated and shattered state of the navigation laws, as they now exist, I find a number of concurrent reasons for the conclusion that those laws cannot stand on their present foundation, but that we must consider them with a view to extensive change.[29]

In what follows we shall be concerned primarily with the imperial aspects of the controversy over the navigation laws.

Canadian petitions and memorials against the navigation laws began in the summer of 1846, as soon as it had become clear that the preference which Canadian wheat and flour had enjoyed in the British market was doomed. A brief and necessarily superficial glance at the peculiar commercial situation of Canada may help to make the Canadian protests intelligible.

It was, and long had been, the ambition and aspiration, as it was the interest, of the Canadian mercantile community to make the St. Lawrence the channel of trade for the entire region of the Great Lakes on both sides of the Canadian-American boundary.[30] It seemed clear to the merchants of Canada that nature had intended the inhabitants of this region to export their surplus produce and import their manufactured goods by way of Montreal and Quebec. Nature's intentions, however, were thwarted to some extent by American tariffs and still more by that monument of Yankee enterprise, the Erie Canal. Opened in 1825, this new artificial waterway was soon supplying the new American communities in northern New York and south of Lake Erie with a much greater volume of merchandise than was coming to them by the St. Lawrence route. In fact, goods transported by the Erie Canal were finding their way in considerable quantities to the settlements in western Canada. In the words of Lord Durham, New York State 'made its own St. Lawrence from Lake Erie to the Hudson.' It was obvious that nature needed some assistance from Canadians.

The St. Lawrence-Great Lakes waterway must be improved. The Welland Canal, connecting Lake Ontario and Lake Erie across Canadian territory, was fully opened by 1832, and smaller canals were constructed to improve navigation on the St. Lawrence above Montreal. The Welland, however, turned out to be more of an auxiliary than a competitor of the Erie, for much of the western produce, Canadian as well as American, which passed through it into Lake Ontario found its way to the Erie by way of the Oswego feeder canal, which was opened in 1828. Thus in 1834 the Welland carried 40,634 bushels of wheat, more than half of it American grown, for Montreal and 224,285 bushels for Oswego.[31] In the 1830's the Erie route was evidently winning at the expense of the St. Lawrence, and New York, not Montreal, was the chief emporium of the western trade.

In the early 1840's, however, after the union of Upper and Lower Canada, the Canadian Government took in hand extensive improvements in the St. Lawrence-Great Lakes waterway, including the enlargement of the Welland and the construction of new canals on the St. Lawrence between Lake Ontario and Montreal, the Imperial Government having guaranteed a loan that was used for this purpose. Canada's improved waterway, which was completed by 1848, possessed distinct advantages over the Erie route. For one thing, its canals were ship canals and could accommodate large lake vessels, which could sail all the way from Lake Huron to Quebec without breaking bulk, whereas the Erie was a barge canal, and therefore cargoes carried by lake vessels, if they were to be sent east by the Erie, had to be trans-shipped at the entrance to the canal, and there was sometimes another trans-shipment at the Hudson. Moreover, the mileage from western lake ports to Montreal was considerably less than to New York, and the canal mileage and canal tolls were very much less. In consequence, transport was quicker and cheaper by the St. Lawrence route.[32] On the other hand, New York had a great advantage over Montreal in trans-Atlantic trade, an advantage that more than counterbalanced Montreal's superiority in inland transport. For reasons that need not be detailed here, freight rates to English ports were much lower from New York than from Montreal.[33] The consequence was that in trade between the Great Lakes region and British ports the Erie enjoyed a competitive superiority over the St. Lawrence.[34]

Before 1846, however, this superiority had been offset to a considerable extent by colonial preferences in the British tariff and high duties in the American tariff. American wheat, excluded by the corn laws from the British market except when the price of wheat in the United Kingdom was very high, could be transported to Canada, ground there, and exported to Britain in the form of Canadian flour, paying only the colonial preferential duty when it entered a British port. On the other hand, wheat grown in western Canada, though it could be transported *via* the Erie route to New York City and exported thence to the United Kingdom in British ships, was subject to the American tariff duty when it entered United States territory in transit. In

1843, as was indicated in the preceding chapter, the Imperial Parliament conferred what was regarded as a great boon upon Canadian trade and agriculture. Following the imposition by the Parliament of Canada of a duty of 3s. per quarter on American wheat imported into the province, it passed an act admitting Canadian wheat and wheat flour into the United Kingdom at merely nominal duties—wheat at 1s. per quarter, and flour at the duty levied upon the quantity of wheat used in its manufacture.[35] Flour milled in Canada was deemed to be Canadian no matter where the wheat had been grown. The effect of these changes in the British and Canadian tariffs upon wheat-growing and the milling industry in Canada, upon the importation of American wheat into Canada, and upon the comparative fortunes of the St. Lawrence and the Erie routes cannot be determined precisely.[36] According to Canadian statistics, the milling capacity of the province was more than doubled during the six years from 1842 to 1848,[37] and there is no doubt that the exceptionally favorable treatment given to Canadian wheat and flour by the British act of 1843 encouraged all those who were interested in improving the St. Lawrence waterway.[38]

American legislation in the interest of the Erie route further stimulated Canadian exertions in behalf of the St. Lawrence. In 1845 Congress provided for the remission of duties on imports into the United States if they were re-exported to Canada, and an act passed in the following year made similar provision for drawbacks when produce imported into the United States from Canada was re-exported to foreign countries. These American drawback laws were a formidable attack on the St. Lawrence trading system, but it suffered an even more serious blow in the repeal of the corn laws, which gave the death sentence to Canada's wheat and flour preferences in the United Kingdom. The year 1846, it has been said,

was the black year of the Canadian commercial system, the year in which the American congress opened the republic to the free transit of Canadian produce destined for exportation abroad. The most ambitious advance of the United States and the final withdrawal of Great Britain had come together in a disastrous coincidence. The British had robbed the St. Lawrence of what was supposedly its greatest attraction at the very moment when the Americans had opened wide the Erie route to the produce of the Canadian commercial state.[39]

In 1846 Canada passed into the grip of a severe depression, which lasted for three or four years and was generally attributed by Canadians to the repeal of the corn laws. Lord Elgin, who arrived in Canada as Governor General in 1847, thought that those responsible for the act of 1843 were to blame for having given 'a false direction to trade,' and that Canadians had a valid grievance against the British Parliament for its inconstancy of purpose.[40] In a letter to Lord Grey, written in November 1848, he said:

Stanley's Bill of 1843 attracted all the Produce of the West to the St Lawrence, and fixed all the disposable capital of the Province in Grinding Mills, Warehouses, and forwarding establishments—Peel's Bill of 1846 drives the whole of this Produce down the New York channels of communication, destroying the Revenue which Canada expected to derive from Canal dues, & ruining at once Mill owners, Forwarders, & Merchants. The consequence is that Private Property is unsaleable in Canada, and not a shilling can be raised on the credit of the Province.[41]

After 1849, Canadian and American wheat and flour were to be admitted into the United Kingdom on equal terms,

and unless something could be done about it, the St. Lawrence must finally succumb to the Erie. Only by cheapening
the Canadian route could economic calamity be averted,
and to that end a movement began in Canada in 1846 for the
removal of restrictions on the navigation of the St. Lawrence.

American lake craft had been allowed to use the Canadian
canals on the same terms as Canadian boats, but under the
navigation laws they could not carry Canadian produce to
Montreal, the head of navigation on the St. Lawrence for
ocean-going vessels, they could not touch at two Canadian
ports without touching intermediately at an American port,
and, though this was not a part of the general British navigation system, they were not permitted to navigate the St.
Lawrence between Montreal and Quebec.[42] Since Quebec
was the only 'free port' in the province of Canada, foreign
vessels were not permitted to ascend the St. Lawrence above
that city, and they could not trade, of course, between Quebec and the United Kingdom or other parts of the British
Empire. The Montreal Board of Trade asserted in 1846 that
the restrictions on the navigation of the St. Lawrence virtually closed the river to American shipping.[43]

The Montreal Free Trade Association, in a petition dated
17 July 1846, addressed to Gladstone as Secretary of State
for the Colonies, made clear the inconsistency between the
restrictions on foreign shipping in the St. Lawrence and the
proclaimed desire of the British Government 'that the trade
of Canada may, in all respects, approach as nearly to perfect
freedom as the dispositions of its inhabitants, and the exi-
gencies of the public revenue there, may permit.' The opening of the St. Lawrence to foreign vessels was emphasized
as a question of paramount importance to Canada. 'That

river is obviously the most essential element of our power, and on the use we make of the natural advantage it affords will mainly depend our future position as a commercial country.' Obstacles to the use of the St. Lawrence had been interposed by 'the energy and enterprise of our neighbors,' and the only way to surmount them was to 'hold out every possible inducement to the inhabitants of the United States to pass their merchandize through our country.' The petitioners professed to have no doubt that if American vessels were allowed the free navigation of the St. Lawrence, subject only to the payment of moderate canal dues, the St. Lawrence route could compete successfully with any other. What was necessary was to make it the cheapest route. As things were, Canada was suffering from an anomaly, the 'removal of protection and prohibition of free trade.' [44] The Montreal Board of Trade, in a memorial of 26 August 1846, similarly expressed its confidence in the future success of the St. Lawrence waterway if the restrictions imposed on navigation were removed. It asked for such a modification of the navigation laws as would leave Canadians free to employ, at their option, the cheapest vessels they could procure, whether British or foreign, and the removal of all the restrictions on the navigation of the St. Lawrence.[45] The Toronto Board of Trade, in a petition of 9 September 1846, indicated the connection between the repeal of the corn laws and the current discontent in Canada with the navigation laws and referred to the combination of private and public interests that felt themselves to be imperilled:

Your petitioners, having carefully considered the operation of the said laws [the navigation laws] upon the commercial and agricultural interests of Canada, feel called on to state, that prior to the alterations in the Corn Laws . . . effected in the last Session of Parliament, Your Majesty's subjects residing in Western Canada did not feel the disadvantages resulting to the colony from the monopoly of the carrying trade conferred on the owners of British ships by the Navigation Laws, as it was found that the prices of their agricultural exports generally equalled those which were observed to obtain in the contiguous sections of the neighbouring States of the republic of America, for the same products destined for shipment to the British market through the Atlantic seaports of the said States . . . The people of Canada now feel convinced that, deprived of that protection formerly extended to their products in Your Majesty's kingdom, by means of which the heavy burthens imposed on their trade by the Navigation Laws were neutralized, they must, in the event of these laws being continued in force, be reduced to a position much inferior to that of the people in the adjacent States of America, and they contemplate, with profound mortification, their only alternative in the conversion of their export trade into a valuable branch of the resources of their republican neighbours . . . Your petitioners further most humbly submit, that Your Majesty's Canadian subjects have incurred a heavy debt in the construction of canals capable of giving passage to vessels of large dimensions, under the expectations that by these improvements of their internal navigation they would not fail to secure to themselves a large share of the carrying trade of the rich agricultural countries bordering on the great lakes of Canada. The repayment of the debt thus incurred is an object from which your petitioners feel convinced no consideration can ever divert the intentions of the people of Canada; but it is quite manifest, that in the event of the export trade of Western Canada, and the states adjacent to the lakes, being forced out of the waters of the St. Lawrence, the outlay upon the improvements, from Lake Ontario to the ocean, will have become a dead weight on the resources and energies of the province, the trade of the recently flourishing cities of Quebec and Montreal will have disappeared, and the mercantile capital of their enterprising citizens will have been transferred to the commercial emporia of the neighbouring country.[46]

Lord Cathcart, who was Governor of Canada when the Canadian demands for drastic changes in the navigation laws began, sympathized with them,[47] and his successor, Lord Elgin, took the same position, both in his official dispatches and in his private letters to Lord Grey, the British Secretary of State for the Colonies.[48] In July 1847, Elgin transmitted to Grey a joint address of the two houses of the Canadian Parliament, asking for imperial legislation 'to repeal the laws of navigation so far as they in any manner relate to or affect this colony,' [49] and soon after his arrival in Canada he was urging that Montreal be made a free port.[50]

From the West Indies, too, came expressions of dissatisfaction with the navigation laws. At a public meeting in Trinidad in September 1846, resolutions were adopted protesting against the Sugar Duties Act of that year, by which the preferences that Great Britain had given to the sugar of her West India colonies ever since the seventeenth century had been put in process of extinction, and calling for a number of measures of relief. One of these was 'such an approximation to the general principles of "free trade," as, by a modification of the existing Navigation Laws, would enable British colonists to avail themselves of the cheapest "bottoms" for carrying their produce to the home market as well as bringing their outward supplies, an advantage at present denied them.' [51] The Governor of Trinidad, in despatches to the Colonial Office, made strong representations to show that a relaxation of the navigation laws would benefit the colony.[52] The planters of Jamaica, smarting under a long accumulation of grievances against the British Government for its measures against slavery and in behalf of the Negro population of the colony, learned with dismay of the Sugar Duties Act, and in April 1847, the Assembly, lamenting the grievous sufferings of their constituents, urged that the navigation laws be relaxed so that the colonists might be permitted 'to enjoy a free commercial intercourse with all nations.'[53] The legislature of Antigua protested against the protection of British shipping as 'entirely indefensible upon the all-powerful principles of free trade.'[54] In far-off Ceylon merchants and planters asked that the importation of rice, the staple food of the laborers on the coffee, sugar, and cinnamon plantations, from the territories of the East India Company, be opened to the vessels of all nations.[55] The eastern colonies in general, however, found little fault with the navigation laws.[56]

*

* *

The repeal of the corn laws did not solve the food problem in the United Kingdom. There were serious crop deficiencies in 1846, and in that year a disastrous blight fell upon the potato plants in Ireland. The years 1846 and 1847 were famine years in that sorely afflicted country. Grain prices in the British market advanced rapidly. Wheat rose from 49s. in September 1846 to 70s. 3d. in January 1847, and abnormally high freight rates hindered importation. Early in the session of 1847 bills were hurried through Parliament to deal with the emergency. The transitional duties on imported grain provided for in Peel's act of 1846 were suspended from 26 January to 1 September 1847, and the navigation laws were suspended for the same period with respect to the importation of grain, flour, meal, rice, and potatoes.[57] These could be imported into the United Kingdom 'from any Country, in any Ship or Vessel of any Country, however navigated . . . any thing in the Law of Navigation to the contrary in anywise notwithstanding.' By later acts passed in the same session these suspensions were continued in effect until 1 March 1848.[58] In the House of Commons, Joseph Hume, veteran champion of retrenchment and reform, urged repeal, instead of mere suspension, of the navigation laws, as well as immediate repeal of all duties on grain and on all articles used in shipbuilding. 'Why should not the noble Lord [Lord John Russell] carry out to their fullest extent the free-trade principles which were now supposed to regulate the policy of this country?' If the Government would only be courageous, 'England would speedily become the manufactury of ships for a great portion of the world—to the same extent as she now supplied so large a portion of it with other manufactured articles.'[59] Protectionist members did not oppose the first suspension of the navigation laws as an emergency measure to facilitate the importation of grain, but they let it be known that they would not countenance a repeal of the laws,[60] and when the question of a second suspension came up, Lord George Bentinck, the protectionist leader in the House of Commons, declared that suspension was nothing but 'a flimsy pretext' for undermining the whole navigation system, and therefore opposed the bill.[61]

In February 1847, Mr. John Lewis Ricardo, an extreme free-trade member of Parliament, secured the appointment of a select committee of the House of Commons 'to inquire into the operation and policy of the navigation laws.'[62] This committee sat from March to June under the chairmanship of Milner Gibson, Vice President of the Board of Trade and a strong advocate of free-trade measures. It examined witnesses and reported to the House from time to time the minutes of evidence which it had taken,[63] but it made no recommendations. The House of Lords later appointed a committee of inquiry on the same subject, which sat from March to July 1848, and similarly reported its minutes of evidence without recommendations.[64] The reports of these committees fill two quarto volumes of parliamentary papers and are storehouses of information regarding the operation of the navigation laws and cognate matters. This is not to say, of course, that the witnesses who appeared before the committees were without preconceptions and biases. Undoubtedly their testimony should be used with great caution; it was, as Disraeli said, contradictory, complicated, and conflicting. The navigation laws were actively canvassed in the press in 1847, pamphlets were published on the subject, and the Queen's Speech in opening Parliament in November indicated that it would be brought forward during the session 'with a view to ascertain whether any Changes can be adopted, which, without Danger to our Maritime Strength, may promote the Commercial and Colonial Interests of the Empire.' [65] Lord John Russell's free-trade Government found much to its liking in the evidence made public by the House of Commons committee, and colonial remonstrances against the navigation laws found a very sympathetic auditor at the Colonial Office in Lord Grey. On the other side, the landed interest, though it had not received the support of the shipping interest in the great battle over the corn laws, now joined with it in opposing the repeal of the navigation laws.

For six months the Government took no parliamentary action with regard to the navigation laws, and it was not until 15 May 1848 that the President of the Board of Trade, Henry Labouchere (afterwards Lord Taunton), presented its proposals to the House of Commons [66] and moved the following resolution:

That it is expedient to remove the restrictions which prevent the free carriage of goods by sea, to and from the United Kingdom and the British Possessions abroad, subject, nevertheless, to such control by Her Majesty in Council as may be necessary, and to amend the Laws for the registration of Ships and Seamen.

The revolutionary character of the changes advocated was unmistakable and was openly avowed. If they were to be carried out, all the prohibitions and restrictions of the old system that had been regarded as essential would be done away with, except the rules that ships, in order to qualify as British, must be British owned, and manned as existing law required. The rule that they must be British built would be abolished. Labouchere proposed, it is true, to continue the legal restriction of the coasting trade of the United Kingdom and of the colonies to British shipping, but inasmuch as the former was naturally protected against foreign competition, the removal of the legal prohibition would have been nugatory; and he proposed to allow any colony that might so desire to open its coasting trade to foreign shipping.

On 29 May Mr. J. C. Herries moved the following resolution for the purpose of testing the sense of the House on the question of whether the principle of the navigation laws should be upheld or abandoned:

That it is essential to the national interests of this country to maintain the fundamental principles of the existing Navigation Laws; subject to such modification as may be best calculated to obviate any proved inconvenience to the commerce of the United Kingdom and its dependencies, without danger to our national strength.

This resolution shows on what ground the protectionists stood throughout the parliamentary debates on the navigation laws in 1848 and 1849. They supported the fundamental principles of the existing system though they constantly professed their willingness to consider modifications and relaxations that might seem desirable in view of the conditions of the time, especially along the lines of reciprocity.

A protracted debate on Mr. Herries' resolution was concluded on 9 June, when it was defeated by a vote of 294 to 177. It would have been impossible to pass a highly controversial measure through Parliament during the current session, and announcement was made that it would be postponed till the following year. The Government had been criticized for having failed to present its proposals at an earlier date, and it now desired to place them before the country as a basis for public discussion. Near the close of the session, accordingly, Labouchere was given leave to bring in a bill for this purpose on condition that there would be no debate on it.[67]

Representations against the navigation laws continued to be made in the colonies while the subject was under discussion in Great Britain. Lord Grey, speaking in the House of Lords on 25 February 1848, said he believed that 'there was not a House of Assembly in the West Indies that had not petitioned Her Majesty to relieve those colonies from the operation of the Navigation Laws.' [68]

Canada remained in the forefront of the colonial movement for repeal, with Lord Elgin encouraging and perhaps even coaching from the side-lines. The Executive Council of the province, in a memorandum drawn up in May 1848, restated familiar Canadian arguments and voiced high hopes of prosperity for Canada if the laws were repealed and the navigation of the St. Lawrence above Quebec opened to American vessels:

That a great portion of the exportable produce of Western Canada, probably by far the greater part, is at this moment on its way to the ports of the United States; that little is expected in Montreal; that the canals constructed on the St. Lawrence are almost idle; that the importing ships coming to Montreal this season are without their usual full freights; that the principal importations into Western Canada are now through the United States; that the trade of the city of Montreal is, in consequence, rapidly decreasing, notwithstanding a rapid increase in the consumption and importation into Canada of the articles formerly imported altogether through that port; and that the opening of the Canadian sea-ports to the vessels of all nations, permitting the produce of the colony to be sent to the United Kingdom in these vessels without distinction, and the permitting the use of the River St. Lawrence above Quebec to Americans, would probably not only restore trade to its original channel, but cause an increase in the commerce and revenues of Canada beyond former precedent,—are facts which the Executive Council of Canada wish to present to the consideration of Her Majesty's Ministers, in the hope of strengthening their hands in bringing about the expected changes.[69]

The Montreal Board of Trade, in memorials and petitions dated 26 May and 14 December 1848, continued to urge the repeal of the navigation laws and the free navigation of the St. Lawrence, and the Quebec Board of Trade, in June of the same year, asked for the removal of 'all restrictions that now exist to the free navigation of the river St. Lawrence . . . or which prevent the free carriage of goods by sea to and from the United Kingdom and its possessions abroad, so far as this colony is concerned, subject to such control by Your Majesty in Council as may be necessary.'[70] In a joint address to the Queen, adopted at the end of January 1849, both houses of the Parliament of Canada declared that delay in removing the existing restrictions on the use of foreign shipping would be 'highly injurious to the carrying trade of the St. Lawrence,' expressed approval of the bill for the repeal of the navigation laws that had been introduced into the British House of Commons in the session of 1848, and asked that foreign vessels be permitted to navigate the St. Lawrence above Quebec.[71]

In New Brunswick, where shipbuilding had begun soon after the establishment of the province in 1784, voices were raised in opposition to repeal. Colonial shipping interests, like those of the mother country, had been accustomed to look upon the navigation laws as their guardian and protector. St. John was the chief center of shipbuilding in British North America, and at a public meeting held there in June 1848 a petition to the Queen was adopted in which it was predicted that the proposals of the British Government would, if carried out, prove 'generally prejudicial to the British Empire, and particularly to this loyal colony.' The petitioners stated that many British subjects in New Brunswick had invested their capital in shipping, that many immigrants were employed in shipbuilding, which supplied the greater part of the exports of the colony, and that if the proposed measure should be passed, it would 'wholly destroy the export trade of this province, in the production of which a very large amount of British manufactures is consumed.' Should it be deemed necessary, in the general interests of the Empire, to alter the navigation laws, they asked the Queen to refuse her assent to any measure that did not secure for her loyal subjects of New Brunswick the opening of other markets for their exports, the privilege of selling their ships in any market, the right of procuring registries in foreign countries, perfect freedom in the employment of foreigners in the navigating of their ships, the privilege of trading to and with all countries, coastwise as well as foreign, and the removal of all restrictions in the conduct of their ships.[72]

Between the parliamentary sessions of 1848 and 1849 the issues raised by the Government's proposals were actively canvassed in the British press and in pamphlets. The Shipowners' Society carried on propaganda against the proposals, and among those who regarded changes in the old system as desirable or inevitable there seemed to be more general support for relaxations on the basis of reciprocity, which had been advocated in Parliament by Gladstone and by several of the protectionist Conservatives, than for absolute and unconditional repeal. Labouchere's bill of 1848 itself seemed to contemplate retaliatory discrimination as a means of securing reciprocity, for it contained provisions empowering the crown to impose differential duties, prohibitions, or restrictions upon the ships of any country which subjected British ships to the like discriminations.

In December 1848, Lord Palmerston, as Secretary of State for Foreign Affairs, addressed a circular dispatch to British diplomatic representatives abroad, accompanied by a statement of the changes proposed to be made in the British navigation system. This the diplomats were to communicate to the governments to which they were accredited, and they were instructed to ascertain whether those governments imposed any restrictions upon British vessels from which the vessels of their own nationals were exempt. 'For,' said Lord Palmerston, while the British Government are prepared to remove nearly the whole of the restrictions of the British Navigation Law in all cases where such a measure shall be met in a spirit of corresponding liberality, it is impossible for them to lay down with any precision the course they may think fit to take, where no such spirit is shown, until they shall be fully informed of all the circumstances which should be taken into their consideration.

The information collected was duly transmitted to the Foreign Office and presented to Parliament in the form of command papers.[73]

The Queen's Speech at the opening of the session of 1849 contained this reference to the navigation laws:

I again commend to your Attention the Restrictions imposed on Commerce by the Navigation Laws.

If you shall find that these Laws are in whole or in part unnecessary for the Maintenance of our Maritime Power, while they fetter Trade and Industry, you will no doubt deem it right to repeal or modify their Provisions.

On 14 February Labouchere presented a resolution substantially the same as the one he had introduced in the preceding session. This having been agreed to, a bill was brought in, and at the second reading, on 9 March, Mr. Herries moved as a destroying amendment that it 'be read a second time this day six months.' On 12 March this was defeated, and the Navigation Bill passed second reading by a vote of 266 to 210. It was amended in committee in a few particulars, and on 23 April passed third reading, 275 to 214.[74]

While the bill was before Parliament, meetings were held of the General Shipowners' Society in London and of local societies in the outports, and many petitions against it were drawn up. The London petition bore some 27,000 signatures and that from Liverpool more than 24,000.[75] The agitation carried on by the shipping interests helps to explain why the majorities given by the House of Commons for the bill of 1849 were smaller than that by which it had defeated the motion for upholding the principle of the navigation laws in 1848.

Shipowners and opponents of the bill in general looked forward hopefully to its rejection by the House of Lords. Grievous disappointment, however, lay in store for them, for the Upper House passed it, though only by a narrow margin. The vote at the second reading was 173 to 163. The bill was saved only by proxy votes, of which about three-fifths were cast in its favor. Of the lords present, 105 supported and 119 opposed it. The dissentient members protested against the second reading on the ground that the repeal of the navigation laws would imperil the safety of the nation and inflict grievous injury upon the shipping interest and the various classes dependent upon it for support. At the third reading, on 12 June, Lord Stanley, the leader of the opposition in the upper house, contented himself with an individual protest.[76] The bill became law on 26 June and went into operation on 1 January 1850.[77]

Entitled 'An Act to amend the Laws in force for the Encouragement of British Shipping and Navigation,' the statute repealed the Navigation Act of 1845 and ten other acts of Parliament in whole or in part. The effect was to sweep away the old navigation system root and branch, except the reservation of trade between different parts of the British Isles and between different parts of the several colonies to British ships and the requirements that British ships must be British owned and navigated by a British master and a crew of which three-fourths (in the coasting trade of the British Isles, the entire crew) were British seamen. It was provided, however, that upon the request of any British colony its coasting trade could be opened to foreign shipping by order in council,[78] authority was given to the Governor General of India in Council to authorize trade between different parts of the possessions of the East India Company in foreign ships, and the proportion of seamen required to be British for the legal navigation of a British ship could be reduced by royal proclamation. Discretionary power was given to the crown to impose restrictions upon the ships of foreign countries so as to place them as nearly as possible on the same footing in British ports as that on which British ships were placed in the ports of those countries, but it was understood that this power of retaliation would not be invoked unless exceptional circumstances should seem to require it.[79]

In the course of the arguments and discussions that preceded the repeal of the navigation laws the colonial phases of the subject received much consideration. 'Justice to the colonies' was an effective argument, and free-traders made the most of it, though their opponents did not fail to point out that they had shown little concern for colonial interests in the measures they had taken against colonial preference. Other phases, however, received a large share of contemporary attention—the question of national defense, of the welfare of British shipping considered as a great economic interest, of the attitude of foreign countries toward the navigation laws, of the foreign trade of the United Kingdom. The most vital question of all was, did national defense require the continuation of the old navigation system in its essentials? As to the paramount importance of national defense, there was no issue. No British Government would have dared, or would have wished, to propose a measure calculated to weaken British sea power, and no British Parliament would have passed such a measure. Even Cobden, much as he disliked 'incessant harping on the string of "Rule, Britannia," ' felt it expedient to express his belief that the repeal of the navigation laws would not weaken the British mercantile marine or 'diminish our naval supremacy.' [80] There was little disposition to question that a large and flourishing mercantile marine was requisite to the maintenance of British sea power. Many of those who supported the bill, however, did deny that the navigation laws had been the cause of the increase of the British mercantile marine.[81] Protectionist predictions that the abandonment of the old system would lead to a decline of British shipping were countered by free-trade prophecies that it would have the opposite effect. The issue, as stated by Gladstone, was, would it give 'a wholesome stimulus' to the mercantile marine, or would the mercantile marine 'dwindle away under the influence of competition'? On that issue he was ready to stake the whole question: 'I am prepared to advocate an alteration in the navigation laws on my conviction, supported by arguments, that the effect of a judicious change will be, not to limit, but to strengthen and extend the commerce, and, with the commerce, the navigation of this country.' [82] The Prime Minister expressed the same conviction, as did the leader of the free-trade Conservatives. 'I cannot have the smallest doubt,' Lord John Russell said, 'that if we abrogate the principal part of the navigation laws, our commercial marine will increase further than it has already done'; and Sir Robert Peel declared that the increase of shipping depended not on navigation laws but on the prosperity of commerce.[83] Some extreme free-traders went so far as to assert that the existing British mercantile marine would actually have been larger than it was if there had been no navigation laws.[84] A reading of the parliamentary debates confirms Professor Clapham's opinion: 'Had complete proof been forthcoming that, as the world stood in the forties, British naval strength really depended on the retention of the navigation system, the system might be living still.' [85] The protectionist minority failed to convince Parliament that the repeal of the navigation laws would result in weakening British naval power.

At the same time, it could not be shown that there was any strong popular demand in Britain for the abolition of the old system. This was admitted by the Prime Minister himself.[86] The free-trade press, of course, supported the Government's bill, but there was no organized agitation on the subject such as had preceded the repeal of the corn laws. Few petitions were presented to Parliament for the repeal of the navigation laws, while many were presented against it. It was stated in the House of Lords that up to 4 May 1849 the petitions against the bill numbered 182, while only 6 had been presented in favor of it. Most of the former came, as would be supposed, from the shipping interests, and it was easy to suggest that the patriotic concern for national defense which they expressed was alloyed with pecuniary motives. A member of Parliament referred to 'those effusions of patriotism which discovered a latent sympathy towards the breeches pocket of the patriots who uttered them.' [87]

*

* *

It would be illogical to impute supreme wisdom to those who brought about the repeal of the navigation laws for the reason that British shipping experienced a phenomenal growth after that event. Such an opinion as that of Dr. Cunningham, granted that he was not predisposed toward over-admiration of *laissez-faire* measures, ought not to be brushed aside lightly, the opinion, namely, that if it had not been for the coming of the iron age in shipbuilding, 'it would hardly have been possible for England to reassert her supremacy in ocean trading.' [88] Few of those who contributed to the overthrow of the old system seem to have foreseen the extraordinary development of iron shipbuilding that was to take place in the near future. W. S. Lindsay, an important shipowner of the time, a member of Parliament, and an opponent of the Act of 1849, was the author of a comprehensive history of British shipping written some years later. In this he expressed the opinion that the situation immediately after the repeal of the navigation laws was critical, and that, had it not been for British resources and energy, 'foreign shipping might then have gained an ascendancy which might not afterwards have been easily overcome.' [89]

The total tonnage, British and foreign, entered and cleared in the ports of the United Kingdom increased from 14,004,388 in 1849 to 14,505,064 in 1850, but the increase was entirely in foreign tonnage, which rose from 4,334,750 to 5,062,520. British tonnage actually fell off from 9,669,638 to 9,442,544.[90] The early 'fifties were years of recovery and prosperity for British shipping, and Great Britain enjoyed a great advantage over all other countries in the building of iron steamships, which, according to Lindsay, 'were the main weapon, whereby we bade defiance to the competition of all other nations, in the general ocean race then just commenced.' [91] British shipping, however, suffered a protracted depression in the late 'fifties, the years immediately following the Crimean War, and many shipowners believed that the situation called for a return to protection.

It is obvious that none of the British free-traders of the 'forties could have foreseen the collapse of Britain's greatest shipping rival, the American mercantile marine, during the Civil War. That collapse, as Professor Clapham has remarked, 'ushered in the generation during which British maritime ascendancy was more conspicuous than it had ever been before, when, consequently, the Navigation Laws and all that pertained to them were almost forgotten.' [92] In 1870 the mercantile tonnage of the British Empire nearly equalled that of all non-British countries, and by 1880 it exceeded it. The figure for British Empire steam tonnage in the latter year (2,949,282) was more than twice that for all other countries. [93]

In arguing that justice to the colonies required that they ought to be freed from the restrictions that the navigation laws imposed upon their trade, now that Parliament had adopted the principle that their produce was no longer to be protected in the British market by differential duties, the Government and its supporters put Canada in the forefront of discussion. In justice to Canada, it was urged, freight rates on the ocean route between the United Kingdom and the St. Lawrence ought not to be kept artificially high by the continued exclusion of foreign, and especially American, ships. The United States had shown great sagacity in passing its drawback laws, which had attracted a large volume of Canadian trade to the Erie Canal route, but what kind of sagacity was Britain showing in deliberately penalizing the St. Lawrence route? If the navigation laws were repealed, American ships, so it was predicted, would engage in trade between Canada and the United Kingdom, freight rates would be lowered, and the St. Lawrence would be able to compete successfully with the Erie. 'We are deeply interested,' Labouchere declared, 'in affording the people of Canada every possible facility by means of cheapening freights . . . to avail themselves of the natural advantages which the St. Lawrence presents.'[94] The opinions of Montreal merchants were publicized to show that western Canada would be supplied with West India produce more cheaply by way of the St. Lawrence than it was then supplied by way of the Erie if the 'obnoxious navigation laws' were repealed. Under existing conditions, according to the merchants, the supply of British vessels in the West Indies available for transporting sugar and molasses to Montreal was inadequate; 'our sugars and molasses,' they said, 'go to New York, there to pay a transit duty . . . and to be subjected to all the costs and delays of an inland communication through the United States to Canada; the result is, that Canadians pay dearer than if the navigation laws did not exist . . . for their sugar; but we cannot see what benefit is conferred upon the British shipowner by the restriction.' It was represented, moreover, that the removal of the restrictions on foreign shipping in Canadian trade would make it possible for Montreal to compete successfully with New York in supplying the American communities south of the Great Lakes.[95] Peel regarded the claims of Canada as unanswerable, and several other opponents of the navigation laws in Parliament went so far as to predict that if justice were denied to Canada, the political connection between that province and the mother country would soon be dissolved.[96] Protectionists, on the other hand, gave warning that the Empire would surely go to pieces if the navigation laws were repealed.[97]

Opponents of repeal contended that the disadvantages of

Montreal and Quebec, as compared with New York, in trade with Europe and the West Indies were the result of natural causes, not of British legislation, and that no changes in the law could overcome those disadvantages. Lord Stanley argued to this effect in an able speech which he delivered in the House of Lords on 8 May 1849.[98] He observed that Canadians had a double interest in cheapening the Canadian-British route, 'as producers and as carriers.' As producers, they naturally desired the cheapest transportation to market for their produce; as carriers, they desired that the transportation should be through their own territory rather than through the United States. But the natural difficulties of navigation on the St. Lawrence were such, he declared, that on the basis of free competition American vessels would not be attracted to trade between Canada and the United Kingdom. 'Montreal and Quebec cannot compete successfully with New York on the principle of entire and unlimited competition; and unless we allow them the protection of a moderate differential duty upon foreign corn . . . you will never be able to transfer the great tide of traffic from the Erie Canal to the St. Lawrence.'[99] As a matter of fact, the tonnage of United States vessels entered at Montreal and Quebec increased from 64,986 in 1849 to 126,981 in 1850, but this increase of 61,995 tons was counterbalanced by a decrease in the tonnage of British vessels of 61,799. The tonnage of non-British shipping, other than that of the United States, increased, but only by about 19,500.[100] The conclusion drawn from shipping statistics by a careful historian is that the repeal of the navigation laws did not increase the shipping resources of the St. Lawrence.

Free competition demonstrated that the St. Lawrence route as a whole, mainly for reasons of geography, was economically in-

ferior to that by way of New York. The Navigation Laws therefore were not responsible for the lack of success of the St.
Lawrence route . . . They constituted a grievance which so far
as the province was concerned was apparent rather than real,
and their repeal proved to be an entirely inadequate remedy for
the failure of the waterway.[101]

Another scholar concludes that the repeal of the navigation laws was 'of little avail in the corn trade (where most
was hoped for it) and consequently no encouragement to the
use of the St. Lawrence canals.' [102]

A good deal was said about the trade of the British West
Indies during the course of the debates in Parliament. The
Jamaica Assembly, it will be remembered, had asked for the
relaxation of the navigation laws, but it was very doubtful
whether the colony would gain anything from a measure
under which foreign ships would be permitted to carry
Cuban and Brazilian, as well as British West Indian, sugar
to the United Kingdom. Opponents of repeal in Parliament
insisted that Cuba and Brazil, where sugar was still grown by
slave labor, would gain more than the British sugar islands,
and would gain at their expense.[103] In Jamaica itself opinion seems to have been divided, and protectionist members
of Parliament were able to point to evidences of opposition
to repeal in other British sugar colonies.[104] The Governor of
Britain's eastern sugar island, Mauritius, reported, however,
that during the year 1850 the amount of foreign tonnage,
chiefly French, entering the colony had nearly doubled,
without any decline in the number of British vessels entering, the result being a marked lowering of the prices of imported commodities.[105] In the Australian colonies there had
been no serious complaint of the navigation laws, and both
in them and in Cape Colony the repeal seems to have had

no important effect on trade and to have aroused little interest.[106]

It may be noted in conclusion that opponents of the navigation laws, anxious to discredit them in all possible ways, professed to see in Great Britain's restrictions upon the trade and navigation of her old colonies the principal cause of the American Revolution. It had been the opinion of William Huskisson and of the classical economists of the early nineteenth century, as has already been pointed out, and of Josiah Tucker before them, that those restrictions were a more important cause of the conflict than parliamentary taxation of the colonies, and Labouchere agreed with them.[107] It was generally supposed, Earl Grey said, that the Revolution arose merely out of the question of taxation, but this, he declared, was not the case. It was 'not merely taxation, it was a question about the navigation laws. It was an attempt to enforce those laws which led to hostilities between the mother country and the States of America.' [108]

THE WITHDRAWAL OF THE IMPERIAL GARRISONS

BRITAIN emerged from the war of the American Revolution shorn of prestige and the larger part of her old Empire. With the coming of peace in 1783 her military forces were reduced, but it was deemed necessary still to maintain some 9500 troops for colonial service.[1] Almost the whole expense of supporting them fell upon the mother country.[2] The disastrous attempts of Grenville and Townshend to extract revenue from colonies for the support of British troops quartered therein was not repeated. On the contrary, Parliament, recognizing, when too late to avert the disruption of the Empire, that 'taxation by the Parliament of Great Britain for the purpose of raising a Revenue in His Majesty's Colonies, Provinces and Plantations in North America has been found by Experience to occasion great uneasiness and disorders,' enacted in the following words what was clearly intended to be a binding pledge:

That from and after the passing of this Act the King and Parliament of Great Britain will not impose any Duty, Tax or Assessment whatever, payable in any of His Majesty's Colonies, Provinces or Plantations in North America or the West Indies; except only such Duties as it may be expedient to impose for the Regulation of Commerce: the net produce of such Duties to be always paid and applied to and for the use of the Colony, Province or Plantation in which the same shall be respectively levied, in such manner as other Duties collected by the authority of the Respective General Courts or General Assemblies of such

Colonies, Provinces or Plantations are ordinarily paid and applied.[3]

This belated concession to the American revolutionists failed wholly as a measure of conciliation, but the pledge which it gave, though not legally binding on succeeding Parliaments, has in fact been observed, not only in respect of the colonies to which the act expressly referred, but as a general principle of British colonial policy.[4] The troops which the Imperial Government saw fit to maintain in the colonies were paid by the British treasury, assisted in some cases by contributions from the colonies.

The outcome of the American Revolution produced a feeling of depression and pessimism in England with regard to colonies in general. This was reflected in the abolition in 1782 of the old Board of Trade, which had been concerned mainly with colonial affairs, and of what was called the American Department, the forerunner of the later Colonial Office, as well as in the political and economic literature of the day.[5] But the war with Revolutionary France, which began in 1793, was accompanied by something of an imperialist revival, and an enlargement of her Empire was the most obvious result of that prolonged conflict so far as Britain was concerned. To guard her scattered dependencies in America, the West Indies, the Mediterranean, Africa, Asia, and Australia, numerous garrisons were deemed necessary. The expense of maintaining them was borne almost wholly by the mother country. Earl Grey, Colonial Secretary from 1846 to 1852, wrote in his *Colonial Policy of Lord John Russell's Administration* (page 44): 'I believe it was not until the time of the great revolutionary war with France, that nearly the whole burden of the defense of the Colonies was undertaken by this country.' And in the course of testimony given before a parliamentary committee in 1861 he observed: 'It is to be remarked that for a very long series of years this country has acted on the principle of taking their [the colonies'] defence entirely upon herself.' [6] To the same effect is a statement made by C. B. Adderley (afterwards Lord Norton), who was under-secretary for the colonies in the Derby-Disraeli ministry, that 'our earliest and most vigorous colonists in North America defended themselves, as in fact they governed themselves, and separated from us in resentment of our interference. Our second Colonial policy was to govern and defend Colonies from home.' [7]

The purposes for which military forces were maintained varied according to the nature and local conditions of the colony. In the case of military and naval stations, Gibraltar and Malta, for example, the primary purpose was imperial defense. In Canada it was precaution against American aggression; in Jamaica, the preservation of law and order among the Negroes; at the Cape of Good Hope, protection against strong and warlike native tribes.[8]

Argument was not wanting to justify the heavy expenditure to which the people of Great Britain were put in consequence of this policy. Many British military men, aware of the traditional opposition to a powerful standing army at home, must have agreed with the Duke of Wellington that it was desirable to maintain strong garrisons in the colonies as reserves; and the statement was often made that the presence of British 'red-coats' in the colonies was an outward and visible sign of imperial unity which it would be dangerous to remove. Then, too, since the colonies might at any time be involved in war because of the foreign policy of the mother country, it was only just, so the argument ran, that they should be protected at her expense from the consequences of that policy. Furthermore, it was held by many that the control of military affairs by the colonial governments might lead to cruelty and violence on their part toward native peoples.[9]

As the years passed, however, the voice of economy and retrenchment began to be heard. During the War of 1812 with the United States British expenditures for the military defense of Canada were exceptionally heavy, and after the war large sums were spent on fortifications at Quebec, Halifax, and elsewhere in British North America. In 1817 a House of Commons committee on finance stated that the value to Britain of colonial possessions 'must be greatly diminished by their continuing a lasting drain on its resources,' and voiced the hope that some means might be found to make them 'more efficient towards defraying the expenses of their own military protection.'[10] Joseph Hume entered the House of Commons in 1819, and for many years one of his favorite themes was the great financial burden which Britain was bearing for the military defense of the colonies.[11]

In 1834 a select parliamentary committee was appointed 'to inquire into the Military Establishment and Expenditure in the Colonies and Dependencies of the Crown.' Lord John Russell, Grote, and Charles Buller were among its members. It was found that the total charges incurred for the year 1832 for the military defense of the dependencies, classified as 'military and maritime stations,' 'plantations and settlements,' and 'penal settlements,' was £2,003,397 and the actual net cost to Great Britain £1,761,505.[12] The committee urged that the strictest economy should be observed in every branch of colonial military expenditure and recommended a few trifling reductions of forces and expenses, but in the following resolution it recognized that an obligation rested on the Imperial Government to provide for the security of the colonies, even in time of peace:

That it is not the Intention of this Committee, by any suggestion which it may offer as to the Amount of Force deemed to be sufficient for the Garrison of any Colony in time of Peace, to relieve the Executive Government from the Duty which constitutionally belongs to it, of providing, on the responsibility of the King's Ministers, a Force sufficient for the Security of His Majesty's Possessions abroad, which Experience has proved is liable to vary in time of Peace, according to several contingencies arising out of internal or external causes.[13]

The system of colonial military defense at the expense of Great Britain continued with but slight modifications until the 'sixties. To quote from the report of an interdepartmental committee appointed in 1859 to investigate the expense of military defenses in the colonies:

. . . the Colonies of Great Britain may be said, speaking generally, to have been free from the obligation of contributing, either by personal service or money payment, towards their own defences—a state of things which we believe to have no parallel or precedent in the case of any other organized community of which the history is known.[14]

This report showed that the total military expenditure in the colonies for the year ending 31 March 1858 was £3,-968,599, toward the defrayal of which the colonies contributed only £378,253, or less than one-tenth, leaving £3,-590,346 as the cost to the Imperial Government. It appeared, furthermore, that of the total colonial contributions about two-thirds were paid by the three colonies of New South Wales, Victoria, and Ceylon, that several colonies contributed nothing, and that only Canada, the Cape of Good Hope, and one or two of the West Indies had organized any militia or other local force.[15] A parliamentary committee on colonial military expenditure, appointed in 1861, found that the Imperial Government had expended on the military defense of the dependencies during the year ending 31 March 1860 £3,225,081, the colonies having contributed £369,224.[16] It may not be superfluous to point out that this system whereby Great Britain held herself responsible for the military defense of the whole Empire was similar to that which still prevails with respect to naval defense. In the former case, as in the latter, initiative and responsibility rested with the Imperial Government, and some of the colonies made financial contributions or raised local forces.

*

* *

The financial burdens which the colonies imposed upon Great Britain was naturally a favorite theme with anti-imperialists. Josiah Tucker and Adam Smith, though attacking the colonial system primarily on commercial grounds, did not fail to touch on the subject of colonial defense. In that remarkable tract, *The True Interest of Great-Britain set forth in regard to the Colonies,* which we referred to in Chapter II, Tucker enumerated the 'manifold advantages' which would accrue to the mother country from the independence of the colonies. One of these was that she would be relieved of an expenditure of between £300,000 and £400,000 a year for their civil and military establishments, 'for which generous Benefaction,' he added, 'we receive at present no other Return than Invectives and Reproaches.'[17]

Adam Smith, in the course of his bold and sweeping indictment of the colonial system as a scheme of monopoly injurious both to colonies and to mother country, included in the cost of the colonies to Great Britain the expenses of naval forces maintained to prevent colonial smuggling and of colonial military establishments.[18] Though he realized that considerations of national pride and prestige, as well as the interest of the governing classes of England, would prevent the voluntary abandonment of the colonies by Great Britain, he said that one of the great advantages to be derived by her from colonial independence would be freedom 'from the whole annual expense of the peace establishment of the colonies.'[19] According to the Father of Free Trade, despite all the attempts that had been made to monopolize colonial commerce, 'no country has yet been able to engross to itself anything but the expense of supporting in time of peace and of defending in time of war the oppressive authority which it assumes over them.'[20]

The teachings of Adam Smith did not, of course, captivate at once the government and ruling classes of Britain.[21] Indeed, after the loss of the American colonies, British colonial policy and administration became, and for a time remained, more rather than less restrictive. The height of imperial interference in the affairs of the colonies came in the third and fourth decades of the nineteenth century. But Adam Smith was never silenced. His free-trade and anti-imperialist doctrines were perpetuated by the classical economists and the Benthamites.

The Manchester School, interested always in governmental economy, was fond of enlarging upon the burdensomeness of colonies to the harassed British taxpayer. England was pictured as a weary Titan struggling under a crushing burden. This view was forcefully expressed by Cobden in the course of a speech delivered in the House of Commons on 22 June 1843:

He was not opposed to the retention of colonies . . . and he believed that colonization, under a proper system of management, might be made as conducive to the interests of the mother country as to the emigrants themselves. But he also believed that the system upon which our colonial affairs were now conducted was one of unmixed evil, injustice and loss to the people of this country . . . He found that the mother country furnished her colonies with an army and a navy, and maintained every description of military defence all over the world; that in some cases this country supplied the colonies with schoolmasters, with bishops, with magistrates; that she built them lighthouses, constructed their canals, and, in fact, the mother country not only did not derive any revenue from her colonies, but that, besides maintaining for them large fleets and armies, she paid almost everything that constituted the governmental expenses of the colonies . . . The distribution of the British forces on the 1st of January this year he found to be this: out of 88,510 rank and file, there were stationed abroad (exclusively of India) 44,529 rank and file, the number left at home being 43,981. Thus, it appeared that more than half of our army was stationed in the colonies. But it had been stated by the authorities at the Horse Guards, and it was also stated by the noble Lord the Member for Tiverton, when Secretary of War, that for every 10,000 men in the colonies, 5000 were wanted in England for the purposes of making the necessary exchanges, and for recruiting the regiments abroad; therefore not merely half, but three-fourths of our army were devoted to the colonies.[22]

The Manchester School always insisted that free trade for the colonies ought to be accompanied by colonial self-defense. In a debate on financial reform in the House of Commons on 26 February 1849, Cobden said that the colonies were 'bound to maintain for themselves those establishments which are necessary for their own defense and their own government.' Two years later he declared that Britain's relations with the colonies had been 'completely changed by the adoption of our free-trade policy,' and that 'if it was folly before to garrison the Colonies, it was now downright insanity.' [23]

The colonial reformers shared the views of the Manchester School with regard to colonial military expenditure, and emphasized the relation of colonial self-defense to colonial self-government. In 1850 a Colonial Reform Association came into existence under the inspiration of Edward Gibbon Wakefield, having for its main objects the promotion of colonial self-government and colonial self-support. In it, Cobden and such zealous colonial reformers as C. B. Adderley and J. R. Godley were fellow-members. The death of Charles Buller in 1848 left Sir William Molesworth as the leading representative of the colonial reform school in the House of Commons. Molesworth warmly commended the grant of responsible government to the British North American colonies, and when it had been conceded to Canada, it 'seemed to him as absurd to pay for troops in the virtually independent colony of the Canadas, as it would be to pay for the military establishments in the independent colony of the United States.' [24] On 10 April 1851, he moved two resolutions in the House of Commons which linked the obligation of colonial self-defense and the privilege of colonial self-government. In the speech in which he opened the debate he said:

I maintain, that if these Colonies were governed as they ought to be governed, no troops ought to be maintained in them at the expense of the United Kingdom, except for strictly imperial purposes, and that the expenses of all troops required for local purposes ought to be paid by the Colonies . . . most of our Colonies, properly so called, do possess representative institutions, and all of them are about to possess those institutions. With such institutions no taxes can be levied in these Colonies without the consent of the representatives of the people; and their inhabitants cannot be constitutionally compelled to contribute out of their taxes to the revenues of the united kingdoms. Therefore, the people of the united kingdoms ought not to be called upon to pay out of their own taxes any portion of the local expenses of such colonies; and, consequently, in such colonies all expenses for local purposes should be paid out of local revenues, while all expenses for imperial purposes should be paid out of imperial revenues.[25]

The substance of Molesworth's resolutions was that the United Kingdom ought to be relieved as quickly as possible of its expenditure for colonies, except those held as military stations or convict settlements, and that their inhabitants ought at the same time to be given ample powers of local self-government and freed from 'that Imperial interference with their affairs which is inseparable from their present military occupation.' [26]

Wakefield sent a memorandum on the military defense of the colonies to Gladstone in March 1851.[27] In it he emphasized what he considered to be the bad effects of keeping British military forces in colonies—its tendency to cause local wars, to make real colonial self-government impossible, and to corrupt the colonists. He went so far as to attribute the Canadian rebellions of 1837 to the presence of British troops. 'The tyrannical rule of the small minority, which provoked the rebellion, was sustained by the presence of a large Imperial force.' In New Zealand 'free institutions' were being sacrificed to a policy toward the Maoris which depended on the presence of British troops there, and by 'a large foreign expenditure' the settlers were 'corrupted into lazy and servile dependents of the miserable government.'

The colonial reformers were convinced, too, that the heavy burden of colonial defense borne by the mother country greatly strengthened the hands of the separatists and was a standing threat to the preservation of the Empire. Adderley expressed this point of view when he said, in the debate on Molesworth's resolutions, that the people of Great Britain, at some moment of indignation, 'would not only throw off the burden of the expenditure, but with it they would cast away the Colonies themselves.' [28]

Anglo-French relations were dangerously strained for several periods during the 1840's and 1850's. British fears of attack by France, mounting at times to the height of panic, may have been unfounded and to a large extent worked up by those who did not share in the delusion, as Cobden believed, but at any rate there was great concern in England over the defense of the British Isles. In 1846 there occurred the affair of the Spanish marriages, which ruptured a so-called *entente* between England and France, and in December of that year the Duke of Wellington, then Commander-in-Chief of the British Army, urged upon Earl Grey, Secretary of State for War and the Colonies in Lord John Russell's Ministry, the need of an increase in the military establishment. Grey, who had already expressed himself as in favor of a large reduction of the British garrisons in the colonies, replied that considerations of economy made an increase of the army impossible, but promised to augment the force at home by reducing colonial garrisons.[29]

So long as Great Britain pursued the policy of commercial restriction which was the essence of the colonial system, the executive governments of the colonies continued to be held

responsible to the Imperial Government. As a writer on colonial administration put it, 'it was obviously impossible for
us to liberalize our system of administration until we should
first have liberalized our commercial policy.' [30] So long,
moreover, as colonial governments were responsible to an
external authority, it could be argued that this authority
was justly chargeable with the military defense of the colonies, not only against foreign powers but against internal
dangers as well. It was no mere coincidence that the advent
of free trade synchronized with the beginning of colonial
self-government. They were related causally, and with them
logically went a change in the system of colonial military
defense. Earl Grey in his work on colonial policy already referred to makes clear the connection between these three
subjects:

> I think it will follow, that when this Country no longer at-
> tempts either to levy a commercial tribute from the Colonies by
> a system of restriction, nor to interfere needlessly in their inter-
> nal affairs, it has a right to expect that they should take upon
> themselves a larger proportion than heretofore of the expenses
> incurred for their advantage . . . Our military expenditure on
> account of the Colonies is certainly very heavy . . . This expen-
> diture ought, I think, to be very largely reduced; and the Colo-
> nies, now that they are relieved from all that is onerous to them
> in their connection with the Mother country, should be required
> to contribute much more than they have hitherto done to their
> own protection.[31]

*

* *

It was Grey who took the first steps in the direction of
modifying the system of colonial defense which had been in
operation during the preceding half century. A beginning

was made with New South Wales, a colony free from the menace of either warlike native tribes or foreign powers. A few months after the Russell Ministry took office, Grey directed the Governor of New South Wales to send all disposable forces in the colony to New Zealand, where the settlers were then having trouble with the Maoris, retaining at Sydney only a small garrison, which, under the circumstances, was all that the Imperial Government deemed necessary. In his dispatch Grey said:

New South Wales may be regarded as being perfectly safe, for the present at least, from any attack from a foreign enemy; there are no native tribes capable of engaging in serious hostilities with the Colonists; and the Convict establishment is now reduced so low . . . that there is no longer the necessity which some years ago existed for maintaining a considerable military force to guard against the risk of an attempt to rise on the part of the convicts . . . Her Majesty's confidential Servants will consider it their duty to take care that the naval and military forces shall afford efficient protection from the attacks of any foreign enemy to so important a part of her dominions as New South Wales; but for the maintenance of internal order and tranquillity it is only reasonable that the Colonists should themselves be called upon to provide, by the formation of an adequate force of Police, or, if necessary, of militia.[32]

Despite local opposition, the policy which Grey outlined was carried out in the case of the Australian colonies. That policy, briefly stated, was that a certain maximum military force should be maintained at the expense of the mother country, and that any additional British troops that might be desired must be paid for by the colony that asked for them. Barracks and other military buildings were transferred to the colonies, which were held responsible for providing quarters for the British troops still remaining. According to testimony given in 1861 by Herman Merivale, one of the leading colonial experts of the day and previously permanent under-secretary of state for the colonies, Grey's plan for the military defense of the Australian colonies worked in a satisfactory manner. It undoubtedly stimulated the formation of volunteer forces. In 1859 there were only some 1,800 British troops in Australia, while the number of local volunteers amounted to about 9,000.[33]

Conditions in Canada, New Zealand, and Cape Colony prevented Grey from applying his policy as fully to those colonies. In New Zealand and South Africa there were war-like natives, and Canada, Anglo-American relations being as they were in 'the roaring forties,' was in more or less constant fear of invasion from the United States. The peaceful settlement of the Oregon dispute in 1846 made possible some reduction in the size of the British garrison in Canada, and Grey hopefully contemplated further reductions. Keenly sensitive to complaints in Britain of the financial burden-someness of colonies, he urged his views on Lord Elgin, who was then preoccupied with a great act of imperial faith—the introduction of responsible government in Canada—and with serious problems related to the severe economic depression which then held the province in its grip, including the question of annexation to the United States. Elgin thought that colonists ought not to be relieved altogether of the responsibility for self-defense, but in view of the state of public opinion in Canada he counseled the utmost caution in adopting new policies for its defense, especially at a time when the United States, having brought to a victorious conclusion its war with Mexico, was believed by Canadians to be in an exceptionally expansionist humor. 'British Statesmen, even Secretaries of State,' he wrote pointedly to Grey,

'have got into the habit lately of talking of the maintenance
of the connexion between Great Britain and Canada with
so much indifference, that a change of system in respect of
military defense incautiously carried out, might be presumed
by many to argue on the part of the Mother Country a disposition to prepare the way for separation.' [34] In a later letter
he remarked that the danger of an American attack on Canada was largely owing to its connection with Britain, and
that Canadian claims on the mother country for military
protection were therefore 'infinitely stronger than those of
any other colony.' [35] He realized, however, that the existing
British forces in Canada (about 5,000 infantry and 600 ar-
tillery in December 1848) would be no better able to cope
with an American invasion than a lesser force, and he told
Grey that a considerable reduction could be made without
increasing the probability of annexation to the United
States, 'provided always that you make no noise about it.' [36]

In an important dispatch to Elgin, dated 14 March 1851,
Grey outlined a military policy for Canada similar to that
already applied to New South Wales. He announced that
the British troops in the province would be confined for the
future to garrisons at two or three fortified posts, probably
only Quebec and Kingston, and that the use of the barracks
would be made over to the provincial authorities if the
Parliament of Canada was prepared to maintain them at its
own expense. If British forces were desired at any of the
other posts previously occupied, they would be supplied by
the Imperial Government, provided the cost was met by the
province. Grey was careful to add that this policy, though
necessary in justice to the people of Britain, was not to be
taken to mean that the connection between Canada and the
mother country could be severed without great injury to

both, or that there was any likelihood that it would be severed.[37] Professor C. P. Stacey, who has gone most fully into the subject of British military policy regarding Canada, says of this 'monumental dispatch' that it 'may be said to have been the theoretical basis of imperial military policy in Canada for years afterwards' and was 'repeatedly referred to as the classic statement of the official position.' [38]

Grey thus described the policy which as Colonial Secretary he had formulated and begun to apply:

. . . we endeavoured to establish, and by degrees to act upon, the principle that the Colonies can only look to the Mother-country for military support in any dangers to which they may be exposed from a powerful foreign enemy; that Her Majesty's troops are not to be expected to undertake the duties of police, and of maintaining the internal tranquillity of the Colonies; and that the Colonies ought to undertake to provide for the expense of barracks for such of Her Majesty's troops as may be stationed in them for their protection.[39]

And later Grey expressed the opinion that the policy had been carried out during his tenure of office (1846-52) as far as it safely and properly could be.[40]

The Anglo-Russian tension which led to the Crimean War caused Britain to withdraw some troops from colonies in order to increase her forces available for use against Russia. In February 1854, it was announced in Parliament that 5,000 men had been withdrawn from British North America, Cape Colony, and the West Indies,[41] and there were some further withdrawals during the course of the war. By the end of the fiscal year 1854-5, the number of British troops in Canada was down to less than 2,000.[42] Increased responsibility for defense was thrown on the province, which had so far made very little contribution to its own defense, and in

1855 the Canadian legislature passed a militia bill that provided for the establishment of a new force of volunteers, or 'active militia.' This was the first step taken by Canada towards the organization of an effective military force of its own, and for the future the main reliance for the military defense of Canada was to be the patriotism and loyalty of the Canadian people.[43]

The British Government, however, was so hard pressed for troops during the Crimean War that efforts were unfortunately made to obtain recruits in the United States, with the result that the British Minister at Washington was dismissed by the American Government, and another crisis arose in Anglo-American relations. In 1856 the Palmerston Ministry sent five regiments to Canada.[44]

In the same year Sir William Denison, Governor of New South Wales, made a proposal which, if adopted, would have shifted the initiative in providing for the military defense of the colonies from the Imperial Government to the colonies. He recommended that, 'whatever may be the mode in which the military force in a Colony may be raised and organized, the mother country and the Colony shall contribute towards its expense in equal proportions, and that the Government of the Colony should have the responsibility of determining the amount of that force, whether in peace or war.' The Imperial Government declined to accede to this proposal on the ground that it could not be carried out 'without compromising the independent action of the central Government of the Empire.'[45]

More important than the Denison proposal was a report of a committee appointed in 1859 to prepare a general plan of colonial military expenditure. Throughout the first half of the nineteenth century, a single minister was at the head of the war and colonial departments. This arrangement, whatever may have been its disadvantages, possessed a certain convenience so far as the military defense of the colonies was concerned. It came to an end, however, at the time of the Crimean War. Thenceforth the secretary of state for war was obliged to defend in Parliament expenditure incurred for the defense of the colonies, of whose needs he had no official knowledge and with whose governments he held no direct communication. He inevitably found himself embarrassed by the lack of any general principle determining questions with which he was called upon to deal. Accordingly, on 14 March 1859, the War Office, at the direction of the Secretary, General Peel, addressed a note to the Colonial Office, suggesting the propriety of adopting arrangements 'which should define the respective liabilities of this Department and the various Colonial Governments, in respect to military expenditure.' It was the opinion of the Secretary

that England should assist in the defence of her Colonies against aggression on the part of foreign civilized nations, and (in a less proportion) of formidable native tribes; but in no case, except where such Colonies are mere garrisons kept up for Imperial purposes, should she assume the whole of such defence . . . [and] that military expenditure, for purposes of internal police, should be defrayed from local funds, there being no grounds for drawing any distinction between a Colony and an independent nation in this respect.

He proposed the appointment of an interdepartmental committee, representative of the Colonial Office, the Treasury, and the War Office, to prepare a general scheme of colonial military expenditure.[46] Such a committee was appointed, consisting of Sir T. F. Elliot of the Colonial Office, Mr.

George A. Hamilton of the Treasury, and Mr. John Robert Godley of the War Office. The report, to which reference has been made, was not signed by the representative of the Colonial Office, who found himself unable to concur with his colleagues and submitted a separate memorandum in the nature of a minority report.[47] The committee found that the total imperial expenditure for colonial military defense for the year ending 31 March 1858 was nearly £4,000,000 and the total colonial expenditure approximately £375,000.[48]

The report attacked the existing policy of colonial defense on two principal grounds: (1) that it imposed an enormous burden on the people of Great Britain, not only in taxes but also by withdrawing a large part of their military forces from home; and (2) that it tended to prevent the development among the colonists of a spirit of self-reliance and to enfeeble their character. It was pointed out that existing arrangements were attended with great inequality and chronic discussions with regard to the respective liabilities of the imperial and colonial governments. There were, it was asserted, 'no recognized principles of mutual relations to which appeal can be made, or upon which a permanent settlement can be founded.' The report did not recommend the adoption as a general policy of Lord Grey's plan for the defense of the Australian colonies. The presence of even small garrisons in the colonies, maintained on the initiative of the mother country, would be taken, it was said, as a symbol of her responsibility for colonial military defense and would 'tend to perpetuate the main evils of the present system, namely, the dependence of the Colonies on the mother country for defense, and their neglect of local efforts.'

What the report proposed was to divide the colonies into two classes: (1) military posts, garrisoned by the Imperial

Government for imperial purposes rather than for local defense; and (2) all other dependencies where troops were stationed primarily for the protection of the inhabitants. In the case of the latter, it recommended that the system of defense should be founded on two simple principles: 'colonial management, and joint contribution at a uniform rate.' It proposed that the Imperial Government should call upon each colony to decide on the nature of its own defenses and should offer to bear a share—one-half was the proportion suggested —of the entire cost. Among the advantages anticipated by the committee from the adoption of its plan were: (1) that it would result in a great saving to the British exchequer without imposing an unduly heavy burden on the colonies; (2) that it would be applicable alike in time of peace and of war; (3) that it would stimulate the patriotism, self-reliance, and military spirit of the colonists by throwing on them responsibility for their own defense; and (4) that 'it would convey, in the most marked and emphatic way, the determination of the mother country, that the colonies should be governed through and for their own people.'

The representative of the Colonial Office dissented from some of the major proposals of the report. In particular, he did not accept the principle that all the colonies should bear a uniform proportion of the expense of their military defense, irrespective of local conditions, such as the degree of exposure to invasion, the character of the colonial population, and the wealth of the colony. Nor did he concur in the position taken by his colleagues that the only ground for military assistance to the colonies was that the Imperial Government controlled the issues of war and peace. On the contrary, he held that the interests of Great Britain were involved, and that they would suffer if certain colonies were lost. He preferred Lord Grey's plan to that recommended by the committee.[49]

This report of 1859 resulted in no radical change in the system of colonial defense. Its principal proposal, which had previously been made by Sir William Denison, that the initiative in providing for colonial defense should be thrown upon the colonies, was not at once adopted. The immediate outcome was fairly stated by Godley, in a criticism of Elliot's memorandum, when he said: 'We have, with trifling exceptions, the same extravagance on our side, the same helplessness on theirs; the same confusion, inconsistence, and disputation which has prevailed more or less for the last century in our military policy towards our Colonies.' [50]

*

* *

But the demand for reform was insistent, and on 5 March 1861, on motion of Arthur Mills, a select committee was appointed by the House of Commons 'to Inquire and Report whether any and what Alterations may be advantageously adopted in regard to the Defence of the British Dependencies, and the Proportions of Cost of such Defence as now defrayed from the Imperial and Colonial Funds respectively.' Mills, who served as chairman of the committee, had long been interested in colonial questions, had published a book on colonial constitutions, and was a member of the colonial reform group. He believed that British colonial policy ought to aim at immediate colonial self-government and self-defense, and eventual colonial independence. The meetings of the committee extended over a period of nearly four months. It examined a number of witnesses who were able to speak with authority on colonial, military, and fiscal questions, notably Earl Grey, Mr. Elliot, Mr. Merivale, General Sir J. F. Burgoyne, Inspector-General of Fortifications, Mr. Gladstone, Chancellor of the Exchequer, and Mr. Godley.[51]

For the purposes of the inquiry the report divided the British dependencies, exclusive of India, into two classes: (1) colonies proper, and (2) military garrisons, naval stations, convict depots, and dependencies maintained chiefly for objects of imperial policy. In the former class it included the North American, South African, and West Indian colonies, Ceylon, Mauritius, New Zealand, and the Australian colonies with the exception of Western Australia; in the latter, Malta, Gibraltar, the Ionian Islands, Hong Kong, Labuan, Bermuda, the Bahamas, St. Helena, the Falklands, Western Australia, Sierra Leone, Gambia, and the Gold Coast. The committee found that for the year ending 31 March 1860 the imperial military expenditure for the colonies proper was £1,715,246 and for the dependencies of the second class, £1,509,835—a total of £3,225,081. For the same year the dependencies, including some of both classes, contributed £369,224.[52] In the case of the dependencies of the second class, the committee agreed that 'the responsibility and main cost of their defence properly devolves on the Imperial Government,' but with respect to the colonies proper, it recommended that 'the responsibility and cost of the military defence . . . ought mainly to devolve upon themselves,' the Imperial Government using its discretion in applying this principle to particular colonies. Not the recommendation of the committee of 1859, but rather an extension of Lord Grey's policy for the defense of the Australian colonies was the solution of the problem urged by the select committee. The principles which it advocated were regarded by successive British ministries of both parties during the 1860's as representing the settled policy of the country.[53]

It will be remarked that the classification of the dependencies adopted by the committee of 1861 is not identical with that which divides them into 'self-governing colonies' and 'crown colonies'; some of the colonies which the committee classed as 'colonies proper' were not self-governing. All of the witnesses examined by the committee agreed that colonies enjoying responsible government should bear the primary responsibility for their military defense.[54] This view was clearly stated by Gladstone when he said: 'The privileges of freedom and the burdens of freedom are absolutely associated together; to bear the burdens is as necessary as to enjoy the privileges, in order to form that character which is the great ornament of all freedom itself.' [55]

On 4 March 1862, the House of Commons adopted the following resolution introduced by Mr. Mills:

That this House (while fully recognizing the claims of all portions of the British Empire to Imperial aid in their protection against perils arising from the consequences of Imperial policy) is of opinion that Colonies exercising the rights of self-government ought to undertake the main responsibility of providing for their own internal order and security, and ought to assist in their own external defence.[56]

This resolution introduced no novel principle, but it is significant that it was agreed to without a division, and was never afterwards called in question.[57]

In 1863 the Australian colonies were notified by the Duke of Newcastle, Secretary of State for the Colonies in Lord Palmerston's Ministry, that thenceforth they must pay for all imperial troops at the rate of £40 a year for every soldier, and that if additional British soldiers were supplied at the request of a colony, the rate would be £70, 'a sum which more nearly approaches the real cost to the Imperial Government of each soldier.' [58] Under Edward (afterwards Lord) Cardwell, who succeeded Newcastle at the Colonial Office in 1864, 10,000 troops were withdrawn from New Zealand, and the non-self-governing colonies of Ceylon, Mauritius, the Straits Settlements, and Hong Kong were required to contribute towards the support of their garrisons. Under Cardwell's successor, Lord Carnarvon, there were some withdrawals from Cape Colony.

Canada, because of peculiar conditions arising from the American Civil War, received exceptional treatment.[59] The Trent affair, which occurred late in 1861, threatened immediate war between Britain and the United States, and the British garrisons in North America, which had numbered little more than 4,000 when the Civil War began, rose to about 18,000 in the spring of 1862.[60] The number was slightly reduced after the passing of the Trent crisis, but Anglo-American relations could not be called harmonious prior to the Treaty of Washington in 1871. The United States at the close of the Civil War was the foremost military power in the world, and though demobilization proceeded rapidly in 1865, it was generally apparent in England that Canada could not be successfully defended by a British garrison. She must depend mainly upon her own exertions. The British Government looked with favor upon the confederation of the North American provinces, consummated in 1867, as a means of strengthening their defenses, and withdrawals of British troops were carried out in 1867 and 1868.

The cost to Britain of the military defense of Cape Colony had long seemed unduly heavy, and in 1867 the colony was notified that the force maintained there would be reduced at once, and that after 1869 all remaining British troops must be paid for at the Australian rate.[61] Troubles with natives and continued friction between the British and the Boers made it impossible to carry out this policy so soon, but the imperial forces were gradually reduced. The dispatch of British troops in great numbers to South Africa during the Boer War was, of course, no part of a permanent colonial policy.

It was while Cardwell was Secretary of State for War in the Liberal Ministry which Gladstone formed in December 1868, that the principles already followed were most fully carried out. Cardwell, a first-rate administrator, had already had wide governmental experience, having served as President of the Board of Trade, Chief Secretary for Ireland, and Secretary of State for the Colonies. Conditions in the army, he was convinced, called urgently for extensive and drastic reforms in the interest of efficiency and economy, and as head of the Colonial Office (1864-6) he had become thoroughly familiar with the problem of the imperial garrisons.[62]

Soon after his appointment to the War Office, Cardwell, in a memorandum submitted to Gladstone and approved by him, indicated the lines along which he thought army reform ought to proceed.[63] One of his proposals was to reduce the imperial forces in the colonies from 50,000 to 26,000. In presenting the army estimates for the year 1869-70, he announced a reduction in expenditure for the colonies proper, distinguishing between them and oversea possessions held as imperial stations, of more than one-third, from £1,643,794 in the budget of the preceding year to £1,070,735. The principal retrenchment was on the force in Canada, which was to be reduced from about 16,000 to 6,000 men. Like his chief, Cardwell was a robust Liberal, with faith in the saving virtues of self-government, self-support, and self-defense:

If, instead of calling upon your colonists to exert themselves and to rely on their own resources, you distribute forces among them in small divisions, you will paralyze their efforts without furnishing them with real strength. I believe that Canada, with 30,000 or 40,000 armed men of her own, occupies a stronger and more independent position than she ever did before . . . the true defence of our colonies is that they live under the ægis of the name of England, and that war with them is war with England.[64]

Cardwell's colleague, Lord Granville, Gladstone's Colonial Secretary, notified the Governor General of Canada that about 2,000 men would be left in Nova Scotia for the time being for the defense of Halifax, which would continue to be regarded as an imperial station, and about 4,000 in the other provinces of the Dominion, adding: 'But this must be considered a temporary arrangement, and I am disposed to concur with Mr. Cardwell in the opinion that it will soon become unnecessary to maintain any British force in those Provinces, beyond what may be required for the training of the Militia and Volunteers and the maintenance of Schools of Instruction.'[65] This was in April 1869. Early in the following year he gave notice that the barracks and fortifications vacated by the imperial forces would be turned over to Canada with the understanding that if, at any future time, troops should be sent to Canada at the request of the Canadian Government, the Dominion would be expected to lodge them 'to the satisfaction of Her Majesty's Government.'[66] Commenting on the decisions taken by the British Government, Professor Stacey remarks that 'close examination of the dispatches revealed in them an alarming air of finality, reflecting an evident determination to effect as complete a severance as possible between the military systems of Britain and Canada, and in particular to relieve the British taxpayer from any liability whatever for that of the Dominion.' [67]

It should be remarked, too, that these decisions were reached at a time when Canada's position was full of peril. Anglo-American relations were still far from cordial, and the dark cloud of annexation to the United States hung low on the Canadian horizon. Charles Sumner, chairman of the American Senate's Committee on Foreign Relations, was publicly urging the cession of Canada to the United States in settlement of the Alabama claims, and Hamilton Fish, the American Secretary of State, was privately discussing annexation with the British Minister.[68] Irish Fenians in the United States had not yet lost their pious and patriotic hope of doing something for 'the old country' by an invasion of Canada that would bring on war between their hereditary enemy and the United States. At the moment, moreover, the Canadian Government had on its hands a revolt that had broken out among French-Canadian half-breeds in the Red River Settlement at what is now Winnipeg, the Riel Rebellion as it is called. It is small wonder that many Canadians came to believe that England desired to be rid of them. 'We do not think,' said the influential Toronto *Globe* in its issue of 14 October 1870, 'that the withdrawal of all the troops in Canada, with the exception of one regiment, was the act of men friendly to the colonial connexion.' [69]

By the end of 1871 the British garrisons had evacuated all the posts previously occupied in Canada except Halifax and Esquimalt on Vancouver Island, which became a part of the Dominion in that year. These two British naval bases continued to be garrisoned by imperial troops until the time of the Boer War. Military installations at the various posts were transferred to the Dominion when the British garrisons were withdrawn. Fortunately for Canada, the danger of American invasion passed away when, in 1871, Great Britain and the United States settled their outstanding disputes by the Treaty of Washington.

From New Zealand, the last of the British troops were withdrawn in 1869 under extraordinary circumstances which will claim our attention in the next chapter.[70] The imperial military evacuation of Australia was completed in the following year.[71]

According to a statement in the House of Commons made by the parliamentary under secretary of state for the colonies on 7 March 1873, British expenditure on account of the colonies had fallen from £3,388,033 in 1869 to £1,708,290, of which amount, he said, £1,205,026 was chargeable to imperial purposes, leaving only about £500,000 for local colonial purposes, and against this should be set £238,600 repaid by various colonies.[72] The cost of the colonies to the mother country, in other words, was down to about £250,000 per annum. A Royal Commission appointed in 1879 to study questions of imperial defense found that small detachments were quartered in some of the less important colonies, notably in British Honduras, 'mainly for the maintenance of peace and order within their borders.' The commission recommended 'that the practice of employing Imperial soldiers in duties hardly distinguishable from those of police—especially in the smaller Crown Colonies—should be discontinued as soon as possible.' [73]

To a great many people in Britain as well as in the colonies the withdrawal of the garrisons carried out by the Gladstone Government was taken as clear evidence of a desire on its part to free the mother country from all responsibility for the colonies and hasten the break-up of the Empire. It cannot be said that the withdrawals were characterized by a high degree of sympathetic consideration for colonial sensibilities, but it is equally true that by diminishing the burdens of empire, of which the anti-imperialists had always made so much, the Government, whatever motives may be ascribed to it, removed the principal argument against maintaining the Empire. In doing so, it helped to pave the way for the rise of a new imperialism.

THE CLIMAX OF ANTI-IMPERIALISM

AT a time when free trade was destroying the old colonial system and Englishmen were complaining loudly of the encumbrances of empire, it was not surprising that some of them openly advocated the independence of the colonies. The free-trade press was distinctly anti-imperialist in tone. There was no ground for supposing, said *The Economist,* that the colonies

would become less valuable customers to us, less open to the reception of our superabundant population, or less friendly to us, if each had its own government, and were a separate state, only bound to us by the ties of a common origin, and a common interest. In fact, there does not seem to be, in general, any doubt whatever on this subject; and it is now stated as the main reason for retaining these colonies, at a great cost, in a state of dependence, that if we permitted them to separate from us they would fall into the possession of some other power and endanger our supremacy . . . The murmurs, the complaints, the distant grumblings, coming from many quarters, indicate demands for reform, and it is only rational to adopt means at once to prepare both the colonies and the mother country for a change that seems in the order of nature.[1]

At a time when it was the habit to regard imperial dominion as a scheme of commercial monopoly, it was difficult to justify heavy expenditures on colonies that were free to trade where and in what ships they pleased. And when these colonies began to impose protective duties on products of the mother country, the quintessence of anomaly seemed to have been reached.[2]

The same era that witnessed the removal of the old restrictions on colonial trade saw the establishment of responsible government in the North American and Australasian colonies, and there were many who regarded this as the prelude to their independence. Lord John Russell, speaking as Government leader in the House of Commons in 1837, argued that the grant of responsible government to colonies would be tantamount to giving them independence,[3] and later, as Secretary of State for the Colonies (1839-41), he opposed full responsible government for Canada.[4] Lord John, to be sure, changed his mind later on, but by no means all of those who had shared his opinion—and it was probably the prevailing opinion among the English governing classes—kept pace with him. The assumed tendency of colonies to separate from their mother countries was invested with the compulsive character of a natural law which the will of man was impotent to check.

The liberal imperialism of the colonial reformers, which received its most celebrated expression in Lord Durham's Report, made rapid progress during the Ministry of Lord John Russell (1846-52), when Earl Grey (formerly Lord Howick) presided over the Colonial Office. Grey was the chief architect of 'the colonial policy of Lord John Russell's administration' as well as the author of a book which bore this title. He was a very able administrator and an enthusiastic, almost passionate, and decidedly dogmatic free-trader. He cherished the illusion, entertained by British free-traders in general, that Britain's commercial liberalism would usher in an age of world-wide free trade and international goodwill.[5] He was also a firm believer in the virtues of colonial

self-government. While he was Colonial Secretary, free trade
was carried practically to completion, and responsible government was established in the British North American
colonies.[6] There were limitations, however, to his devotion
to colonial self-government, as was true in the case of other
colonial reformers of his day. If colonial self-government
should come into conflict with his other ideal, free trade, if
a colony, even a colony to which responsible government
had been granted, should be so unwise as to prefer protection to the new and 'sound' commercial policy which the
Imperial Government and Parliament, in their wisdom, had
adopted as the policy of the Empire, Grey had no doubt that
free trade ought to prevail,[7] and he believed that the Imperial Government ought to disallow colonial laws which
were repugnant to free-trade principles.[8] But here the tendency was against Grey, and a few years after his retirement
from the Colonial Office it was established as a principle of
colonial policy that it was within the powers of a self-governing colony to impose protective duties on imports, British
as well as foreign.[9]

The most important official statement on colonial policy
made by any member of the Russell Ministry is to be found
in a speech delivered in the House of Commons on 8 February 1850, by Lord John himself.[10] An authoritative declaration seemed to be called for, since Britain's new free-trade
policy had caused discontent in some of the colonies and at
home had raised the question of whether it was worth while
to keep the colonies. In the body of the speech the Prime
Minister came out strongly against separation—'I consider
it to be our bounden duty to maintain the colonies which
have been placed under our own charge'—and laid down two

cardinal principles on which his Government intended to proceed. The first of these was free trade—'that you shall trade with your colonies on the principle that you are at liberty to obtain productions from other countries where they may be produced better or cheaper than in the colonies, and that the colonies should be at liberty to trade with all parts of the world in the manner which may seem to them most advantageous.' The second principle was colonial freedom—'that . . . you should, as far as possible, proceed upon the principle of introducing and maintaining political freedom in all your colonies. I think whenever you say political freedom cannot be introduced, you are bound to show the reasons for the exemption . . . that you must show the colony is not formed of the British people, or even that there is no such admixture of the British population as to make it safe to introduce representative institutions.' A confession of faith, this seemed to be, in liberal imperialism. But then came this peroration:

I anticipate indeed with others that some of the colonies may so grow in population and wealth that they may say—'Our strength is sufficient to enable us to be independent of England. The link is now become onerous to us—the time is come when we can, in amity and alliance with England, maintain our independence.' I do not think that that time is yet approaching. But let us make them as far as possible, fit to govern themselves—let us give them, as far as we can, the capacity of ruling their own affairs—let them increase in wealth and population, and whatever may happen, we of this great empire shall have the consolation of saying that we have contributed to the happiness of the world.

Lord Elgin, keenly conscious of the crisis through which Canada was then passing in its relations with the mother country, and aware of the rising tide of separatist sentiment in Britain, regarded those concluding sentences—'the sting in the tail,' as he called them—with dismay. He wrote to Grey:

I much fear that when the liberal and enlightened sentiments, the enuntiation of which by one so high in authority is so well calculated to make the Colonists sensible of the advantages which they derive from their connexion with Great Britain, shall have passed away from their memories, there will not be wanting those who will remind them that on this solemn occasion the Prime Minister of England amid the plaudits of a full Senate declared that he looked forward to the day when the ties which he was endeavouring to render so easy & mutually advantageous would be severed! . . . I have never been able to comprehend why, elastic as our constitutional system is, we should not be able, now more especially when we have ceased to control the trade of our Colonies, to render the links which bind them to the British Crown at least as lasting as those which unite the component parts of the [American] Union . . . One thing is however indispensable to the success of this or any other system of Colonial Gov^t—You must renounce the habit of telling the Colonies that the Colonial is a provisional existence.—You must allow them to believe that without severing the bonds which unite them to Great Britain they may attain the degree of perfection and of social and political development to which organized communities of freemen have a right to aspire.[11]

'The sting in the tail' was widely commented upon at home and abroad. The London *Times* observed: 'When a colony feels itself really independent . . . it will undoubtedly aspire to the dignity as well as convenience of absolute self-government . . . It is the order of nature, and we cannot fight against it, except to our disappointment, loss, and disgrace.' [12]

In a private letter to Elgin, Grey thus interpreted the Prime Minister's words:

I do not think he Meant to say more than the time *might* come
in wh. the Colonies w^d wish to dissolve the connection & that
when it did so we ought to allow the separation to take place
amicably, & in the Mean time to take all the means in our power
to prepare them for self Gov^{nt}—It seems to me that this clearly *is*
our policy tho' with you I deprecate all reference that can possibly be avoided to eventual separation—.[13]

He deprecated public reference to it, but his private correspondence with Elgin shows that it was constantly in his
mind. He himself was far from being a separatist. He believed that much of Britain's influence and power depended
on her colonial empire, and he had an acute sense of the
imperial responsibilities she had undertaken and of her
obligation to discharge them. Disastrous consequences would
follow in many parts of the Empire, he was convinced, if
British authority should be withdrawn.[14] He was a liberal
imperialist, with an almost mystical conception of the British
Empire as a mighty and beneficent instrument, under Providence, for the maintenance of peace and justice and the
spread of Christianity and civilization throughout vast regions of the earth. In the history of imperial trusteeship as
a principle of British colonial policy, Grey deserves an hon-
orable place. At times, however, 'the lamp of faith burned
dim' within him.[15] Its flickerings can be detected in his private letters to Elgin:

You have I know observed how great a leaning there is in a
party wh. is becoming very numerous to seek to get rid of our
Colonies representing them to be merely a burthen & incum-
berance to us, & this most mistaken & shortsighted policy (as I
consider it) has received too much encouragement from persons
who occupy a prominent position in public life— . . . unfortunately there begins to prevail in the H. of Commons & I am
sorry to say in the highest quarters, an opinion (wh. I believe

to be utterly erroneous) that we have no interest in preserving our Colonies & ought therefore to Make no sacrifice for that purpose, Peel, Graham, & Gladstone if they do not avow this opinion as openly as Cobden & his friends, yet betray very clearly that they entertain it, nor do I find some Members of the Cabinet free from it . . .[16]

*

* *

Separatism was distinctly a British, not a colonial, phenomenon. In Canada, to be sure, there was a movement which involved this issue, though separation was not advocated by any considerable number of people there except as a preliminary to annexation to the United States. The Canadian Annexation movement, which reached its culmination in 1849, was not a movement for colonial independence.[17] In Canada, moreover, support for separation came not, as in England, from reformers and free-traders, but principally from Tories, especially in Montreal, who detested reform and free trade and looked back with nostalgia to the good old days of protection and imperial preference. Their argument was that the adoption of free trade by Britain made the continuance of the British connection useless to Canada. Canadian free-traders, on the other hand, saw important advantages to Canada in remaining within the Empire.[18] The Annexation movement has received careful and comprehensive treatment at the hands of a number of scholars, and no detailed account of it will be attempted here.[19]

From 1846 to 1850, Canada, as we saw in Chapter v, was suffering from a severe commercial depression of which there was no single and simple cause, but the human mind craves simple explanations, and the *post hoc ergo propter hoc* argument, however fallacious, is easy to grasp and almost sure to be popular. The repeal of the corn laws was generally regarded in Canada as the chief, if not the only, cause of the depression.[20] Many remedies were proposed, including the repeal of the navigation laws, commercial reciprocity with the United States, a federal union of the British North American colonies, a protective tariff for Canada, and the building of railways.[21] But for a time Annexation was the popular panacea. In March 1849, Elgin wrote to Grey,

no matter what the subject of complaint, or what the party complaining; Whether it be alleged that the French are oppressing the British, or the British the French,—that Upper Canada Debt presses on Lower Canada, or Lower Canada claims on Upper; whether merchants be bankrupt, stocks depretiated, roads bad, or seasons unfavourable—annexation is invoked as the remedy for all ills imaginary or real.[22]

Of all the arguments employed by the annexationists, the most difficult to refute, according to Elgin, was the assertion that England was indifferent to the maintenance of the colonial connection.[23] He complained that when he protested against Canadian proposals for dismembering the Empire he always met with this response: 'The most eminent statesmen in England have over and over again told us that whenever we chose we might separate—Why then blame us for discussing the subject?' [24]

An Annexation Association was formed in Montreal, the Tory press of the city campaigned vigorously for the cause, and on 11 October 1849 the celebrated Annexation Manifesto was published.[25] First among the causes of the evils from which Canada was suffering was placed 'the reversal of the ancient policy of Great Britain, whereby she withdrew

from the colonies their wonted protection in her markets.'
Remedies that had been proposed were reviewed, and the
conclusion was reached that the only effective one was a
'friendly and peaceful separation from British connexion,
and a union upon equitable terms with the great North
American confederacy of sovereign States.' Separation without the consent of Britain was disavowed and rejected as
impracticable and undesirable, but the conviction was expressed that the mother country had determined to compel
the people of Canada 'to assume the burdens of independence,' and as evidence of this, reference was made to the
policy of withdrawing British troops from the colonies.

It is impossible to make an accurate estimate of the
strength of Annexation sentiment in Canada. Montreal was
the center of the movement, and such leadership as it enjoyed was supplied by discontented Tories there and in the
Eastern Townships of Lower Canada, whose sense of grievance against the British Government for its new commercial
policy had been heightened by the working of the recently
established system of responsible government, under which
their political opponents had come to power. They feared
and dreaded French Canadian domination and resented
Lord Elgin's cordial relations with French Canadian political leaders; and his recent action in assenting to the Rebellion Losses Bill, which they denounced as a measure for re-
warding treason, was in their eyes an unforgivable sin. Some
support was given to the movement by Americans resident
in Montreal and elsewhere in Canada, and among the Irish
element in the province, heavily reinforced by the famine
migration of 1847, fishing in waters troublesome to Britain
was a traditionally popular occupation. Among French Ca-

nadians there were some annexationists, especially within the anti-British, anti-clerical, and pro-republican *Rouge* party headed by the former rebel leader, L. J. Papineau. The great bulk of the French Canadians, however, looked with no favor upon incorporation in a predominantly Protestant republic, and the Roman Catholic Church in Canada was strongly opposed to it. The movement made no headway in Upper Canada in spite of economic distress.

Lord Elgin looked upon the Annexation Manifesto as the work of 'a knot of violent protectionists and disappointed party men,' [26] but he did not make the mistake of underestimating the extent of the economic distress, and he believed that if remedies were not applied, separation would probably come about. The two remedies on which he laid chief stress in his private correspondence with Lord Grey were the repeal of the navigation laws and reciprocity between Canada and the United States. [27] Before the Annexation movement reached its climax he was writing to Grey that among the commercial classes of the province the belief was almost universal that they would be better off if Canada were annexed to the United States, and that unless the American market were opened to Canadian producers, it would be 'quite hopeless to attempt to maintain the connexion with G^t Britain under our present system of Commercial Policy.' [28] The British Parliament, as we know, passed the bill for the repeal of the navigation laws in June 1849, but this did not put a stop to the Annexation agitation. Elgin hoped that if the repeal was followed by reciprocity, Canada would remain contentedly within the Empire. [29] To this end, however, he considered it absolutely indispensable that British statesmen should 'renounce the habit of telling

the Colonies that the Colonial is a provisional existence.' [30]
'There cannot,' he wrote to Grey in March 1850, 'be peace,
contentment, progress, or credit in this Colony while the
idea obtains that the connexion with England is a millstone
about it's neck which should be cast off, as soon as it can be
conveniently managed.' [31]

The Annexation movement died during the year 1850.
Lord Grey in his private letters to Lord Elgin had referred
to the growth of separatist sentiment in high political quarters in England and expressed pessimistic views about the
maintenance of the British connection with Canada, but no
trace of this appeared in the official dispatch which Her
Majesty's Secretary of State for the Colonies sent to the Governor General of Canada in response to the Annexation
Manifesto:

Her Majesty confidently relies on the Loyalty of the great
majority of Her Canadian Subjects, and She is therefore determined to exert all the authority which belongs to her for the
purpose of maintaining the connection of Canada with this
Country, being persuaded that the permanence of that connection is highly advantageous to both . . . Your Lordship will
therefore understand that you are Commanded by Her Majesty
to resist, to the utmost of your power, any attempt which may
be made to bring about the separation of Canada from the British Dominions . . .[32]

Clearly, then, the annexationists could look for no encouragement to the British Government of the day, and by 1850
the depression in Canada had run its course. With the advent of better times, Annexationism lost whatever vitality it
had had. Writing to Grey in October 1850, Elgin was able
to say that he believed 'there never was before in Canada
such general contentment,' and during the election of 1851

he detected 'few if any attacks on the *connection with England.*' [33] Annexationism was dead before reciprocity came to bury it.[34]

＊

＊ ＊

The decade 1861-70 may fairly be called a critical period in British imperial history, for it was during those years that tendencies in Britain toward the disruption of the Empire reached their climax. The doctrines of the Manchester School were at the height of their influence. Free trade, having justified itself by its fruits, had been accepted by all parties as the settled policy of the nation, and the Anglo-French Commercial Treaty of 1860 was taken to herald it as the future policy of all nations. Prosperity, peace, and progress were about to supplant the unholy trinity of protectionism, militarism, and imperialism. So at least it seemed, for untoward events had not yet shown this faith of Manchester to be unwarranted. Were free-trade principles to be followed to the limit of logic; was the Empire to be dissolved? There was much to indicate that the answer to this question would be in the affirmative. The subject has received little or no notice, however, in the standard histories of England or in the biographies of the leading British statesmen of the day. Sometimes when an English historian has vouchsafed to touch upon the anti-imperial sentiment of the mid-Victorian era, the reader gets the impression that a regrettable episode is being glossed over.

Probably the foremost advocate of the dismemberment of the Empire was Goldwin Smith. While Regius Professor of Modern History at Oxford, he wrote a series of letters that appeared in *The Daily News* in 1862 and 1863 and were published in the latter year in a volume entitled *The Empire*. He pointed out that conditions were very different from what they had been when the old colonial system was established.

The time was [he said] when the universal prevalence of commercial monopoly made it well worth our while to hold colonies in dependence for the sake of commanding their trade. But that time has gone. Trade is everywhere free, or becoming free; and this expensive and perilous connection has entirely survived its sole legitimate cause. It is time that we should recognize the change that has come over the world.

Every hour that an adult colony was kept in a state of dependence, an injury was done to its political character. If Canada was unable to stand by itself, it must eventually join with the United States. As things were, Great Britain's dominion there kept her constantly on the brink of war with the American Republic. The West Indies had become 'a mere burden.' The case of India was different; there England had assumed responsibilities which she must discharge if possible, but if she could not transform India from a dependency into a colony by settling there as a governing and civilizing class, the days of her rule were numbered. Even military dependencies like Gibraltar had been rendered to a great extent unnecessary by the triumph of free trade. There was no longer any need for the British to post themselves all over the globe in order to make way for their commerce; trade had become its own protection. British policy had of late become favorable to colonial self-government, 'and, therefore, theoretically favorable to emancipation,' but it would be difficult for statesmen to take the decisive step of freeing a colony unless urged on by public opinion. Like other anti-imperialists of the day, Goldwin Smith hoped that the independence of the colonies would be achieved peacefully, without the rancor and animosity that had accompanied the separation of the United States from the Empire and survived to mar Anglo-American relations for a hundred years. He believed that what was best in the colonial relationship—the ties of blood, sympathy, and ideas—would not be affected by political separation, and he looked forward to the time when, the colonies having become independent nations, something in the nature of an Anglo-Saxon federation might develop spontaneously out of 'affinity and natural affection.'

Goldwin Smith's letters provoked a debate in the press and attracted attention not only in England but throughout the Empire. The London *Times* poured ridicule upon his ideas by comparing them with 'projects for general disarmament or for equalizing the political rights of the sexes.' [35] Disraeli alluded to him in a contemptuous reference which he made in the House of Commons to 'prigs and pedants.' [36] He was referred to as the apostle of anti-imperialism, and the dissolution of the Empire came to be spoken of as his 'colonial policy.' [37] The colonial press in general, and especially that of Australia, was bitterly hostile to his proposals.[38] In his *Reminiscences,* published in 1911, Goldwin Smith wrote of his *Daily News* letters: 'The whole series was Anti-Imperialist, advocating the concession of independence to adult Colonies so that England might become indeed the mother of free nations.' [39] Though his doctrines were submerged in the tide of imperialism that began to flow in the early 'seventies, he himself seems never to have wavered in his opinions.[40]

In 1865, Henry (afterwards Lord) Thring published a pamphlet entitled *Suggestions for Colonial Reform,* in which he urged that the independence of the colonies ought to be looked forward to and prepared for as the natural termination of a temporary connection. His views are not to be regarded as those of a visionary, remote from the realities of practical politics. He was at the time Home Office Counsel and as such was called upon to draft all important Government measures; probably no man knew more of the inner history of parliamentary legislation than he. For years he had taken an interest in colonial questions, and in 1850 he had prepared a plan of colonial reform for Sir William Molesworth, which the latter introduced into Parliament as a series of amendments to a bill for the government of New South Wales.[41] In the tract of 1865 Thring proposed a comprehensive scheme defining the relations between the mother country and the colonies at every stage of their existence. It included rules regulating the conditions on which adventurers might settle in unoccupied territory, provisions for their temporary subjection to the authority of the Crown and their subsequent organization as a colony with representative institutions, and arrangements by which a colony, having arrived at maturity, might declare its desire for independence. The author was strongly influenced by current events. He believed that the union of the British North American provinces, then pending, would be followed by their independence, and the War of Secession in the United States, then in progress, confirmed him in his belief that the British colonies would eventually secede from the Empire.

As an expert parliamentary draftsman Thring naturally threw his scheme of colonial reform into the form of a parliamentary bill, which was printed in an appendix to his pamphlet. It consists of four parts, of which only the last, entitled 'Independence of Colony,' concerns us here. This outlined the procedure to be followed by a colony when it desired to withdraw from the Empire. It provided that if a resolution asking for independence should be adopted by the legislature of a colony, by a two-thirds majority of both houses, and confirmed after an interval of not less than three months by a similar resolution passed during the same session by a like majority, the governor should notify the secretary of state for the colonies, whereupon it should be lawful for the Queen to grant or withhold her assent to the petition. If the assent were given, it should be proclaimed in the colony, which should thereupon become independent. A colony, when it had become independent, would be in all respects in the same situation as an independent state, but it should be deemed to have entered into a treaty with the former mother country providing (1) that no law should be passed in the former colony impairing the obligation of any contract made before the date of the colony's independence; (2) that no differential duty should be laid on imports from or exports to any part of the British dominions; and (3) that no privilege should be conferred on the subjects of any foreign power that was not equally conferred on British subjects.[42]

Shortly after the publication of Thring's pamphlet there appeared a work by Viscount Bury, entitled *Exodus of the Western Nations*. Though the book was historical, the author, in a concluding chapter, turned his eyes to the future. He was firmly convinced that the separation of the colonies was a matter of time only, and that it should be prepared for with prudence and foresight so that it might take place peacefully and with mutual good-will. 'The wisest statesman,' he said, 'is not he who would by any shift postpone the inevitable day, but he who most clearly recognizes signs of maturity and seizes the right moment for separation.' He proposed to supplement Thring's bill, of which he approved, by a treaty between Great Britain and a seceding colony. Believing that the British North American colonies, then about to confederate, would be the first to become formally independent, he submitted, as an indication of his views, a draft treaty in the form of 'Articles of Separation' between Great Britain and British North America, the latter being referred to as the 'New Nation.' This provided, among other things, that the Imperial Government might at any time, either with the consent of Parliament or at the request of the colonists of the New Nation, give twelve months' notice of its intention to discontinue the exercise of authority over the New Nation and to recognize its independence; that Great Britain, to the utmost of her power, should protect the New Nation if the latter were attacked by an external enemy; that neither should discriminate against the other's commerce; and that citizens of each should enjoy the rights of citizenship in the other.[43]

In 1868 there was published in London a two-volume book of travel entitled *Greater Britain,* which rapidly ran through three editions and had a large sale in the United States.[44] It is the record of a tour around the world which its author, Charles Dilke, then at the threshold of his political career, had just completed, and in it he indulged in various observations and reflections on British imperial relations. Dilke's thought on questions of empire was colored by the fact that his patriotism was cultural, not political. His supreme allegiance was not to Great Britain or to the British Empire as political entities, but to 'Anglo-Saxondom.' He included the United States in 'Greater Britain,' an expression that he coined, and looked upon the American

Republic as an amplifier for England's voice to the world, offering to the English race 'the moral dictatorship of the globe, by ruling mankind through Saxon institutions and the English tongue.' He had no doubt that English laws and institutions were essential to the freedom and welfare of humanity, but the future of any one branch of the English race was to him a matter of slight importance compared with its triumph as a whole.[45]

It is not strange, therefore, that Dilke saw little objection to the political separation from Great Britain of those colonies that were English in speech and culture. In the case of Canada he thought that it would be distinctly beneficial. 'At bottom,' he said, 'it would seem as though no one gained by the retention of our hold on Canada.' Separation would mean, for Canada, an end of the danger of Fenian raids and a removal of the menace of American invasion in the event of war between Great Britain and the United States. For Great Britain it would result in improvement in her relations with the United States as well as in relief from heavy expenditure for Canadian defense.[46] With regard to Australia his view was somewhat different, for here Britain's dominion did not imperil her good relations with a foreign power. He was in favor of an Australian federation, which he believed would tend toward independence, and he was wholly opposed to a continuance of what he called 'the existing one-sided tie,' which bound England to defend Australia; but he believed that in a healthier state of imperial relations separation would not be to the interest of Great Britain, though it might be morally beneficial to Australia.[47]

Dilke distinguished sharply between colonies proper, 'English-speaking, white-inhabited, and self-governed,' and dependencies like India, Ceylon, and the West Indies. In the case of the former he dwelt upon what he deemed to be the defects of the existing system of defense, which placed a heavy financial burden upon Britain and prevented the colonies from forming habits of self-reliance. Since in trade with the colonies the mother country no longer enjoyed advantages that were not accorded to foreigners, he saw no greater reason why she should defend them than why they should assist her in European wars, and he conjectured that 'Australia would scarcely feel herself deeply interested in the guarantee of Luxembourg, nor Canada in the affairs of Servia.' He looked upon the United States as a better colony, for commercial purposes, than Canada, and he thought it unlikely that British trade with a colony would be affected by its political independence. As an outlet for the surplus population of the British Isles, the colonies, as independent states, would be as useful as they had been, and might be more so. He estimated that of every twenty people who emigrated from the United Kingdom, one went to Canada, two to Australia, and sixteen to the United States. The imperialist argument of prestige from far-flung dominion he dismissed as an absurdity; if extent of territory measured power, China was twenty-six times as powerful as France!

It is unfair to mid-Victorian Englishmen who were not averse to the dismemberment of the Empire to represent them as wholly controlled by considerations of profit and loss.

> And that true North, whereof we lately heard
> A strain to shame us, 'keep you to yourselves;
> So loyal is too costly! friends—your love
> Is but a burthen: loose the bond, and go.'
> Is this the tone of empire? here the faith
> That made us rulers? this, indeed, her voice

And meaning, whom the roar of Hougoumont
Left mightiest of all peoples under heaven?
What shock has fool'd her since, that she should speak
So feebly? wealthier—wealthier—hour by hour!
The voice of Britain, or a sinking land,
Some third-rate isle half-lost among her seas?

This may have been good imperialist propaganda, but sober history must record that some of those upon whom Tennyson heaped his scorn had their fair share of idealism, that they saw, indeed, a vision not vouchsafed to him, and rose to the conception of a new type of empire, purged of the dross of the old imperialism. 'After all,' wrote Dilke, 'the strongest of the arguments in favour of separation is the somewhat paradoxical one that it would bring us a step nearer to the virtual confederation of the English race.' [48]

It should be added that so far as the dependencies were concerned Dilke was not in the least anti-imperialist. No Little Englander of the Manchester School would have said, 'The possession of India offers to ourselves that element of vastness of dominion which, in this age, is needed to secure width of vision and nobility of purpose; but to the English our possession of India, of the coasts of Africa, and the ports of China offers the possibility of planting free institutions among the dark-skinned races of the world.' Dilke found much to criticize in the British administration of India, but he considered British rule justifiable from the point of view both of the dominant power and of the dependency. For India he saw no prospect of self-government, and the only alternatives to British rule seemed to him to be Russian dominion or anarchy. In either case India would be the loser, and England would be injured commercially. If she withdrew from Australia or the Cape of Good Hope, she would continue to trade with them. If she abandoned India or Ceylon, 'they would have no customers at all; for falling into anarchy, they would cease at once to export their goods to us and to consume our manufactures.' He thought that the annexation of Afghanistan and Abyssinia would be beneficial to the natives if not to England, since in those countries there was no sentiment of nationality to be outraged, and the worst imaginable form of British government would be better for the governed than the best conceivable native rule. Though some of the dependencies did not pay the cost of their defense—this was not true of India—their retention by England stood, in Dilke's mind, upon a wholly different footing from that of the colonies.[49]

The British public at large was uninterested in the colonies and ignorant of colonial conditions. The popular apathy, of which the colonial reformers of the 'thirties and 'forties had complained, was still general. Relatively trifling matters of home politics outweighed the gravest problems of colonial policy. Scarcely any of the campaign speeches made during the General Election of 1868 touched upon colonial questions; and even in Parliament they evoked, as a rule, little if any debate.[50] In discussing British anti-imperialism we are concerned, therefore, not with 'the man in the street' but with the limited circle of those who had opinions on matters of colonial policy. How general, among such, were the views of Goldwin Smith, Lord Thring, and Lord Bury? In his *Reminiscences,* Goldwin Smith tells us that his opinions on the colonial question were prevalent in influential circles. 'Some of our statesmen avowed them, more were inclined to them.'[51] Let us test the truth of this assertion.

In March 1862, Arthur Mills introduced in the House of Commons the resolution relative to colonial defense of which mention was made in the preceding chapter. In referring to the inquiry into this subject which had recently been made by a committee of which he was chairman, he used somewhat ambiguous language. It had been assumed, he said, not only that 'Great Britain desired to maintain her Colonial Empire, but that she aimed at developing the resources of her colonies and qualifying them for present self-government and eventual independence.' In seconding Mr. Mills's motion, Mr. Buxton said: 'He supposed there was no statesman who would not allow that the prudent as well as the right way to deal with the colonies was to let them feel that they were free to cancel the bond if they chose, and that the evils resulting to us from the severance would be infinitely less than the disadvantages which would accrue to them.' [52]

In a debate on the army estimates in March 1865, John Bright thus expressed what may be taken as the view of the Manchester School:

I suspect, from what has been stated by official Gentlemen in Government and in previous Governments, that there is no objection to the independence of Canada whenever Canada may wish it. I have been glad to hear those statements, because I think they mark an extraordinary progress in sound opinions in this country . . . I do not object to that separation [of Canada from Great Britain] in the least; I believe it would be better for us and better for her.[53]

Sir George Cornewall Lewis was one of the few English politicians who had given systematic attention to questions of colonial government. His *Essay on the Government of Dependencies,* first published in 1841, was a standard treatise on its subject. In that work he wrote:

If a dominant country understood the true nature of the advantages arising from the relation of supremacy and dependence to the related communities, it would voluntarily recognize the legal independence of such of its own dependencies as were fit for independence; it would, by its political arrangements, study to prepare for independence those which were still unable to stand alone; and it would seek to promote colonization for the purpose of extending its trade rather than its empire, and without attempting to maintain the dependence of its colonies beyond the time when they need its protection.[54]

In a private letter, written in 1849, he gave it as his judgment that responsible government could not be worked successfully in a colony unless the people of England recognized that it meant virtual independence.[55] In 1862, when Secretary of State for War, he said in the House of Commons: 'I, for one, can only say that I look forward without apprehension—and, I may add, without regret—to the time when Canada might become an independent state.'[56]

Robert Lowe (later Lord Sherbrooke), who was afterwards Chancellor of the Exchequer in Gladstone's first Ministry, said in the House of Commons in 1865 that Canada ought to be given to understand that she was quite free to establish herself as an independent republic if she desired to do so.[57]

In 1865 a select committee of the House of Commons was appointed to inquire into the state of the British establishments on the West Coast of Africa. These settlements, which were on the Gambia, at Sierra Leone, on the Gold Coast, and at Lagos, were maintained primarily in the interest of British commerce and for the suppression of the slave trade. After taking evidence from civil, military, and naval officers, merchants, and missionaries, and examining official papers, the committee reported that in its opinion all further extension of territory or assumption of Government, or new treatises offering any protection to native tribes, would be inexpedient; and that the object of our policy should be to encourage in the natives the exercise of those qualities which may render it possible for us more and more to transfer to them the administration of all the Governments, with a view to our ultimate withdrawal from all, except, probably, Sierra Leone.[58]

It need not be supposed that mid-Victorian statesmen were more indifferent than their successors of today to the welfare of the natives of Africa, but the international scramble for African territory had not yet begun, and there was no need for the doctrine of 'the white man's burden' to justify British imperialism in the Dark Continent.

In defending his Government against the charge that it had adopted a new policy of imperial dismemberment, Gladstone, in April 1870, made the following statement:

If you look back to the history of the colonial connection between European Powers and trans-Atlantic possessions you find that it is the nature of those possessions to grow, and so to grow as to alter essentially, in obedience to laws stronger than the will of man, the conditions of their relation to the countries with which they were originally connected, until they arrive at that stage of their progress in which separation from the mother country inevitably takes place. It is impossible, however, to look back with satisfaction to the mode in which that separation has occurred. In every instance it has been brought about by war and bloodshed, involving an inheritance of pain, hatred and shame; whereas in reason there ought to be nothing to preclude the hope, when the growth of a colonial possession is such as to make separation from the mother country a natural and beneficial result, that the separation, so far from being effected by violence and bloodshed, might be the result of a peaceful and friendly transaction. Surely it is a great object to place, if possible, our colonial policy on such a footing, not for the purpose of bringing about a separation, but of providing a guarantee that, if separation should occur, it should be in a friendly way. That is the sense, the principle, and the secret of our policy with regard to colonial reform . . .[59]

Earl Granville, who was Colonial Secretary in Gladstone's first Ministry, at a time when imperial relations reached their most critical stage, undoubtedly shared the views of his leader if he did not go beyond them. In June 1869, he sent a confidential dispatch to Sir John Young, Governor General of Canada, which contained the following sentence: 'You will also be good enough to bring to my notice any line of policy or any measures which without implying on the part of Her Majesty's Government any wish to change abruptly our relations, would gradually prepare both Countries for a friendly relaxation of them.' [60] A month after this dispatch was written, the Governor General of Canada, in a speech at Quebec, declared that the Dominion was now 'in reality independent' and that it was for Canadian statesmen to decide whether to maintain the connection with the mother country 'or in due time of the maturity of the Dominion to change it for some other form of alliance.' [61]

Granville's colleague Lord Clarendon, the Foreign Secretary, expressed himself privately as in favor of the annexation of Canada to the United States. In 1870, Lord Lyons, who had been British Minister to the United States during the Civil War and had been obliged to study Canadian questions, wrote in a letter to Clarendon that it seemed to be 'in the nature of things' that the influence and prestige of the United States should increase throughout North America. In reply Clarendon said, 'I agree in every word you say about our possessions in North America, and wish that they would propose to be independent, and to annex themselves. We can't throw them off, and it is very desirable that we should part as friends.' [62]

Disraeli, in a famous party pronouncement made in 1872, asserted that the Liberal party had been striving for forty years, continuously, subtly, and energetically, to bring about the disruption of the British Empire.[63] Surely his imperialism must have been above reproach. Yet twenty years before, in 1852, he had written in a private letter to Lord Malmesbury, then Foreign Secretary: 'These wretched colonies will all be independent too in a few years and are a millstone round our necks.' [64] Nor does this seem to have been an outburst of mere momentary irritation, as we are assured by Disraeli's biographers.[65] Sir William Gregory, a veteran parliamentarian, who knew Disraeli well, tells us that his expressions with regard to the colonies 'were always those of contempt and a contented impression that we should sooner or later be rid of them.' [66] No doubt real empire, such an *imperium* as Britain wielded over India, appealed to Disraeli, but the conception of a British Commonwealth of Nations does not seem to have stirred his imagination.[67] In September 1866, when he was Chancellor of the Exchequer in Lord Derby's Ministry and as such concerned about the heavy expenditure that Britain was then bearing for colonial, and especially Canadian, defense, he wrote to his chief:

It can never be our pretence or our policy to defend the Canadian frontier against the U.S. . . . Power and influence we should exercise in Asia; consequently in Eastern Europe, consequently also in Western Europe; but what is the use of these colonial dead-weights which *we do not govern?* . . . Leave the Canadians to defend themselves; recall the African Squadron; give up the settlements on the West Coast of Africa; and we shall make a saving which will, at the same time, enable us to build ships and have a good Budget.[68]

Canadian statesmen visiting England during the American Civil War and the years immediately following, when the question of the defense of Canada against aggression from the United States was causing grave anxiety in the colony and serious concern in governmental circles in the mother country, were disturbed by evidences of what they took to be widespread separatist sentiment. In December 1864, after the Quebec Conference held in that year had agreed upon the essentials of the plan of confederation which was to issue in the British North America Act of 1867, George Brown, writing from England to John A. Macdonald, his colleague in the Canadian Ministry, spoke regretfully of 'a manifest desire in almost every quarter that, ere long, the British American colonies should shift for themselves, and in some quarters evident regret that we did not declare at once for independence.' [69] Alexander Galt, another of the 'fathers' of the Dominion of Canada, was in London in 1866-7, attending the conference which put the substance of the Quebec Resolutions into the form of a bill to be introduced into the British Parliament. Galt was forcibly impressed by the desire of British politicians to wash their hands of Canada. In a letter written in January 1867 he said: 'I cannot shut my eyes to the fact that they want to get rid of us . . . I much doubt whether Confederation will save us from Annexation. Even Macdonald is rapidly feeling as I do.' [70]

No one who recalls Charles Buller's sarcastic invective against the Colonial Office is likely to underrate the influence on colonial policy exerted by the permanent officials of the department. Long tenure of office and thorough familiarity with the routine of official business enabled the permanent under-secretary as a rule to guide his official superior, who was selected mainly for party reasons and whose tenure of office was usually brief.

Sir James Stephen, the *bête noire* of the colonial reformers and the target of their abuse, unquestionably exercised great influence for many years at the Colonial Office, where he served in various capacities under a succession of secretaries of state from 1813 to 1847.[71] From 1836 to 1847 he was permanent under-secretary, and according to Sir Henry Taylor, who was long associated with him in the work of the department, he 'virtually governed the Colonial Empire' for more than twenty-five years, 'not,' says Taylor, 'that he was otherwise than profoundly subordinate; but he found the way to bring men to his own conclusions.' [72] Stephen shared the widely accepted view that Canada would soon be independent, and when, in 1846, Lord Elgin was appointed Governor General of the province, he recorded privately his opinion that this was not unlikely to be the last such appointment that would be made.[73] A few years later he seems to have thought that under the more liberal colonial policy which Britain had adopted, the separation of Canada from the Empire might be postponed, though hardly averted permanently. In 1850, after his retirement from the Colonial Office, he expressed approval of the course which had been taken with relation to Canada.

It was that of cheerfully relaxing, one after another, the bonds of authority, as soon as the colony itself clearly desired that relaxation—so substituting a federal for a colonial relation, the change being real, not nominal—no national pride wounded, or national greatness diminished, or national duty abandoned. It remains for the Canadians to cut the last cable which anchors them to us. But it is for them, not for us, to take that step, and to assume the consequent responsibility.

He thought that the Australian colonies were moving along the same road.[74]

Stephen was succeeded as permanent under-secretary for the colonies by Herman Merivale, who, while professor of political economy at Oxford, had delivered a course of lectures on colonies which made a great impression and led to his appointment to the Colonial Office. Merivale believed that the colonies would ultimately become independent,[75] as did his successor, Sir Frederic Rogers (afterwards Lord Blachford), who held the office of permanent under-secretary from 1860 to 1871, during the entire decade under review. Goldwin Smith's statement that Rogers shared his views on colonial policy is certainly not an exaggeration.[76] In some autobiographical notes which he left, Rogers wrote:

I had always believed—and the belief has so confirmed and consolidated itself that I can hardly realize the possibility of anyone seriously thinking the contrary—that the destiny of our colonies is independence; and that, in this point of view, the function of the Colonial Office is to secure that our connection, while it lasts, shall be as profitable to both parties, and our separation, when it comes, as amicable as possible. This opinion is founded first on the general principle that a spirited nation (and a colony becomes a nation) will not submit to be governed in its internal affairs by a distant Government, and that nations geographically remote have no such common interests as will bind them permanently together in foreign policy, with all its details and mutations.[77]

So strong were Rogers's convictions that he was not swept into the imperial reaction of the 'seventies and 'eighties.[78]

An intimate friend of Rogers's was Sir Henry Taylor, an

author and playwright. Taylor served in the Colonial Office in subordinate positions for nearly fifty years, from 1824 to 1872. His anti-imperialism was clear and emphatic. In 1852 he wrote to Earl Grey, then Colonial Secretary, that he regarded the British North American colonies as 'a most dangerous possession for this country, whether as likely to breed a war with the United States or to make a war otherwise generated more grievous and disastrous.' He added: 'I do not suppose the provinces to be useless to us at present, but I regard any present uses not obtainable from them as independent nations to be no more than the dust of the balance as compared with the evil contingencies.'[79] Twelve years later, in 1864, he wrote in a letter to the Duke of Newcastle, then Colonial Secretary:

As to our American possessions, I have long held and often expressed the opinion that they are a sort of *damnosa hæreditas;* and when your Grace and the Prince of Wales were employing yourselves so successfully in conciliating the colonists I thought that you were drawing closer ties which might better be slackened if there were any chance of their slipping away altogether. I think that a policy which has regard to a not very far off future should prepare facilities and propensities for separation.[80]

Some anti-imperialists feared that an independent Canada would be annexed to the United States, but Taylor saw nothing to be alarmed at even in this eventuality.[81]

*

* *

The anti-imperial movement reached its climax in the early part of Gladstone's first Ministry, which was formed in December 1868. Lord Granville, Bright, and Lowe, whose anti-imperial utterances have been quoted, were members of the Cabinet, the first-mentioned presiding over the Colonial Office. Certain events soon occurred to create a belief, which became widespread in the colonies and in England, that the Government was contemplating, if it had not positively decided upon, the dissolution of the Empire.

In the first place a crisis was reached in the relations between the Imperial Government and the colony of New Zealand. For some years before the Gladstone Ministry took office, successive Governments, as we know, had been carrying out a policy of withdrawing imperial military forces from the self-governing colonies. In May 1868, at a time when hostilities were in progress between the colonists of New Zealand and some of the native tribes, the Duke of Buckingham, then Colonial Secretary, notified the Governor of New Zealand that the last of the British troops would soon be removed; and even after a massacre of some thirty colonists had occurred at Poverty Bay in the North Island, the Colonial Office declined to grant the colony's request that the recall of the troops should be delayed. Lord Granville, upon taking office, announced that he would adhere to his predecessor's policy.[82] Early in February 1869, a representative of the New Zealand Government asked for an imperial guarantee of a loan to aid the colony in borrowing money to cover contemplated war expenditure, but this request also was peremptorily refused by Lord Granville in a dispatch to the Governor of New Zealand (21 March 1869), which aroused the deepest indignation throughout the colony and no little hostile criticism in England. A protest signed by Sir George Grey, formerly Governor of New Zealand, and several other persons who had held office in the colony, declared that the policy of the Imperial Government was calculated to drive New Zealand out of the Empire.[83] Lord Granville's dispatch was reprinted in the New Zealand and Australian newspapers, which strongly resented its content, and especially its tone; and part of the New Zealand press went so far as to advocate openly the annexation of the colony to the United States.[84] A later dispatch of the Colonial Secretary (7 October 1869) still further embittered the feeling of the New Zealand colonists. In this, although he had been informed that the New Zealand Parliament had passed an act binding the colony, in the event of the Imperial Government's sanctioning the retention of the troops, to pay whatever contribution might be demanded, Lord Granville stated that under no conditions would the recall of the troops be further delayed.[85] The New Zealand ministers officially recorded their conviction that the 'tone and purport' of this document would be taken in the colony to indicate a desire on the part of the Imperial Government to sever the colony's connection with the Empire.[86] Writing from New Zealand in January 1870, the *Times* correspondent said:

As the immediate consequence of Earl Granville's expressions and his declaration of the Imperial policy towards New Zealand, the expediency of declaring the independence of the colony, of refusing to maintain the Viceregal establishment, and even of annexation with the United States has been freely discussed, and it is only because the case of the colony appears to have attracted considerable attention and called forth the sympathy of a large and influential section of the English people that no decided steps have been taken in one of these directions.[87]

The conduct of the Imperial Government gave rise to a long debate in the New Zealand Parliament, in the course of which bitter resentment was expressed at the tone of Granville's dispatches, and the view was freely voiced that the dissolution of the Empire was at hand.[88]

In England the alarm was sounded in the press by the Liberal *Spectator,* the Conservative *Standard,* and the Roman Catholic organ, *The Tablet.* They professed to see in the dispatches of the Colonial Secretary and the utterances of supporters of the Ministry, evidence that the Government had adopted a policy of dismembering the Empire. 'It is clear,' said *Spectator* (24 July 1869), 'that Mr. Goldwin Smith's colonial "policy" . . . has not only been accepted by the existing Government, but that they are acting on it. It is not only New Zealand which is to be dismissed, but Australia, not only Australia, but the Canadian Dominion.' Attention was called to the New Zealand crisis in Parliament, and opposition was expressed to the withdrawal of all imperial protection from the colony. Lord Bury said that 'considering all the circumstances of New Zealand, he did not think that this was the time to convey to the settlers that it mattered not to this country whether they were eaten up by the savages or not.'[89] The Government's course was defended by the parliamentary under-secretary for the colonies, and no member of the Cabinet participated in the debate. Official denials by the Government of any intention to bring about the separation of New Zealand from the Empire failed to satisfy the colony or to silence critics of the Government in England.[90]

The attitude of the Imperial Government in its relations with New Zealand led to a meeting of colonists then in London at the Palace Hotel, Westminster, early in August 1869, at which it was decided by those present to enter into communication with the colonial governments on the subject of the relations between the colonies and the mother country. A few days later letters were sent to the governments of the self-governing colonies expressing the opinion that British policy seemed to point to the disintegration of the Empire and proposing that a conference of representatives of the self-governing colonies should be held in London early in the following year in order to consider such changes in colonial administration and imperial relations as might seem desirable.[91] Agitation was continued in a series of weekly meetings held at the Cannon Street Hotel from November to January. At the first meeting resolutions were adopted, one of which stated that 'this meeting deprecates the colonial policy of Her Majesty's Government as illustrated by Lord Granville's dispatches.'[92] According to the *Times*, these meetings 'set politicians talking everywhere about the colonies and their relations with England.'[93] The Colonial Office, however, discountenanced the project of a colonial conference, and the responses of the colonial governments were not favorable to it. The conference was never held, though the proposal evoked considerable interest and discussion.

It was not the New Zealand crisis alone that lent support to the view that the Imperial Government was aiming at the dissolution of the Empire. There was at this time some sentiment in Canada in favor of independence, and though it was caused principally by the friction between the United States and Great Britain during and after the American Civil War and a belief among Canadians that the British connection subjected them to constant danger from their southern neighbor, it was certainly not diminished by the conviction of many Canadians that Great Britain would welcome the separation of the Dominion from the Empire.[94] The course taken by the Imperial Government, far from allaying the movement for independence in Canada, was calculated to strengthen it.

Early in 1869, Lord Granville, through the Governor General of Canada, offered Alexander Galt the Order of St. Michael and St. George. Feeling that it would be improper to accept the honor without informing the Imperial Government precisely of his political views, Galt wrote in reply: 'I regard the Confederation of the British North American Provinces as a measure which must ultimately lead to their separation from Great Britain . . . I believe the existing relations would be safer if the future state were clearly recognized, and, if possible, a term fixed therefor.' [95] In spite of this plain statement of his views, the distinction was conferred upon him; and when in February 1870, in a debate in the Canadian Parliament, his opinions were spoken of as disloyal, he replied that, inasmuch as the honor had been bestowed upon him, he did not consider himself more disloyal than Her Majesty's ministers.[96] It was natural to draw the conclusion that the Imperial Government and Galt were at one in their desire for the political future of Canada, especially as Lord Granville refused to permit the publication of one of the letters which he had written in the course of the correspondence.[97]

The decision of the Government to withdraw almost all of the few British troops still left in Canada seemed to many to point to the same conclusion. The question was not so much the fact of the withdrawal as the motive for it, and many Canadians undoubtedly believed that the motive was to show them that they could stand alone. Lord Carnarvon, who as Colonial Secretary in a preceding Government had himself been instrumental in withdrawing some British troops from the colonies, seems to have been convinced that

Lord Granville desired to bring about the separation of Canada from the Empire and professed to see nothing but disaster in what he called the 'shabby policy' which the Government was pursuing. 'I hope,' he said in the House of Lords (14 February 1870), 'that Her Majesty's Government are serious in the belief that the course they are now taking will not lead to the dismemberment of the Empire; but I warn them—as everyone who stands calmly and impartially by must warn them—that, whatever may be their meaning, they are doing the very acts, they are taking the very steps which must accomplish that result.' It was important, he added, that the policy of the Government should be publicly announced. 'There are whispers abroad that there is a policy on foot to dismember this Empire . . . If there is such a policy, in God's name let us know it; if there be not, let it be disavowed.' [98] As tending to confirm the rumors, he referred to a public meeting at Halifax in the preceding summer at which the Governor General of Canada threw out what was taken to be an intimation that the time had perhaps come for the Dominion to consider whether it was not ripe for independence, and to a recent dispatch of Granville's which, he said, might lead to the inference that the Government wished to be rid of British Columbia.[99] In a letter to Lord Carnarvon written in April 1870, Sir John Macdonald, a staunch supporter of the British connection and at the time Prime Minister of Canada, showed his suspicions of British colonial policy:

We are glad to know that we have in you a friend, I may almost say a friend in need—for we greatly distrust the men at the helm in England, who cannot, I fear, be considered as appreciating the importance of maintaining the Empire as it is, intact. We indulge the belief here, however, that Messrs. Bright,

Lowe, and Gladstone (shall I add Lord Granville?) are not true exponents of the public opinion of England. We may perhaps be obliged to appeal from the Government to the people of England.[100]

Early in General Grant's first term as President of the United States it was seriously urged by members of his Administration, and especially by Senator Sumner, chairman of the Senate Committee on Foreign Relations, that the claims of the United States against Great Britain for damages sustained during the Civil War should be settled on the basis of the annexation of Canada to the United States and the withdrawal of Great Britain from the western hemisphere. Charles Francis Adams, in an illuminating essay on the Treaty of Washington, showed that this grandiose project, in view of the anti-imperialist sentiment expressed by the British Minister in Washington and by the British press of the day, was not as preposterous as it would otherwise appear to have been. 'Mr. Sumner,' said Adams, 'certainly had grounds for assuming that a not unwilling hemispheric flag-withdrawal by Great Britain was more than probable in the early future.' [101] In December 1869 and early in 1870 Hamilton Fish, the American Secretary of State, in conversations with the British Minister, Sir Edward Thornton, urged the complete withdrawal of Great Britain from Canada. Thornton replied that this was impossible. Fish recorded in his diary that Thornton said: 'The Canadians find great fault with me for saying as openly as I do that we are ready to let them go whenever they wish, and declare they do not desire it.' And later Thornton reiterated that his Government was willing and even anxious to have the colonies become independent.[102] According to Sir John Macdonald, Thornton, in a dispatch of 8 January 1870, informed Lord Clarendon, the British Foreign Secretary, that Fish had actually asked him to ascertain 'whether Her Majesty's Government would offer any objection to a free vote being taken in Canada, or in any portions of it, whether the people desire to join the United States or not, and stated his conviction that if the vote were taken a large majority, nine-tenths he said of the people, would vote for Annexation.' [103] Fish's reported estimate of Canadian sentiment in favor of Annexation is ludicrous, though many Canadians, no doubt, believed that separation from the Empire was in store for their country, and the withdrawal of the British troops from Canada by the Gladstone Government was quite generally regarded in the Dominion as evidence that separatism had triumphed in the mother country.

To the Australian colonies the recall of imperial troops was not so vital a matter as it was to New Zealand, since Australia was not vexed with warlike native tribes. Australian public opinion, however, was naturally affected by what was happening in New Zealand, and many Australians believed that independence was the ultimate destiny of their country. There was certainly a widespread impression that such an outcome would be welcomed by the British Government.[104]

At the Cape of Good Hope it was openly stated in the Parliament that independence was impending in Canada, Australia, and New Zealand. 'In North America,' said Sir Philip Wodehouse, formerly governor of the colony, 'we have unmistakable indications of the rapid establishment of a powerful independent State. In Australia it is probable that its several settlements, with their great wealth and homogeneous population, will see their way to a similar coalition. *In New Zealand the severance is being accomplished*

under very painful circumstances.' [105] *Spectator,* in an article
on 'The New Colonial Policy' (26 March 1870), remarked
that in view of Wodehouse's declarations and Galt's declarations and the 'unparalleled severity' of the Government's
dealings with New Zealand, 'any politician of ordinary sagacity will draw the inference that a deliberate colonial
policy of no insignificant moment has been, at all events,
provisionally adopted by the present Cabinet, which they are
not willing to confide to Parliament and to have discussed
in Parliament as yet.' It was the duty of the Government,
Spectator insisted, to take the sense of the nation 'on the
boldest and most startling innovation in modern statesmanship.' [106]

*

*   *

There are evidences that even before the formation of
Gladstone's Ministry a revival of imperialism was at hand.
In the summer of 1868 a Colonial Society, later named the
Royal Colonial Institute, was organized in London to arouse
interest in colonial questions; the advantages of closer union
between England and the colonies were beginning to be
canvassed; and there are other indications that a change in
public opinion was at hand.[107] The imperial movement was
naturally strengthened by the suspicions entertained of the
intentions of Gladstone's Government. The earlier public
apathy passed away. Relations between the mother country
and the colonies became a subject of lively discussion in the
press and in public meetings, and questions of colonial
policy were seriously debated in Parliament.[108]

It was quickly apparent that the country would not sanction any policy of cutting the colonies adrift. Nor must it

be supposed that the ministers, whatever the individual opinions of some of them may have been, had, collectively, as a Government, adopted such a policy. Had they done so, Mr. W. E. Forster, who openly stated his conviction that public opinion would not permit the dismemberment of the Empire, could not have remained a member of the Ministry.[109] The imperial question must have been discussed at Cabinet meetings, though what was said upon it we do not, of course, know. In view, however, of the anti-imperial sentiments of some of the ministers, and the declarations of Lord Granville and Lord Kimberley, who succeeded him at the Colonial Office in July 1870, to the effect that the Government was not seeking to dismember the Empire,[110] it seems not unreasonable to surmise that it was left an 'open' question, on which members of the Government were not bound to unanimity. In an article entitled 'Greater or Lesser Britain,' published in *The Nineteenth Century*, in July 1877, Sir Julius Vogel, who had been a member of the New Zealand Ministry at the time of the crisis in the relations between the colony and the Imperial Government, conjectured that a decision was reached by the British Cabinet to the effect that, whatever might be the opinions of individual ministers, the Government should not commit itself to the dismemberment policy. 'But without any policy of the kind,' he added, 'a strong conviction might have been entertained that the colonies would in course of time be detached from the Empire, and that the sooner that result ensued the better.' [111]

In May 1870, an accommodation was reached in the New Zealand dispute, which was taken to indicate, both in the colonies and by critics of the Government in England, that the Imperial Government had changed its attitude, not only toward New Zealand but on the imperial question in general. The Government of New Zealand sent special commissioners to England to negotiate for the retention of the troops and for assistance to the colony in creating a colonial military force. One great object hoped for from the mission, as stated by the New Zealand Premier, was the re-establishment of harmonious relations between the Imperial and the New Zealand Governments. The commissioners were unable to induce the Colonial Office to yield on the question of the withdrawal of the troops, but they offered to accept an imperial guarantee of a loan of £1,000,000 to cover expenditures incurred in aid of immigration and the construction of public works in the colony 'as a measure of conciliation which would be taken throughout New Zealand as proof of the continued goodwill of the Imperial Government, and of its desire that the relations between the Imperial and Colonial Governments should be maintained on the most friendly footing.' The knowledge in New Zealand that such an agreement had been reached would, the commissioners informed Lord Granville, 'put an end to irritation and discontent.' The Colonial Office, which had previously refused so peremptorily to accede to a like request, now yielded and agreed to introduce the necessary legislation in Parliament. 'If we have not been able to induce your lordship to regard in the same light as the Assembly [of New Zealand] did, the question of military assistance,' wrote the commissioners in a letter to Granville thanking him for the concession that had been made, 'still the chief object of our mission has been gained. It is not a mere matter of money that has been arranged; a lasting tie has been made between the two Governments by their engaging together in objects in which the nation has a common interest with her Dependency . . .'

In a reply, in which graciousness of language took the place of the blunt uncompromising tone of his earlier dispatches, Granville wrote: 'I trust that the decision of Her Majesty's Government to waive the objections which attach to the guarantee of Colonial loans will be received by the colonists of New Zealand as a proof of the deep interest which they feel in the welfare and prosperity of this great possession of the Crown.' [112] In New Zealand the concession made by the Imperial Government was regarded as a peace offering, and the colonial legislature resolved to let bygones be bygones.[113]

Spectator was jubilant, insisting that nothing less than a revolution in British colonial policy had taken place. 'Ministers have changed their policy, have changed it very abruptly, and have changed it for the best of all reasons,— because they had begun to discover that their line was not the line of the people of England, and would, if pushed to its logical results, end in events which would bring down the bitter displeasure of the people of England . . .' The Liberal press, which was supporting the Government through thick and thin, might try to show that the concession to New Zealand was in harmony with the previous course taken by the Colonial Office, but that, according to *Spectator,* was all nonsense, and it was important for the people of New Zealand to know that it was all nonsense. The difference between military aid and financial aid was merely administrative; there was no difference in policy.[114] Nor was *Spectator* alone in its opinion that a change in colonial policy had occurred. 'I am happy to see,' said Earl Russell in the House of Lords,

that my noble Friend, the present Secretary of State for the Colonies (Earl Granville) seems in some respects to have changed his opinion; and I always thought that when he had further studied colonial questions and the position of this country, he would be of opinion that it was necessary not only to allow the Colonies to pay their allegiance to this country, but to give them from time to time such encouragement as to make them pay that allegiance happily and contentedly.[115]

The years 1869-70 seem clearly to mark a turning point in the attitude of public opinion in Britain toward the colonies. When confronted with what looked like an imminent dissolution of the Empire, the British people, it was evident, were not ready to follow the doctrinaire disciples of the Manchester School, whatever some of the political leaders might wish.

From the summer of 1870 onward, anti-imperial sentiment waned rapidly. When in July Lord Granville was transferred to the Foreign Office, all imperialists breathed more easily. His successor at the Colonial Office, Lord Kimberley, was not suspect to imperialists as he had been, and official assurances that the Government cherished no separatist designs carried greater conviction. In May 1871, a debate took place in the House of Commons on a motion for the appointment of a committee of inquiry to consider what changes should be made in the relations between the colonies and the mother country with a view to 'the permanent maintenance of the best and most cordial interconnection between all parts of the Empire.'[116] The motion was withdrawn, but imperialists were gratified by a speech made by Mr. Knatchbull-Hugessen, under-secretary of state for the colonies, in which he stated that it was the policy of the Government 'to retain and preserve the connection between the mother country and the Colonies, basing always that connection on the sure and sound foundation of mutual good and the promotion of mutual interests.' There were those, it was true, who emphasized the burdensomeness of colonies to the mother country, but separatist opinions had never been avowed—and he hoped they never would be avowed—by a British Government. Another member of the House said that this speech would go far to remove the impression which had certainly existed in the country that the Government looked upon the colonies with indifference and would regard their separation with little regret. The spirit of the under-secretary's remarks was in sharp contrast with the brusque and unsympathetic tone of Lord Granville's New Zealand dispatches of 1869.

In March 1873, a Conservative member of the House of Commons raised the question of colonial contributions toward the defense of the Empire. It is evident that he was thinking of the self-governing colonies, though he did not distinguish explicitly between them and the others. The resolution which he moved went beyond the principle of colonial responsibility for local defense. He rejected the view that the expenses of imperial, as distinguished from local, defense ought to be borne exclusively by the taxpayers of the United Kingdom, maintaining, on the contrary, that they should be borne by the whole Empire. His resolution was opposed by the Government and was not adopted.[117] Mr. Knatchbull-Hugessen, who was still under-secretary for the colonies, took the position that the colonies were doing all that they could fairly be called upon to do in the matter of defense, voiced a strong sense of their value to the mother country, and expressed fear that the resolution, if adopted, might 'awaken misgiving in the Colonies.' Gladstone himself took part in the debate:

What we wish is, not that the Colonies should under pressure from this country be brought to make, probably not insignificant, but at any rate grudging, contributions towards the expenses of the Empire; what we wish is to see the growth of the true spirit of freedom in the colonial communities which would make them not only willing, but eager, to share all the responsibilities of freedom and to take a part in the common burdens.

Here was a suggestion of a future British Commonwealth of Nations.

Disraeli skillfully, if not too scrupulously, seized upon imperialism as a party issue, and probably no part of his political program appealed more strongly to the British electorate than his pledge to maintain the integrity of the British Empire. The Conservative victory in the General Election of 1874 drove separatism completely from the field of practical politics. 'Who talks now of casting off the colonies?' W. E. Forster asked in 1875. 'What more popular cry than the preservation of our colonial empire?' [118]

*

* *

Since the new British imperialism which took shape during the seventies and eighties of the last century does not come within the scope of this book, a careful analysis of the complex of conditions which underlay it would be superfluous.[119] Its earliest conspicuous manifestation is to be seen in the reaction against what was widely believed to be a desire on the part of the Gladstone Government to liquidate the British Empire, but this reaction cannot be understood without taking account of changing circumstances within the British Empire and in the outside world and their effects on British public opinion. A brief consideration of some of these changes may serve as an appropriate epilogue to our study.

For one thing, improvements in means of communication tended to counteract the devisive effects of distance in weakening imperial ties. Three thousand miles of ocean lay between England and America, as Burke in a famous speech reminded his hearers. 'No contrivance,' he went on to say, 'can prevent the effect of this distance in weakening government. Seas roll and months pass between the order and the execution.' A hundred years later the seas were still rolling, but human contrivances undreamed of by Burke had mitigated the effects of distance. By 1870 the progress of steam navigation had greatly shortened the length of time required for oceanic voyages, telegraphic communication across the Atlantic had been established in 1866, and the Suez Canal, opened in 1869, brought Australia and New Zealand, as well as India, much nearer to Britain. James Anthony Froude, one of the leading exponents of the new imperialism, in an article published in 1870 in *Fraser's Magazine,* of which he was then editor, said:

The problem now is but to reunite the scattered fragments of the same nation, and bridge over the distance which divides them from us. Distance frightens us; but steam and the telegraph have abolished distance . . . St. George's Channel at the time of the union with Ireland was harder to cross in stormy weather than the Atlantic is at present.[120]

The fact that there was no considerable sentiment in the self-governing colonies in favor of separation had its effect on opinion in Britain. Many Englishmen had looked upon the confederation of the British North American colonies as a prelude to their secession from the Empire, but it was highly significant that in the debates on confederation in the Canadian Parliament in 1865 the strongest expressions of Canadian nationalism were accompanied with explicit declarations of a desire to remain within the British Empire. When confederation came, in 1867, it was not followed by anything that could be called a separatist movement in the new Dominion of Canada; and at the time of the New Zealand crisis it was made clear that in the self-governing colonies generally the predominant opinion was opposed to separation. If colonies refused to grasp at sovereign independence when it was within their reach, might there not be something wrong with the time-honored view that separation from the mother country is the natural and inevitable result of colonial development? Perhaps, after all, enlightened statesmanship could give permanence to imperial relations.

A revival of interest in emigration was an important factor in the beginnings of the imperial movement. Toward the close of the 'sixties a period of remarkable prosperity was followed by a serious depression in British trade and industry, and this was accompanied by a marked increase in unemployment and pauperism. There had been a lull in the emigration movement in the ten years from 1858 to 1868 as compared with the preceding decade, but emigration from England alone rose from 58,000 in 1868 to 95,000 in 1869. Many voices were raised in advocacy of state-aided emigration. Froude, in the article which has been referred to, denied that it made no difference to Britain whether her redundant population settled in British or in foreign territory, as apostles of *laissez-faire* had been fond of asserting. He remarked that during the twenty-five years preceding 1870 nearly four million British subjects had become citizens of the United States and declared that this emigration had weakened the British Empire and correspondingly strengthened a rival power. He said:

We have no longer land enough in England commensurate with our present dimensions . . . Other nations, once less powerful or not more powerful than ourselves, are growing in strength and numbers, and we too must grow if we intend to remain on a level with them. Here at home we have no room to grow except by the expansion of towns which are already overgrown . . . Once absolutely our own, and still easily within our reach, are our eastern and western colonies, containing all and more than all that we require. We want land on which to plant English families . . . The land lies ready to our hand. The colonies contain virgin soil sufficient to employ and feed five times as many people as are now crowded into Great Britain and Ireland . . . What more simple than to bring the men and the land together? . . . Once established on a great scale emigration supports itself . . . It would cost us money—but so do wars; and for a great object we do not shrink from fighting. Let it be once established that an Englishman emigrating to Canada, or the Cape, or Australia, or New Zealand did not forfeit his nationality, that he was still on English soil as much as if he was in Devonshire or Yorkshire, and would remain an Englishman while the English empire lasted; and if we spent a quarter of the sums which were sunk in the morasses at Balaclava in sending out and establishing two millions of our people in those colonies, it would contribute more to the essential strength of the country than all the wars in which we have been entangled from Agincourt to Waterloo.

In February 1870, a petition to the Queen, signed by more than 100,000 workingmen, was presented to the Government. It asked that measures be taken to enable 'those who are willing to work to go to those parts of Your Majesty's dominions where their labour is required, and where they may prosper and may increase the prosperity of the whole Empire.' The petitioners, it was stated, had 'heard with alarm that Your Majesty has been advised to give up the colonies, containing millions of acres which might be employed profitably both to the colonies and to ourselves as fields of emigration.' [121] The question of state aid for emigration was debated in the House of Commons in March 1870 on a motion introduced by R. R. Torrens, a former prime minister of New South Wales, affirming the expediency of adopting measures 'for facilitating the emigration of poor families to British colonies' in order to check the increase of pauperism in Britain and relieve distress among the working classes.[122]

The formation of larger political entities had its influence on British opinion. The trend of the times seemed to be distinctly in the direction of political unification—in Germany, in Italy, and (within the British Empire itself) in British North America. In the United States the forces of disruption had been defeated in the most bloody and expensive civil war of history. 'These,' said Froude,

are not days for small States . . . The German States gravitate into Prussia, the Italians into Piedmont. While we are talking of dismembering our empire, the Americans have made enormous sacrifices to preserve the unity of theirs. If we throw off the colonies, it is at least possible that they may apply for admittance into the American Union; and it is equally possible that the Americans may not refuse them.

This fear that Britain's losses would be her rivals' gains was from the outset an important element in the new imperialism.

Perhaps, however, the most important factor in the beginnings of the imperial movement was a realization on the part of many Englishmen that the position of their country in the world was changing. Increasing doubt came to be cast upon the validity of the assumptions of the Manchester School. Fond hopes that the adoption of free trade by Brit-

ain would usher in an era of world-wide free trade and universal peace were proving to be delusive. Other countries
were not following Britain's example, and it seemed questionable to many whether she could afford to persevere in
one-sided free trade. In the depression year of 1869 a group
of Englishmen calling themselves 'The Association of "Re-
vivers" of British Industry' agitated for tariff revision as a
means of retaliation which would force foreign countries to
lower their duties on British goods.[123] The vision of Britain
as the permanent workshop of the world was growing per-
ceptibly dimmer, for other countries were showing unmistakable signs of a determination to set up workshops of their
own, notably the United States, whose Republican protective tariff was profoundly discouraging to all orthdox free
traders. The development of industry in other countries was
beginning to undermine the supremacy which priority in
industrialization had given to Britain. Nor was it easy to believe, in the light of the growth of armaments on the continent of Europe, that the age of great wars was approaching
its end. The Franco-Prussian War in particular gave British
pacifism a decided shock, and pacifism had been inextricably
linked with free trade in the gospel of Manchester. On the
eve of the Franco-Prussian War Froude was writing:

Are our arms so irresistible that we have no longer an enemy
to fear? Is our prosperity so overflowing and the continuance of
it so certain, that we can now let it flow from us elsewhere because we can contain no more? Our national arrogance will
scarcely presume so far. Is it that the great Powers of the world
have furled their battle-flags? Is the parliament of man on the
way to be constituted, and is the rivalry of empires to be confined for the future to competition in the arts of peace? Never
at any period in the world's history was so large a share of the

profits of industry expended upon armies and arms. Is it so certain that we shall never be entangled again in the quarrels of the Continent?

It would be correct to infer from what has been said that the imperial movement in its beginnings was not imperialistic in an aggressive sense. Its object was the preservation of the existing imperial union, not further imperial expansion. Aggressive imperialism and jingoism in international relations originated during the Disraeli Ministry of 1874-80. To many imperialists of the earlier type it seemed that the Empire could be preserved only by some process of constitutional reconstruction—hence the many proposals that were presented to the public during the early 'seventies for what was called Imperial Federation.

NOTES

CHAPTER I

1. Philip W. Buck, *The Politics of Mercantilism*, p. 63. For an informing discussion of mercantilism and the English colonies, see Charles M. Andrews, *The Colonial Period of American History*, IV, chap. x.

2. Schmoller's essay appeared in an English translation in the Economic Classics series, edited by W. J. Ashley, in 1896, with the title *The Mercantile System and its Historical Significance*.

3. This work was first published in Swedish in 1931. The English translation by Mendel Shapiro (*Mercantilism*) was prepared from a German edition and revised by the author.

4. F. W. Maitland, *The Constitutional History of England*, p. 142.

5. *The Wealth of Nations*, Book IV, Introduction. Elsewhere, it is true, Smith does say that 'the great object of the political economy of every country is to increase the riches and power of that country' (Book II, chap. v; Everyman's Library ed., I, 333), but he did not conceive of the mercantile system as a system of power.

6. For references to a number of such statements, see Buck, op. cit. pp. 202-3.

7. 'As every individual, therefore, endeavours as much as he can both to employ his capital in the support of domestic industry, and so to direct that industry that its produce may be of the greatest value; every individual necessarily labours to render the annual revenue of the society as great as he can. He generally, indeed, neither intends to promote the public interest, nor knows how much he is promoting it . . . he is in this, as in many other cases, led by an invisible hand to promote an end which was no part of his intention.' *The Wealth of Nations*, Book IV, chap. ii; Everyman's Library ed., I, 400.

8. Charles Woolsey Cole thinks that in Colbert's day private interests had less influence, on the whole, in France than in England in shaping mercantilist policies and measures; *Colbert and a Century of French Mercantilism*, II, 553-4.

9. Buck, op. cit. p. 88.

10. *The Petition and Remonstrance of the Governour and Company of Merchants of London trading to the East Indies* (London, 1641), p. 16, quoted in Buck, op. cit. p. 114.

11. Heckscher, *Mercantilism*, II, 31.

12. Hakluyt, the foremost Elizabethan student of maritime discovery and exploration, wrote this Discourse to boom colonization at the time when Raleigh was about to plant his ill-fated colony on Roanoke Island. It was first published in 1877 in Volume II of the second series of *The Collections of the Maine Historical Society*. Selections from it can be found in Dunham and Pargellis, *Complaint and Reform in England*, pp. 293-339. It is often cited as *Discourse concerning Western Planting*.

13. *Mercantilism*, II, 175.

14. W. J. Ashley's ed. (London, 1903), p. 7.

15. *The Origins of the British Colonial System*, p. 57.

16. Beer, *The Old Colonial System*, I, 38.

17. Beer, *The Origins of the British Colonial System*, p. 72.

18. For a brief account of experiments down to the seventeenth century, see Lawrence A. Harper, *The English Navigation Laws*, chap. iii.

19. *A New Discourse of Trade* (London, 1693), p. 183. Child was a director of the East India Company and one of the leading mercantilist writers.

20. Beer, *Origins*, chaps. iv-viii.

21. *The Old Colonial System*, I, 11.

22. 12 Car. II, c. 18, § i.

23. 13 & 14 Car. II, c. 11, § vi. 'Under this law it was held that foreign-built ships were not excluded from trades where they were hitherto legally employed, but merely were subject to all duties to which alien ships were liable.' Harper, op. cit. pp. 389-90. Cf. Beer, *The Old Colonial System*, I, 65-7.

24. 'The Effect of the Navigation Acts on the Thirteen Colonies,' in *The Era of the American Revolution*, ed. by Richard B. Morris, pp. 8-10.

25. 12 Car. II, c. 18, § xviii.

26. For a table showing additions to the original list, see Harper, op. cit. pp. 398-9, and for a detailed account of the whole subject, Charles M. Andrews, *The Colonial Period of American History*, IV, chap. iv. The enumerated articles could not be exported to Scotland until the Union in 1707. Their exportation to Ireland was forbidden in 1671 (by 22 & 23 Car. II, c. 26).

27. 12 Car. II, c. 18, § vi.

28. Ibid. §§ iii, iv.

29. Ibid. §§ viii, ix.

30. Harper, op. cit. p. 53.
31. The name 'Staple Act' was given to certain provisions of 'an act for the encouragement of trade' (15 Car. II, c. 7), which related to the importation of European products into the colonies.
32. Ibid. § v.
33. 25 Car. II, c. 7, § 2.
34. Ibid. § 3.
35. Beer, *The Old Colonial System*, I, 284. For the customs service in the colonies, see ibid. 272 ff., and Andrews, op. cit. IV, chap. vii.
36. Beer, *The Old Colonial System*, I, 106.
37. 12 Car. II, c. 4.
38. Beer, *Origins*, chap. iv.
39. Beer, *The Old Colonial System*, I, 136.
40. Ibid. 42.
41. Beer, *Origins*, chap. ii.
42. Beer, *The Old Colonial System*, I, 18 ff. The government was not opposed, however, to emigration from Scotland and Ireland to the colonies; ibid. 31.
43. Ibid. 52.
44. *British Colonial Policy*, 1754-1765, p. 138.
45. Ibid. p. 139. For an interesting discussion of British attitudes toward tropical and continental colonization during the Seven Years' War, see ibid. chap. viii.
46. 6 Geo. II, c. 13.
47. 4 Geo. III, c. 15.
48. 6 Geo. III, c. 52.
49. Beer, *The Old Colonial System*, I, 108 ff.; *British Colonial Policy*, 1754-1765, pp. 6-8.
50. Beer, *The Old Colonial System*, I, 119.
51. *British Colonial Policy*, 1754-1765, pp. 9-10. Stanley M. Pargellis attributes to Walpole, more than to any other individual, responsibility for failure to put colonial defense on a satisfactory basis. *Lord Loudoun in North America*, p. 11.
52. Pargellis, op. cit. pp. 6 ff.
53. For an excellent account of the Albany Plan, see Lawrence Henry Gipson, *The British Empire before the American Revolution*, V, *Zones of International Friction* . . . 1748-1754, chaps. iv and v.
54. *Writings of Benjamin Franklin*, ed. by A. H. Smyth, I, 388-9.
55. Clarence E. Carter, 'The Office of Commander-in-Chief: A Phase of Imperial Unity on the Eve of the Revolution,' in *The Era of the American Revolution*, ed. by Richard B. Morris, pp. 170-213.

56. Robert Livingston Schuyler, *Josiah Tucker,* pp. 34, 321 ff., 395 ff. For Huskisson's opinion; see p. 124, above.
57. *British Colonial Policy, 1754-1765,* pp. 206, 208, 305-6.
58. *The Triumph of American Capitalism,* pp. 160-61.
59. 'Mercantilism and the American Revolution,' *Canadian Historical Review,* XXIII, 1-15.

CHAPTER II

1. E.g. Goldwin Smith, *The Empire,* p. 21. For a recent and illuminating exposition of Adam Smith's ideas concerning colonial trade and colonies, see Klaus E. Knorr, *British Colonial Theories,* 1570-1850, chap. vi. In view of the efforts of certain modern British imperialist writers (e.g. J. Shield Nicholson in *A Project of Empire*) to show that Smith was opposed to the separation of the American colonies from the mother country, Dr. Knorr's critical study of Smith's own words is distinctly refreshing. It is true, and well known, that Smith believed no British Government would ever voluntarily adopt a separatist policy and that he proposed a plan of imperial reform, but it is fallacious, as Dr. Knorr demonstrates, to reason from this that Smith was opposed to separation.
2. E.g. the elder Mirabeau, *Philosophie rurale* (Amsterdam, 1763), III, 224; *Œuvres de Turgot,* ed. by E. Daire, II, 551 ff. Lord Brougham thus contrasted the attitude of the mercantilists and the physiocrats towards colonies: 'The disciples of the Mercantile System found, in these distant branches of the state [colonies], an unlimited field for the trial of their theory, by imposing such restraints as might render the industry of the inhabitants subservient to the wealth of the mother country, and by opening for her produce a market of growing extent, in which positive regulations might secure an exclusive preference, or fix a high price. They have, accordingly, viewed such establishments with a decided partiality . . . The œconomists [physiocrats], on the other hand, have viewed, with more than common jealousy, those distant settlements, which are peopled and cultivated at the mother country's expense, and which hold out the temptations of foreign trade, to allure capital and industry from the great source of national riches—the improvement of the productive powers of the land.' *An Inquiry into the Colonial Policy of the European Powers* (Edinburgh, 1803), I, 5-6.

3. *A Series of Answers to Certain Popular Objections against Separating from the Rebellious Colonies* (Gloucester, 1776), p. 40. For a sketch of Tucker's career, see Robert Livingston Schuyler, *Josiah Tucker*, Introduction.

4. James Bonar, *A Catalogue of the Library of Adam Smith*, p. 115.

5. P. 51.

6. *Industry and Trade*, p. 719 n.

7. *Œuvres de Turgot*, IX (Paris, 1810), 367-8. On Tucker and Turgot, see Walter Ernest Clark, *Josiah Tucker: Economist*, pp. 226-8, and Henry Higgs, *The Physiocrats*, pp. 31, 67.

8. Tucker's writings are listed in Clark, op. cit. pp. 241-58, and in Schuyler, op. cit. pp. 555-8.

9. The *Elements* was first published in 1931 in Schuyler, op. cit. pp. 51 ff.

10. The account of Tucker's economic and anti-imperial ideas that follows is taken from the introduction to Schuyler's *Josiah Tucker*, where supporting references to Tucker's writings will be found.

11. Tucker was by no means the first British economic thinker to reject this cardinal mercantilist doctrine. It had been repudiated by several earlier writers and by Tucker's contemporary, David Hume, in his essays on money and on the balance of trade, published in Part II of his *Essays, Moral, Political, and Literary* (1752). It is probable that Tucker owed a good deal to Hume, with whom he corresponded for several years. For French criticism of the precious-metals doctrine of wealth in the late seventeenth century, see Charles Woolsey Cole, *French Mercantilism*, 1683-1700, chap. v.

12. Adam Smith and Tucker never referred to each other's writings or opinions. Tucker had an admiration for the 'literati' of Scotland (*A Treatise concerning Civil Government*, p. 376), but he made no mention of Smith. As an economist he could not have been indebted to his younger contemporary, for his own economic ideas were formed, and his principal economic tracts were written, long before the publication of the *Wealth of Nations*. Regarding Smith's indebtedness to Tucker there is room for conjecture.

13. G. S. Veitch, *The Genesis of Parliamentary Reform*, p. 43. On the eighteenth-century English radical movement and its leaders, see C. B. R. Kent, *The English Radicals*, and Dora Mae Clark, *British Opinion and the American Revolution*, chap. vi.

14. For Cartwright's career, see *The Life and Correspondence of Major Cartwright*, ed. by F. D. Cartwright, 2 vols., London, 1826.

15. For Sharp, see E. C. P. Lascelles, *Granville Sharp and the Freedom of Slaves in England.*

16. For Price, see Roland Thomas, *Richard Price,* and W. Morgan, *Memoirs of the Life of the Rev. Richard Price.*

17. For Anderson, see Donald O. Wagner, 'British Economists and the Empire,' *Political Science Quarterly,* XLVI, 254-6.

18. This was published in French in order to promote discussion of the idea on the continent.

19. *History of the Public Revenue of the British Empire,* 3rd ed., London, 1803, II, 100-123.

20. Brougham, op. cit. I, 262-3.

21. J. R. McCulloch, *A Dictionary, Practical, Theoretical, and Historical, of Commerce and Commercial Navigation,* ed. by A. J. Wilson, p. 1244.

22. Arthur Young, *Travels in France,* ed. by M. S. Betham-Edwards, pp. 261-2. For the colonial ideas of Arthur Young and other British physiocrats, see Klaus E. Knorr, op. cit. pp. 236 ff.

23. *The Parliamentary History of England, from the Earliest Period to the Year* 1803 (36 vols., London, 1806-1820, printed by T. C. Hansard), XXII, 721; XXIII, 193, 549. This series is referred to hereinafter as *Parl. History.*

24. Imperialists of later times felt the need of refuting this opinion; e.g. Lord Elgin (*The Elgin-Grey Papers,* 1846-1852, ed. by Sir Arthur G. Doughty, II, 609) and Sir J. R. Seeley (*The Expansion of England,* Course I, lecture viii).

25. Witt Bowden, 'The English Manufacturers and the Commercial Treaty of 1786 with France,' *American Historical Review,* XXV, 18 ff.

26. Bowden, *The Rise of the Great Manufacturers in England,* 1760-1790, chap. iii; also the same author's *Industrial Society in England towards the End of the Eighteenth Century,* chap. iii.

27. *The Journal and Correspondence of William, Lord Auckland,* I, 92-3.

28. J. Davidson, 'England's Commercial Policy towards her Colonies since the Treaty of Paris,' *Political Science Quarterly,* XIV, 45.

29. E.g. Hugh Gray, *Letters from Canada* (London, 1809), pp. 75-6: 'Some people pretend to say that we are better without America, and very ingenious arguments have been brought forward to prove it . . . We are very glad to find palliatives for evils we cannot remedy. I suppose no one will pretend to say that the loss of our

North American colonies, and consequently of our Newfoundland trade, would not be a very serious evil to Great Britain.'

30. Leslie Stephen, *The English Utilitarians,* II, chap. i.
31. Also an article on 'Colonies' in McCulloch's *Dictionary* (referred to above, n. 21), pp. 308-41, and his *Statistical Account of the British Empire* (1837), I, 593 ff.
32. These writings are published in *The Works of Jeremy Bentham,* ed. by John Bowring, vols. II, III, IV.
33. Ibid. III, 56. Some observations on Bentham's anti-imperialism can be found in Elie Halévy, *The Growth of Philosophic Radicalism* (trans. by Mary Morris), pp. 114-16, 173, 510.
34. Many of the works which pass under Bentham's name were prepared for publication from his manuscripts by his followers, who were obliged to exercise no little discretion as well as patience in their endeavors to present his thought to the public. His penmanship and methods of composition were such as to put a severe strain on any editor. Graham Wallas, *Life of Francis Place,* pp. 83-5.
35. According to John Stuart Mill (*Autobiography*), the elder Mill exercised a greater personal ascendancy in the Utilitarian movement than Bentham did.
36. *Autobiography,* p. 98. *The Morning Chronicle* was also a vehicle of Utilitarian opinion.
37. *Westminster Review,* XII, 403 (April 1830).
38. Articles on Canada in ibid. VIII and XIII (July 1827 and July 1830).
39. See, e.g. *The Parliamentary Debates from the Year* 1803 *to the Present Time,* published under the superintendence of T. C. Hansard, XL, 1077-1081. The first 18 vols. of this series are entitled *Cobbett's Parliamentary Debates.* The whole series is in 46 vols. (London, 1804-20) and is referred to hereinafter as *Parl. Deb.*
40. *Parl. Deb.,* new series, VIII, 250. This series is entitled *The Parliamentary Debates, New Series,* and was published under the superintendence of T. C. Hansard in 25 vols. (London, 1820-30). It is referred to hereinafter as *Parl. Deb.,* new ser.
41. Chap. xv.
42. *Parl. Deb.,* 3rd series, XL, 213-15. This series is entitled *Hansard's Parliamentary Debates, Third Series,* and was published in 356 vols. (London, 1831-91). It is referred to hereinafter as *Parl. Deb.,* 3rd ser.
43. Ibid. 60.

44. Ibid. 310.

45. Ibid. 107-8.

46. Ibid. LV, 228.

47. Ibid. 261-2.

48. Sir Howard Douglas, *Considerations on the Value and Importance of the British North American Colonies* (London, 1831); Edward Gibbon Wakefield, *A View of the Art of Colonization* (London, 1849), p. 38; *Quarterly Review*, XXXIII, 410 ff.; R. C. Mills, *Colonization of Australia*, pp. 21-2.

49. See, e.g. S. G. Reid, *Life and Letters of the First Earl of Durham*, II, 137-42.

50. *The Durham Papers*, Report on Canadian Archives, 1923, p. 327.

51. For an example of anti-imperial idealism the reader is referred to J. A. Roebuck's *The Colonies of England*. The author was one of the leading Philosophical Radicals.

CHAPTER III

1. John Reeves, *The Law of Shipping and Navigation*, 2nd ed. (London, 1807), p. 62. Klaus E. Knorr, op. cit. p. 148.

2. 6 Geo. III, c. 49.

3. *The History, Civil and Commercial, of the British Colonies in the West Indies* (Philadelphia, 1806), I, 253. The first edition of this work was published in London in 1793.

4. 27 Geo. III, c. 27.

5. 45 Geo. III, c. 57.

6. Dorothy Burne Goebel, 'British Trade to the Spanish Colonies, 1796-1823,' *American Historical Review*, XLIII, 290.

7. Ibid. p. 291.

8. *The Growth of English Industry and Commerce in Modern Times*, 3rd ed., II, 583-4.

9. 26 Geo. III, c. 60.

10. Edwards, op. cit. III, 224.

11. A brief statement regarding this trade on the eve of the Revolution can be found in Edwards, op. cit. Book VI, chap. iv.

12. 16 Geo. III, c. 5, and 17 Geo. III, c. 7.

13. Francis Wharton, *Revolutionary Diplomatic Correspondence of the United States*, V, 807.

14. *Parliamentary Papers*, House of Commons (referred to hereinafter as *Parl. Papers*), 1783, XIII, Nos. 426, 427. The text of this bill is printed in Edwards, op. cit. III, 262-4.

15. A recent brief discussion of the controversy precipitated by Pitt's bill can be found in Gerald S. Graham's *Sea Power and British North America,* 1783-1820, chap. ii.
16. For the debates on Pitt's bill, see *Parl. History,* XXIII, 602-15, 640-46, 724-30.
17. 23 Geo. III, c. 26 and c. 39.
18. The best sketch of Knox's career is to be found in Margaret Marion Spector's *The American Department of the British Government,* pp. 102-5.
19. Ibid. p. 154.
20. *Extra Official State Papers,* II, 54.
21. Ibid. p. 56.
22. Historical Manuscripts Commission, *Report on Manuscripts in Various Collections,* VI, 199.
23. For evidence, see ibid. pp. 191, 199, and *Extra Official State Papers,* II, Appendix No. XVIII.
24. *Extra Official State Papers,* II, 57.
25. Ibid. Appendix No. XIII.
26. Ibid.
27. The order in council of 2 July 1783 is printed in ibid. Appendix No. XVI.
28. Edward Gibbon, *The History of the Decline and Fall of the Roman Empire,* with Notes by Dean Milman, M. Guizot, and Dr. William Smith, I, 191-2.
29. Historical Manuscripts Commission, *Report on Manuscripts in Various Collections,* VI, 191.
30. This committee was appointed on 5 March 1784, by virtue of authority given by an act of Parliament of 1782 (22 Geo. III, c. 82), which abolished the old Board of Trade. It was succeeded in 1786 by a new committee of the council known as the Committee for Trade or Board of Trade. Anna Lane Lingelbach, 'The Inception of the British Board of Trade,' *American Historical Review,* XXX, 701-27.
31. Public Record Office, Board of Trade Papers, 5:1.
32. Edwards, op. cit. III, 267.
33. On the West India organizations in London, see Lillian M. Penson, 'The London West India Interest in the Eighteenth Century,' *English Historical Review,* July 1921, pp. 373 ff.
34. Edwards, op. cit. III, 268.
35. His *Thoughts on the Late Proceedings of Government respecting the Trade of the West India Islands with the United States of*

America was one of the many pamphlets in this controversy that were published in 1784.

36. An admirable study of his career is Grace Amelia Cockroft's *The Public Life of George Chalmers.*

37. The titles of many of the pamphlets published during the course of this controversy are listed in Lowell Joseph Ragatz, *A Guide for the Study of British Caribbean History, 1763-1834, including the Abolition and Emancipation Movements,* Part VIII. For a brief account of the controversy see Ragatz, *The Fall of the Planter Class,* pp. 173 ff.

38. Anna Lane Lingelbach, op. cit. *American Historical Review,* xxx, 707.

39. Edwards, op. cit. III, 275.

40. Herbert C. Bell, 'British Commercial Policy in the West Indies, 1783-93,' *English Historical Review,* xxxi, 439.

41. 28 Geo. III, c. 6. For the orders in council see Reeves, op. cit. pp. 278 ff. For a good general account of the regulation of British West India trade during the ten years after the Revolution, see Bell, op. cit. The act of 1788 sanctioned one slight departure from the rule excluding American ships from trade with the British West Indies. In order to encourage the making of salt on Turks Islands in the Bahamas, American vessels coming in ballast were permitted to enter the ports of those islands in order to take cargoes of salt, but for no other purposes.

42. 'The restraints which this twelfth article would have placed on American exportations of West Indian products, would have cut off the reëxportation not only of English but of French and all other foreign West Indian products, and incidentally it would have prevented for the period of the war then in existence between England and France the development of American domestic cotton export, the prospective importance of which nobody then appreciated.' Samuel Flagg Bemis, *Jay's Treaty,* pp. 258-9. Article XII was to remain in force during the continuance of the war in which England was then engaged and for two years after the date of the signature of articles of peace.

43. Reeves, op. cit. p. 283.

44. The principles of the navigation laws were not applied to trade by inland navigation between the United States and Canada, then organized as the Province of Quebec. The governor of the province, Lord Dorchester (formerly Sir Guy Carleton), took the posi-

tion that the prohibition of imports from the United States applied only to sea-borne imports, and in 1787 he permitted the importation of specified American products by way of Lake Champlain. Article III of Jay's Treaty, which related to trade between Canada and the United States, 'represents the first unqualified recognition of a community of economic interest between the inland colony and the United States' and indicates that 'the old colonial system could not be successfully translated from its native element, salt water.' Gerald S. Graham, op. cit. p. 89. In a dispatch to the Secretary of State for the Colonies, the Lieutenant Governor of Upper Canada wrote with regard to the navigation laws in 1818: 'I find, that, either from inattention to their provisions, or from a persuasion that they did not apply to the inland Navigation of the Waters which separate this Province from the United States of America, they have been hitherto so little regarded, that Vessels of American build, and owned and navigated by subjects of the United States, have been permitted without interruption to import, and carry from port to port in this Province, in the same manner as our own shipping.' *Select Documents in Canadian Economic History*, 1783-1885, ed. by H. A. Innis and A. R. M. Lower, p. 325.

45. 37 Geo. III, c. 117.

46. For Brougham's speech and the ensuing debate, see *Parl. Deb.*, XXXV, 1004 ff.

47. This petition is printed in full in *Parl. Deb.*, new ser., I, 179-82, and in *The Annual Register*, 1820, Part II, 770-72.

48. *The Speeches of the Right Honourable William Huskisson*, II, 475.

49. *A History of Prices*, 6 vols., London, 1838-57. Volumes V and VI were written in collaboration with William Newmarch. Appendix I in Vol. VI contains the text of the petition and Tooke's account of its origin and history.

50. *Parl. Deb.*, new ser., I, 165 ff.

51. Ibid. 576. Charles Duke Yonge, *The Life and Administration of Robert Banks, Second Earl of Liverpool*, III, 5 ff. Lord Liverpool was the son of Charles Jenkinson, First Earl of Liverpool, referred to above.

52. Ibid. p. 8.

53. This report is to be found in *Parl. Papers*, 1820, vol. III.

54. Ibid. vol. ii. The report can also be found in *The Annual Register*, 1820, Part ii, pp. 773 ff.

55. *Parl. Deb.*, new ser., viii, 104, 105.

56. Spencer Walpole, *A History of England from the Conclusion of the Great War in 1815*, 2nd ed., ii, 84-5.

57. *Parl. Deb.*, new ser., ii, 548.

58. 3 & 4 Anne, c. 10. The bounties of 1704 were continued by an act of 1729, which remained in effect till the American Revolution; 2 Geo. ii, c. 35. Robert Greenhalgh Albion, *Forests and Sea Power*, pp. 250 ff.

59. 49 Geo. iii, c. 98; 50 Geo. iii, c. 77; 51 Geo. iii, c. 93; 52 Geo. iii, c. 117; 53 Geo. iii, c. 33. Albion, op. cit. chap. viii.

60. By 46 Geo. iii, c. 117; 54 Geo. iii, c. 125; 55 Geo. iii, c. 86.

61. Graham, op. cit. p. 150. See chap. ix of this work for a brief account of the colonial timber trade.

62. First Report of the Select Committee of the House of Commons on Foreign Trade, 1821, *Parl. Papers*, 1821, vol. vi.

63. *Parl. Deb.*, new ser., i, 848.

64. For Marryat's speech, ibid. i, 846 ff.

65. Ibid. ix, 800.

66. Graham, op. cit. p. 152.

67. *Parl. Deb.*, new ser., vi, 1500.

68. Ibid. v, 1289 ff.

69. 3 Geo. iv, c. 41.

70. 3 Geo. iv, c. 42.

71. 3 Geo. iv, c. 43.

72. 48 Geo. iii, c. 11.

73. *Parl. Deb.*, new ser., vi, 1416.

74. Graham, op. cit. pp. 198 ff., 226 ff.

75. 3 Geo. iv, c. 44.

76. F. Lee Benns, *The American Struggle for the British West India Carrying Trade*, 1815-1830, p. 53.

77. Lowell Joseph Ragatz, *The Fall of the Planter Class in the British Caribbean*, pp. 352 ff.

78. See Graham, op. cit. chap. xiii, on the end of the Atlantic entrepôt.

79. *Speeches*, ii, 315.

80. The legality of this order in council was questionable, but an act of Parliament validating it was passed in 1824, 5 Geo. iv, c. 1.

81. Benns, op. cit. p. 188.

82. 3 Geo. IV, c. 45.

83. *The Annual Register*, 1822, p. 122.

84. *Speeches*, II, 320-21.

85. Ibid. p. 344.

86. Ibid. pp. 483-4.

87. Anna Lane Lingelbach's 'William Huskisson as President of the Board of Trade' (*American Historical Review*, XLIII, 759-74) is an excellent article based mainly on the minutes of the Board of Trade. Other studies of Huskisson are Alexander Brady, *William Huskisson and Liberal Reform*, and G. S. Veitch, *Huskisson and Liverpool*. The Huskisson Papers are in the Manuscripts Department of the British Museum. A selection from this voluminous collection, edited by Lewis Melville, has been published with the title *The Huskisson Papers*. A biographical memoir in the first volume of *The Speeches of the Right Honourable William Huskisson* (3 vols., London, 1831) and the article on Huskisson in the *Dictionary of National Biography* are useful for his career in general.

88. 4 Geo. IV, c. 77.

89. The dates of the several reciprocity treaties concluded by the United Kingdom pursuant to 4 Geo. IV, c. 77, are given in Appendix No. 4 to the Report from the Select Committee on British Shipping, *Parl. Papers*, 1844, vol. VIII. The texts of the treaties and of the British orders in council can be found in Hertslet's *Commercial Treaties*.

90. *Speeches*, II, 205-6. For Ricardo's opinion, see *Parl. Deb.*, new ser., IX, 801.

91. *Speeches*, III, 29.

92. 5 Geo. IV, c. 21.

93. Report from the Select Committee on Import Duties, p. 188, *Parl. Papers*, 1840, vol. V.

94. 5 Geo. IV, c. 95 and c. 97.

95. 6 Geo. IV, c. 105.

96. 6 Geo. IV, c. 109.

97. 6 Geo. IV, c. 104, 106, 107, 108, 110, 111, 112, 113, 114.

98. Alexander Brady, *William Huskisson and Liberal Reform*, p. 113.

99. *Speeches*, II, 427.

100. Ibid. pp. 327-62.

101. 6 Geo. IV, c. 76.

102. *Speeches*, II, 304-27.

103. Ibid. III, 9-10.
104. 6 Geo. IV, c. 109, c. 73, and c. 114.
105. Harper, op. cit. p. 396; Hertslet, Commercial Treaties.
106. It did apply, however, to imports into the colonies in America and the West Indies and Mauritius if produced within the Empire outside of the United Kingdom, those colonies, and Mauritius.
107. *Parl. Deb.*, new ser., IX, 1544; X, 1-2.
108. *The Greville Memoirs,* ed. by Lytton Strachey and Roger Fulford, I, 154. For a brief account of the crisis see Leone Levi, *The History of British Commerce,* Part III, chap. iv.
109. For Lord Liverpool's opinions, see W. R. Brock, *Lord Liverpool and Liberal Toryism,* pp. 201 ff.
110. *Speeches,* II, 465 ff.; III, 1 ff., 77 ff.
111. Ibid. III, 92.
112. Ibid. III, 119.
113. Ibid. II, 318.
114. *On Financial Reform,* p. 74.
115. Ibid. p. 238.
116. Ibid. p. 246.
117. The Report from the Select Committee on Import Duties, with the minutes of evidence, is printed in *Parl. Papers,* 1840, vol. v.
118. Report, pp. 93, 198, 202.

CHAPTER IV

1. John Morley, *The Life of Cobden,* I, 230.
2. *Select Documents on British Colonial Policy,* 1830-1860, ed. by Kenneth N. Bell and W. P. Morrell, pp. 325-6.
3. *Parl. Papers,* Reports from Committees, 1840, II, No. 2, pp. 196-7.
4. For much testimony to this effect, see ibid. No. 2, *passim.* The writer of a pamphlet entitled *The Preference Interests* (London, 1841) estimated that the differential duties on sugar, coffee, and timber amounted to a tax of £5,000,000 annually on British consumers.
5. W. P. Morrell, *British Colonial Policy in the Age of Peel and Russell,* p. 167.
6. Returns laid before the House of Commons in 1847 showing itemized revenues of the colonies for the latest year available indicate that in every colony except South Australia the largest item was the customs. *Parl. Papers,* 1847, XXXVII, H. C. 740.

7. W. P. Morrell, op. cit. pp. 168, 188-9.

8. Bernard Holland, *The Fall of Protection*, p. 104.

9. *Parl. Deb.*, 3rd ser., LXIII, 513.

10. Ibid. 546.

11. Ibid. 541-2, 549.

12. 5 & 6 Vict., c. 47. In 1840 a select parliamentary committee on import duties had recommended revision of the whole system of differential duties and reduction of colonial preference. Their recommendation was not followed in framing the tariff of 1842.

13. *Parl. Deb.*, 3rd ser., LXIII, 1305.

14. *Parl. Deb.*, 3rd ser., LX, 150-56.

15. 5 & 6 Vict., c. 49.

16. A 'possessions act' was passed in 1845, but it made no material changes in the rates of duty; 8 & 9 Vict., c. 93.

17. *Parl. Deb.*, 3rd ser., LXXIV, 1286, 1288.

18. Ibid. 1288-90.

19. Ibid. 1286.

20. Ibid. LXXX, 321. The gross importation of wool into the United Kingdom from the British possessions increased from 21,132,352 pounds in 1843 to 37,333,104 pounds in 1847; *Parl. Papers*, 1905, Cd. 2394, pp. 106-7.

21. *Parl. Deb.*, 3rd ser., LXXIV, 1271, 1273-4.

22. Ibid. 1279-80.

23. *Parl. Papers*, 1846, XLIV, no. 1, p. 2; ibid. 1847, LIX, no. 1, p. 2. For the years 1843-7, inclusive, the gross importation of colonial coffee, expressed in pounds, was 18,277,335; 24,099,613; 23,235,102; 24,286,464; 34,301,316. For the same years the gross importation of foreign coffee was: 20,665,134; 22,423,575; 27,142,813; 27,527,-187; 21,052,728. *Parl. Papers*, 1905, Cd. 2394, pp. 106-7.

24. 6 & 7 Gul. IV, c. 26. This act equalized the duties on East Indian and West Indian sugar at 24s. per cwt.

25. *Parl. Deb.*, 3rd ser., LXXV, 161, 167.

26. Ibid. 170.

27. 7 & 8 Vict., c. 28. The duties referred to above were those on unrefined brown sugar, described as 'muscovado or clayed.'

28. 8 & 9 Vict., c. 5.

29. *Parl. Papers*, 1846, XLIV, no. 1; ibid. 1847, LIX, no. 1; ibid. 1905, Cd. 2394, pp. 126-7.

30. It is impossible within the compass of this chapter to explain the precise effects upon the preferential system of all the numerous changes in the British customs made during Peel's ministry.

31. 9 Geo. IV, c. 60. The sliding scale was applied also to the duties on foreign barley, oats, rye and other grain.

32. Spencer Walpole, *The Life of Lord John Russell,* I, 368.

33. 5 & 6 Vict., c. 14.

34. *Canada and its Provinces,* ed. by Shortt, V, 190.

35. Raw materials brought into the colonies and manufactured there were treated in the British customs as colonial products.

36. *Provincial Statutes of Canada,* 6 Vict., c. 31.

37. 6 & 7 Vict., c. 29.

38. *Parl. Deb.,* 3rd ser., LXIX, 630-31.

39. *Parl. Papers,* 1846, XLIV, no. 130, p. 9.

40. *Canada and its Provinces,* V, pp. 196-7; Allin and Jones, *Annexation, Preferential Trade and Reciprocity,* pp. 12-13; Earl Grey, *Colonial Policy of Lord John Russell's Administration,* I, 220-21.

41. D. L. Burn, 'Canada and the Repeal of the Corn Laws,' *Cambridge Historical Journal,* II, 252 ff.

42. *Parl. Deb.,* 3rd ser., LXXX, 295, 340.

43. Ibid. 340-42.

44. *Parl. Deb.,* 3rd ser., LXXXIII, 262-3. The degree of protection which Peel proposed to leave against foreign grain during the interval from 1846 to 1849 was much less than that afforded by the corn law of 1842. On foreign wheat the duty was to vary from 9s. to 4s. as prices rose from 48s. to 53s.; it was to remain fixed at 4s. for all prices above 53s., and at 10s. for all below 48s.

45. For the years 1846 to 1849, inclusive, the annual gross importation of colonial wheat, expressed in quarters, was as follows: 888,114; 100,780; 32,560; 25,401. From foreign countries for the same years it was: 1,343,777; 2,555,673; 2,548,398; 3,819,977. The repeal of the corn laws led to no abrupt fall in the price of wheat in England. For the decade ending in 1850 the average price was less than that for the preceding decade by only 3s.8d., while for the next decennial period it rose by 1s.4d. See Holland, *The Fall of Protection,* pp. 361-2.

46. *Parl. Deb.,* 3rd ser., LXXXVI, 1165.

47. Ibid. LXXXVII, 963. The anti-imperial character of the legislation of 1846 was dwelt upon by the writer of a contemporary pamphlet, *Our Free Trade Policy Examined* (London, 1846). He predicted the loss of Canada and the West Indies as a consequence of free trade.

48. *Parl. Deb.,* 3rd ser., LXXXIII, 850.

49. Ibid. LXXXVI, 1167-8.
50. Ibid. LXXXVI, 553-67.
51. Ibid. LXXXVI, 1170.
52. Ibid. LXXXIII, 1036-7.
53. Ibid. LXXXVI, 685.
54. Ibid. LXXXVI, 1307-9.
55. See William Cunningham, *Wisdom of the Wise,* Lecture II.
56. 9 & 10 Vict., c. 22.
57. 9 & 10 Vict., c. 23.
58. The duty referred to was that imposed upon undressed timber per load (50 cubic feet). Laths, battens, deals, *etc.* were subject to special duties.
59. *Parl. Deb.,* 3rd ser., LXI, 459.
60. Ibid. LXI, 1113.
61. 5 & 6 Vict., c. 47, Table A, Class 5.
62. *Parl. Deb.,* 3rd ser., LXXXIV, 1290.
63. Ibid. LXXXIV, 1313-27.
64. Allin and Jones, op. cit. chap. i.
65. *Letters and Journals of James, Eighth Earl of Elgin,* p. 60.
66. 8 & 9 Vict., c. 93.
67. The extent to which colonial sugar monopolized the British market may be seen from the following quantities of muscovado sugar imported into the United Kingdom in 1845: British colonial, 4,908,969 cwts.; foreign, the produce of free labor, 168,606 cwts.; foreign slave-grown, 743,315 cwts. The slave-grown sugar, however, was not imported for British consumption, but in bond for re-exportation; *Parl. Papers,* 1905, LXXII, Cd. 2394, pp. 126-7.
68. Unless otherwise stated, the duties on sugar mentioned in this chapter were those imposed on unrefined muscovado sugar; other and higher duties were levied upon white clayed, refined, and double-refined sugar.
69. *Parl. Deb.,* 3rd ser., LXXXVIII, 93-4.
70. Ibid. LXXXVII, 1316-17. Prior to 1846 the sugar duties had been levied annually. Russell proposed to make them permanent, believing that a final settlement would be to the interest of the public and the sugar trade. But constitutional practice required that a considerable amount of revenue should be dependent upon annual grant. He therefore promised the House of Commons that some other source of revenue would be proposed for yearly vote,

but never announced what the substitute was to be! Ibid. LXXXVII, 1304, 1323; Disraeli, *Life of Lord George Bentinck*, pp. 232-3.

71. *Parl. Deb.*, 3rd ser., LXXXVII, 1327.

72. Ibid. LXXXVIII, 44-5, 119, 501, *et seq.;* Disraeli, op. cit. p. 374.

73. *Parl. Deb.*, 3rd ser., LXXXVIII, 93-103.

74. Ibid. 53.

75. Ibid. 180.

76. Ibid. 34, 497-8.

77. Ibid. 127, 495, 545.

78. Ibid. 115-16.

79. Ibid. 117, 545.

80. Ibid. 520.

81. Ibid. 543.

82. Ibid. 495.

83. Ibid. 494.

84. The cry of 'cheap food' won support for free trade among the working classes of Great Britain in much the same way that the familiar 'American standard of living' has enlisted American workingmen under the banner of the protective tariff. Many British manufacturers who were ardent free-traders, however, no doubt accepted Ricardo's theory that whatever lowered the laborer's cost of living would ultimately result in the reduction of his wages. Karl Marx, in his *Discourse on Free Trade,* took pleasure in laying bare what he considered the hypocrisy of the 'cheap food' argument of the British free-traders. Gladstone, in a speech delivered in 1860, thus distinguished between the real and the putative benefits of free trade to the British workingman: 'Take the great change in the corn laws; it may even possibly be doubted whether up to this time you have given them [the working class] cheaper bread—at best it is but a trifle cheaper than before; that change, however, is one comparatively immaterial; but you have created a regular and steady trade which may be stated at £15,000,-000 a year; by that trade you have created a corresponding demand for the commodities of which they are the producers . . . and it is the price their labor thus brings, not the price of cheapened commodities, that forms the main benefit they receive'; *Parl. Deb.*, 3rd ser., CLVI, 831-2. Had the interests of the masses been the controlling factor in British free trade, the duties would, perhaps, have been taken off tobacco, spirits, tea, and coffee; Fuchs,

The Trade Policy of Great Britain and her Colonies, since 1860, p. 15.

85. *Parl. Deb.*, 3rd ser., LXXXVII, 1324-5. Prior to the publication of Lord Durham's Report in 1839, Russell had not been notably liberal in colonial policy. In 1838 he upheld the commercial principles of the old colonial system, and opposed the grant of responsible government to Canada; Holland, *Imperium et Libertas*, pp. 109-11.

86. This argument was dwelt upon at length by the free-trade press. For example, the London *Times*, in an editorial of 20 July 1846, said: 'The severity of the present system is chiefly directed against some of our very best customers in the world, who, if we took their sugar, would quickly take twice as much of our own manufactures, and so give twice as much employment for our poor people.'

87. 9 & 10 Vict., c. 63. Under the operation of this act the gross importation of foreign sugar rose from 1,197,672 cwts. in 1846 to 2,408,981 in 1847; for these two years the gross importation of colonial sugar was, respectively, 4,424,819 and 5,800,539 cwts.; *Parl. Papers*, 1905, Cd. 2394, pp. 126-7.

88. *Parl. Deb.*, 3rd ser., XCVI, 8-9, 172, 189.

89. Ibid. 42, 168.

90. Ibid. XCVI, 9, 184; CI, 692-3. In 1847 Disraeli, soon to succeed Bentinck in the leadership of the Conservative party in the House of Commons, professed the conviction that after a fair trial of free trade the country would return to protection; Monypenny and Buckle, *Life of Disraeli*, III, 23, 26.

91. The committee's report, together with minutes of evidence taken by it, fills four volumes of the *Parliamentary Papers* (*Parl. Papers*, 1847-8, XXIII, parts I-IV) and gives extensive information respecting conditions in the sugar colonies.

92. *Parl. Deb.*, 3rd ser., XCIV, 730, 738, 740. He proposed, furthermore, to encourage the immigration of laborers into the West Indies by assisting the colonies to give bounties on such immigration; to lower the duty on colonial rum to which the West India interests objected as an unfair discrimination against them in favor of the British and Irish distillers of spirits; and to permit the distillation of spirits from sugar and molasses in the United Kingdom. His plan, apart from the alteration of the sugar

duties, was embodied in the following legislation of 1848; 11 & 12 Vict., c. 38, 60, 100, and 130.

93. 11 & 12 Vict., c. 97.

94. *Parl. Deb.*, 3rd ser., cxxv, 1357. The sugar duties remained an important source of revenue, and were modified from time to time to suit the fiscal needs of the government. In 1854 the duty on unrefined sugar was fixed at 11s. (17 & 18 Vict., c. 29), but in 1855, on account of the Crimean War, it was raised to 13s.9d. (18 & 19 Vict., c. 21). In 1857 it was put at 12s.8d. (20 Vict., c. 15), at which amount it was retained by the great customs act of 1860.

95. *Parl. Deb.*, 3rd ser., cxvi, 183.

96. 14 & 15 Vict., c. 62.

97. *Parl. Deb.*, 3rd ser., lxxxvii, 1320.

98. 9 & 10 Vict., c. 94; *Parl. Deb.*, 3rd ser., lxxxviii, 746-7. Bentinck protested against hurrying through so important a measure, 'when half of the House were gone to the moors, and another fourth were gone to the Continent.'

99. *Parl. Deb.*, 3rd ser., lxxxviii, 738.

100. Ibid. 743-4.

101. Ibid. 678-9.

102. *Parl. Deb.*, 3rd ser., lxxxviii, 683.

103. Ibid. 907.

104. Earl Grey, *The Commercial Policy of the British Colonies and the McKinley Tariff*, pp. 13-14. He believed that the policy later adopted by the Imperial Government of permitting the colonies to set up protective systems of their own was unwise in the extreme, and that it was in direct violation of the imperial policy of free trade; ibid. pp. 14, 16-17. Like Lord Durham, he believed that colonial self-government should not extend to the regulation of trade and, like later advocates of imperial reciprocity, he held that the only secure bond of empire was a sense of community of interest, though he disagreed with them entirely as to the means of preserving it; ibid. p. 20.

105. Ibid. p. 14.

106. 13 & 14 Vict., c. 59, sec. 27.

107. 36 & 37 Vict., c. 22.

108. *Journals of the Legislative Assembly of the Province of Canada*, vi, Appendix no. 1 (K).

109. Ibid. p. 7.

110. *Provincial Statutes of Canada*, 11 Vict., c. 31.

111. See, e.g. Acts of the General Assembly of Nova Scotia, 1847, 10 Vict., c. 12 and 13; Acts of the General Assembly of New Brunswick, 1847, 10 Vict., c. 54; Journals of the House of Assembly of Prince Edward Island, 1847, pp. 93, 120; Laws of Jamaica, 1846-1847, 10 Vict., c. 22; Laws of Barbados, no. 238; Laws of Antigua, no. 102.

112. *Parl. Deb.*, 3rd ser., cxxiv, 1036. By 1849 Disraeli had become convinced that Great Britain was committed to free trade, and his budget speech as Chancellor of the Exchequer in April 1852 was intended to rid his party of the incubus of a lost cause. In March 1853 he voted with the radical free-traders in support of a motion which contemplated the repeal of the remaining protective duties; Monypenny and Buckle, op. cit. iii, chaps. viii, xi; *Parl. Deb.*, 3rd ser., cxxiv, 1012-13, 1040-41. By this time the working classes, for whose support Disraeli was coquetting, had become strenuous free-traders, as they were not in 1846; Morley, *Life of Gladstone*, i, 425.

113. *Parl. Deb.*, 3rd ser., cxxv, 1415-16.

114. 16 & 17 Vict., c. 106.

115. 23 Vict., c. 22. This tariff left 48 articles subject to revenue duties, of which only those on spirits, wine, sugar, tea, coffee, tobacco, grain, and timber were of importance.

116. *Parl. Deb.*, 3rd ser., clvi, 834, 837.

117. There was an elaborate classification of timber for purposes of the tariff. The duties referred to were those imposed on undressed hewn wood.

118. Haliburton is still remembered as the author of a number of humorous and descriptive works, of which *The Clockmaker* enjoyed the greatest vogue. In the House of Commons, to which he had been elected in 1859, he regarded himself as peculiarly the spokesman of the people of British North America. The strong advocacy of imperial unity that runs through his writings no doubt had its influence in producing a reaction against the clearly marked tendencies of the 'sixties toward the disintegration of the Empire; *Haliburton* (Toronto, 1897), pp. 33-6, 77 *et seq.*

119. *Parl. Deb.*, 3rd ser., clvii, 2098-9.

120. Ibid. 241. In 1858, for the first time since colonial lumber had enjoyed a high degree of protection in Great Britain, the importation from foreign countries exceeded that from British posses-

sions; this excess naturally continued under the operation of the act of 1860; *Parl. Papers*, 1905, Cd. 2394, pp. 144-5, 160-61, 166-7.

121. *Colonial Policy of Lord John Russell's Administration*, vol. 1, p. 18. The concession of full 'responsible government' to Canada, though recommended by Lord Durham in his famous Report published in 1839, was not actually made until 1848, after the victory of free trade seemed assured by the legislation of 1846.

CHAPTER V

1. 6 June 1848, *The Elgin-Grey Papers*, 1846-1852, I, 181.

2. Some reasons to account for this are suggested by J. H. Clapham, *An Economic History of Modern Britain: The Early Railway Age*, 1820-1850, 2nd ed., p. 501.

3. The traditional view was thus expressed by a prominent representative of the shipping interest in 1847: 'It appears from historical records that the immediate effect of the passing of the Navigation Act of Charles the 2nd was, that the shipping engaged in the mercantile navigation of the country was within 20 years more than doubled. At the commencement of the last century, the mercantile tonnage of the country amounted to 216,000 tons. At the conclusion of the last war it had reached 2,600,000 tons, and it has now attained the enormous magnitude of 3,800,000 tons, all during the continuance and under the operation of the Navigation System; and it is, to my humble perceptions, as clearly demonstrated as the solution of any mathematical problem, that it has been chiefly in consequence of the practical operation of those laws by which, through the immense mercantile tonnage which has been created, the genius of the peoples inhabiting our maritime districts has been directed towards maritime pursuits, the Royal Navy has been kept effectively manned, and those naval triumphs have been achieved to which, I believe, under Providence, this country owes its independence and its safety.' Fourth Report from the Select Committee on Navigation Laws, pp. 65-6, *Parl. Papers*, 1847-8, xx, Part I.

4. Adam Smith, *An Inquiry into the Nature and Causes of the Wealth of Nations*, Book IV, chap. ii.

5. *Parl. Deb.*, 3rd ser., CIV, 1361. The British public gave no attention to the navigation laws until they came under attack. Joseph Allen, *The Navigation Laws of Great Britain, Historically and Practically Considered* (London, 1849), p. vi.

6. J. H. Clapham, 'The Last Years of the Navigation Acts,' *English Historical Review*, xxv, 687.

7. 8 & 9 Vict., c. 88. A commentary on the provisions of the act may be found in the evidence given by Mr. Shaw Lefevre, an official of the Board of Trade and an expert on legal questions connected with the navigation laws, before a select committee of the House of Commons on the navigation laws; *Parl. Papers*, 1847-8, xx, Part i, pp. 1-19. A condensed summary is given by W. S. Lindsay, *History of Merchant Shipping and Ancient Commerce*, iii, 107-9.

8. Shaw Lefevre said that he had never seen an explanation of why exportation was not restricted; he supposed that it was because of a desire to do nothing to impede exportation. Mercantile policy, in general, favored the encouragement of exports.

9. A difference is to be noted between the foreign ships that were permitted to import the enumerated products of Europe into the United Kingdom and those that were permitted to import the products of Asia, Africa, and America. In the case of the former the ship could belong to either the producing country or the country from which the products were imported, supposing that the two countries were not the same. In the case of the latter, the ship must belong to the producing country, which must also be the country from which the products were imported. Thus, for example, a Portuguese ship could carry Spanish wine from Lisbon to London, but a United States ship could not carry Cuban sugar from New York to London.

10. 8 & 9 Vict., c. 89.

11. Report from the Select Committee on British Shipping, Appendix No. 3, *Parl. Papers*, 1844, viii. George Frederick Young, chairman of the Shipowners' Society, thus described the protection then enjoyed by British shipping: 'The great protection we at present enjoy in navigation may be classed under three heads. The first is, the entire restriction of importation from the colonies for consumption in this country to British ships, together with a similar restriction in the coasting trade. The second is, the prohibition on the importation of all articles the produce of distant quarters of the world, Asia, Africa, and America, from any of the ports of Europe, in any ships. The third is, the limitation of importations of the produce of foreign countries to British ships, or ships belonging to the countries in which the articles are produced, or

ships belonging to a country in Europe in which the produce, if European, may be found.' Ibid. p. 45.

12. *Parl. Deb.*, 3rd ser., CIV, 1389.

13. Appendix No. 3, cited in note 11.

14. *Parl. Papers*, 1849, LI, H. C. 181, pp. 2-3.

15. Report from the Select Committee on British Shipping, pp. 16, 72, 82, *Parl. Papers*, 1844, VIII.

16. Fourth Report of the Select Committee of the House of Commons on the Navigation Laws, pp. 143, 145, *Parl. Papers*, 1847-8, XX, Part I.

17. Report from the Select Committee on British Shipping, pp. 86-7, *Parl. Papers*, 1844, VIII.

18. Third Report from the Select Committee of the House of Commons on the Navigation Laws, p. 136, *Parl. Papers*, 1847-8, XX, Part I.

19. First Report from the Select Committee of the House of Lords appointed to inquire into the Policy and Operation of the Navigation Laws, *Parl. Papers*, 1847-8, XX, Part II, p. 193. J. H. Clapham, 'The Last Years of the Navigation Acts,' *English Historical Review*, XXV, 707.

20. Ibid. 706.

21. *Parl. Papers*, 1847-8, XX, Part II, pp. 466, 899. The colonial ships were built mainly in New Brunswick and Canada. They had a bad name with British shipowners, who regarded them as very inferior in quality. Report from the Select Committee on British Shipping, pp. 9, 24, 30, 60 ff., *Parl. Papers*, 1844, VIII.

22. *Parl. Papers*, 1847-8, XX, Part II, p. 670.

23. Report from the Select Committee on British Shipping, p. 52, *Parl. Papers*, 1844, VIII.

24. Ibid. p. 57.

25. Ibid. pp. 164, 190.

26. Ibid. p. 170.

27. *Parl. Papers*, 1847-8, XX, Part II, p. 23.

28. Fourth Report from the Select Committee on the Navigation Laws, p. 21, *Parl. Papers*, 1847-8, XX, Part I.

29. *Parl. Deb.*, 3rd ser., XCIX, 630. History, of course, can never weigh with precision the relative strength of motives, but it may be noted that some of the opponents of the repeal of the navigation laws attributed the attack on the old system to a desire to increase the sale of British manufactures abroad, to what one writer called the

'Manchester interest.' J. Houston Browne, *The Navigation Laws: Their History and Operation* (London, 1847), pp. iv, 42-3. J. L. Ricardo, in his *Anatomy of the Navigation Laws* (London, 1847), pp. 221-2, enumerated as the classes injured by the navigation laws: colonists, merchants, manufacturers, working classes, merchant seamen, and the whole community considered as consumers.

30. On this subject generally, see D. G. Creighton, *The Commercial Empire of the St. Lawrence,* 1760-1850. For early British hopes that Canada would become the 'vestibule of commerce' between Great Britain and the western settlements of the United States, see Gerald S. Graham, *British Policy and Canada,* 1774-1791, chap. viii, and the same author's *Sea Power and British North America,* 1783-1820, chap. v.

31. Creighton, op. cit. p. 251.

32. Gilbert Norman Tucker, *The Canadian Commercial Revolution,* 1845-1851, chaps. ii and iii.

33. *Parl. Papers,* 1847-8, xx, Part II, p. 921. Tucker, op. cit. pp. 58 ff. 'It was, generally, represented that the high rate of freight between Montreal and the United Kingdom was owing to the limited number of ships employed in the import trade of Canada. . . . The rate of freight is said to have fluctuated in Montreal in one and the same season between 3s.6d. and 7s.6d. per barrel; and it is stated that the higher rate, from 6s. to 7s.6d. per barrel, had been paid in Montreal, while freights were offered in foreign ships at New York as low as 1s. and 1s.6d. per barrel.' W. S. Lindsay, *History of Merchant Shipping and Ancient Commerce,* III, 123-4.

34. According to a memorandum of the Executive Council of Canada drawn up in May 1848, the costs of transporting a barrel of flour from Cleveland, Ohio, to New York and to Montreal were, respectively, 4s.6d. and 2s.9d., a difference in favor of the St. Lawrence route of 1s.9d. But this was more than offset by the advantage enjoyed by New York over Montreal in trans-Atlantic freight, for here the difference in favor of the New York-Liverpool route over the Montreal-Liverpool route was estimated at 3s. Correspondence between the Governor-General of Canada and the Secretary of State for the Colonial Department upon the Operation of the Navigation Laws, pp. 4-5, *Parl. Papers,* 1847-8, LIX. A brief account of the two rival trade routes can be found in Alexander

Mackay's *The Western World; or, Travels in the United States in* 1846-47, Vol. III, chap. v.

35. See above, p. 143.
36. Tucker, op. cit. p. 90.
37. Ibid. pp. 93-4.
38. D. L. Burn has argued that the influence of the British act of 1843 in stimulating wheat growing and milling in Canada was greatly exaggerated. Undoubtedly other factors ought to be taken into account. 'Canada and the Repeal of the Corn Laws,' *Cambridge Historical Journal*, II, 252 ff.
39. Creighton, op. cit. p. 361.
40. *The Elgin-Grey Papers*, 1846-1852, I, 178.
41. Ibid. I, 256. For criticism of Elgin's diagnosis, see Burn, op. cit. in *Cambridge Historical Journal*, II, 266.
42. *Parl. Papers*, 1847-8, XX, Part II, pp. 280, 912, 922. The repeal of the navigation laws in 1849 did not open the St. Lawrence to foreign shipping between Montreal and Quebec. This part of the river had been definitely closed to American ships by Jay's Treaty. The Elgin-Marcy Reciprocity Treaty of 1854 secured for American vessels the privilege of navigating the St. Lawrence between Montreal and Quebec. George W. Brown, 'The Opening of the St. Lawrence to American Shipping,' *Canadian Historical Review*, VII, 4-12.
43. *Parl. Papers*, 1847-8, XX, Part II, p. 922.
44. Ibid. pp. 913-16. *The Canadian Economist*, a free-trade journal, regarded the restrictions imposed on Canadian commerce by the navigation laws as the heaviest burden under which Canada was laboring. *Select Documents in Canadian Economic History*, ed. by H. A. Innis and A. R. M. Lower, pp. 349-50.
45. *Parl. Papers*, 1847-8, XX, Part II, p. 923.
46. Ibid. pp. 925-6.
47. Ibid. pp. 923-4.
48. See, e.g. Correspondence between the Governor-General of Canada and the Secretary of State for the Colonial Department upon the Operation of the Navigation Laws, p. 15, *Parl. Papers*, 1847-8, LIX, and *The Elgin-Grey Papers*, 1846-1852, I, 177-9.
49. *Parl. Papers*, 1847-8, XX, Part II, p. 946.
50. Ibid. pp. 940, 943.
51. Ibid. pp. 951-2.
52. Ibid. pp. 952-4.

53. Ibid. pp. 947-8.
54. Ibid. p. 949.
55. Ibid. p. 957.
56. *Parl. Deb.*, 3rd ser., CIII, 613.
57. 10 & 11 Vict., c. 1 and c. 2. Lord Elgin pointed out that this temporary modification of the navigation laws did not enable foreign vessels to load cargoes of grain at Montreal, because Montreal was not a free port and hence could not be reached by foreign vessels from the ocean. *Parl. Papers*, 1847-8, XX, Part II, p. 940. To meet this difficulty foreign ships were permitted to sail in ballast to Montreal and there take cargoes of grain and flour for the United Kingdom. Tucker, op. cit. p. 128.
58. 10 & 11 Vict., c. 64 and c. 86.
59. *Parl. Deb.*, 3rd ser., LXXXIX.
60. Ibid. LXXXIX, 246, 276, 277.
61. Ibid. XCIII, 1136.
62. Ibid. LXXXIX. 1058-9. Ricardo's *The Anatomy of the Navigation Laws* (London, 1847) was based mainly on the evidence of witnesses examined by this committee.
63. *Parl. Papers*, 1847-8, XX, Part I.
64. Ibid. Part II. In moving the appointment of this committee Lord Hardwicke said that the House of Commons' committee on the navigation laws had not been impartial, that it had examined twenty-five witnesses in favor of repealing the navigation laws and only nine who wished to maintain them, and that it had left only 'a very one-sided collection of evidence.' The Government did not oppose the appointment of the Lords' committee, though it did not consider further parliamentary inquiry necessary. *Parl. Deb.*, 3rd ser., XCVI, 1316-17, 1326. A condensation of the evidence of the witnesses who appeared before the Lords' committee can be found in Joseph Allen, *The Navigation Laws of Great Britain, Historically and Practically Considered* (London, 1849), pp. 65-244.
65. *Parl. Deb.*, 3rd ser., XCV, 14.
66. Ibid. XCVIII, 992 ff.
67. Ibid. XCIX, 9 ff., 179 ff., 510 ff., 573 ff.; CI, 56-60.
68. Ibid. XCVI, 1327.
69. Correspondence between the Governor-General of Canada and the Secretary of State for the Colonial Department upon the Operation of the Navigation Laws, p. 7, *Parl. Papers*, 1847-8, LIX.

The Executive Council proposed that the free navigation of the St. Lawrence be conceded to American vessels in return for the repeal by Congress of the existing duty on Canadian wheat in the United States.

70. Ibid. pp. 8-9, 14; same title, pp. 3 ff., *Parl. Papers*, 1849, LI.

71. Further Correspondence between the Governor-General of Canada and the Secretary of State for the Colonial Department upon the Operation of the Navigation Laws, pp. 3-4, *Parl. Papers*, 1849, LI.

72. Copies of Extracts of any Correspondence, Petitions or Memorials relative to the Repeal of the Navigation Laws, which may have been sent Home by the Governor of New Brunswick, pp. 4-5. *Parl. Papers*, 1847-8, LIX.

73. *Parl. Papers*, 1849, LI.

74. *Parl. Deb.*, 3rd ser., CII, 699, 741; CIII, 464 ff.; CIV, 702-5.

75. Ibid. CIII, 466.

76. Ibid. CV, 177 ff.; CVI, 48-9. There had been talk of the Government's resigning if the Navigation Bill should be defeated by the Lords. *The Later Correspondence of Lord John Russell*, ed. by G. P. Gooch, I, 193-4.

77. 12 & 13 Vict., c. 29.

78. The coasting trade of the United Kingdom was opened to foreign ships in 1854, without opposition from British shipowners, by 17 & 18 Vict., c. 5.

79. *Parl. Deb.*, 3rd ser., CIII, 552; CIV, 686-7. Two years after the repeal of the navigation laws, Lord Stanley asked whether the power of retaliation which Parliament had given to the Government would be exercised; Lord Granville, replying for the Government, gave little ground for expecting that this would be done. *Parl. Deb.*, 3rd ser., CXVII, 857, 861-2, 871. In 1858, at a time when British shipping was experiencing another depression, the General Shipowners' Society asked that retaliation be resorted to against those foreign countries which did not admit British shipping to equal privileges with their own ships. The Board of Trade expressed the opinion that the Government would be justified in retaliating against the ships of such countries—there were only a few of them—but that it would not actually be worth while to do so. Copies of an Address to the Queen from the Owners of British Ships . . . and of the subsequent Correspondence in reference thereto, pp. 1-2, 6-7, *Parl. Papers*, 1859, XXV.

80. *Parl. Deb.*, 3rd ser., XCIX, 619.

81. Lord Grey, for example. See his speech on the bill in the House of Lords, ibid. CIV, 683-4. Professor Lawrence A. Harper, who has made a detailed and very valuable study of the navigation laws, takes his stand with those who have contended that the laws were efficacious in increasing British shipping rather than with later free-trade critics of the laws: 'Whether we study the tonnage owned by Englishmen and engaged in foreign trade, the number of English entries at London, the ratio of English participation in entry and clearance figures, or the number of English ships passing the Sound, we reach the same conclusion—that English shipping developed more rapidly under the Navigation Acts than it had before the days of Cromwell, and that the development did not follow, but outstripped, the growth of commerce . . . The survival of English shipbuilding after 1850 offers no ground for believing that the English yards of 1651 could have successfully challenged the then supreme Dutch without parliamentary aid . . . English ingenuity eventually asserted itself in all fields of construction when steam and iron became the order of the day, but it is merely wishful thinking to assume that such or similar developments would have occurred two centuries earlier if English shipwrights had not been protected . . . The Navigation Acts should be judged as we would judge any physical mechanism—with relation to the end it is designed to accomplish. Judged by this standard, the Acts were successful . . . The evidence demonstrates that they benefited England's shipping, seamen, and shipbuilding.' *The English Navigation Laws: A Seventeenth-Century Experiment in Social Engineering*, pp. 368-78.

82. *Parl. Deb.*, 3rd ser., XCIX, 257. Gladstone did not approve of all the provisions of the bill of 1849, but he supported it. Ibid. CIII, 540 ff.

83. Ibid. XCIX, 663, 667.

84. For example, Joseph Hume; ibid. XCIX, 606.

85. 'The Last Years of the Navigation Acts,' *English Historical Review*, XXV, 689.

86. *Parl. Deb.*, 3rd ser., CIV, 688.

87. Ibid. CIII, 590. Lord Grey tried to discredit the petitions against the bill—'they all knew the machinery by which petitions, of late years, were got up . . . That machinery had gone so far as to destroy in a great measure the value of the right of petition. But he had never known that machinery to be worked more

vigorously than on the present occasion.' Ibid. cv, 79. According to J. L. Ricardo, who may be said to have launched the parliamentary movement against the navigation laws, the opponents of the old system deliberately refrained from arousing public excitement. It would have been easy, he said, to work up a popular agitation against the navigation laws and the shipping interests. Ibid. ciii, 602. In a schedule of petitions presented to the House of Lords in reference to the navigation laws during the session of 1847-8, printed as an appendix to Joseph Allen's *The Navigation Laws of Great Britain, Historically and Practically Considered*, there are listed 36 petitions against any alteration of the navigation laws, 5 against any alteration without inquiry, 50 praying that before any alteration is permitted a select committee be appointed to inquire into the policy of the navigation laws, and only one petition for the immediate repeal of the laws—this last from the citizens of Montreal.

88. *The Growth of English Industry and Commerce in Modern Times*, p. 832.

89. W. S. Lindsay, op. cit. iii, 290.

90. Copies of an Address to the Queen from the Owners of British Ships . . . and of the subsequent Correspondence in reference thereto, p. 11, *Parl. Papers*, 1859, xxv.

91. Lindsay, op. cit. iii, 359.

92. 'The Last Years of the Navigation Acts,' *English Historical Review*, xxv, 707.

93. *Proceedings of the Colonial Conference*, 1887, ii (Appendix), 306, *Parl. Papers*, 1887, lvi.

94. *Parl. Deb.*, 3rd ser., xcviii, 1002.

95. Ibid. cii, 685-7.

96. Ibid. xcix, 660-61; civ, 669; cv, 73-4.

97. Ibid. xcix, 51 ff.

98. Ibid. cv, 84 ff.

99. John MacGregor, a secretary of the Board of Trade and the author of a monumental four-volume digest of commercial statistics, had expressed the opinion in evidence given before the House of Commons' committee on the navigation laws that the difficulty of navigation from the Atlantic ports of the United States to Quebec would prevent American ships from going to the St. Lawrence to any extent. First Report from the Select Committee on Navigation Laws, *Parl. Papers*, 1847-8, xx, Part i, pp. 71-2.

100. The Reports made for the year 1850 to the Secretary of State having the Department of the Colonies, p. 12, *Parl. Papers*, 1851, XXXIV.

101. Tucker, op. cit. p. 135.

102. Burn, op. cit. *Cambridge Historical Journal*, II, 269. The author thinks that the Quebec lumber merchants gained something from the repeal of the navigation laws, ibid. p. 269.

103. *Parl. Deb.*, 3rd ser., XCVIII, 1038; XCIX, 600, 635-6; CIII, 470-71, 594.

104. Ibid. CIII, 488, 514-15; CII, 730; CV, 43.

105. The Reports made for the year 1850 to the Secretary of State having the Department of the Colonies, p. 274, *Parl. Papers*, 1851, XXXIV.

106. *Parl. Deb.*, 3rd ser., CIII, 613; W. P. Morrell, *British Colonial Policy in the Age of Peel and Russell*, p. 216.

107. J. R. McCulloch, *The Edinburgh Review*, XLII, 282; *Parl. Deb.*, 3rd ser., XCVIII, 1000.

108. Ibid. CV, 76-7.

CHAPTER VI

1. Sir John Fortescue, *History of the British Army*, III, 499.

2. This statement does not apply to India. The expense of defending India, as indeed of conquering and governing it, has been defrayed out of Indian revenue; cf. Seeley, *Expansion of England*, Course II, lecture iii. On the anomaly of the distinction between Indian and colonial defense, cf. *Parl. Papers*, 1861, XIII, 'Report from the Select Committee on Colonial Military Expenditure,' pp. 126, 141.

3. 18 Geo. III, c. 12. This statute also repealed the memorable tea duty.

4. 'We attempted to tax the North American colonies, *not for imperial*, but *for colonial* objects. Rebellion made us recoil from the attempt, and the 18 Geo. III, c. 12, gave assurance to the colonies that the attempt would not be repeated. It never was repeated with these colonies, nor has it been repeated by the imperial parliament with any other colony, except perhaps during the short period during which the constitution of Canada was suspended. No doubt, what the imperial parliament did not venture to do, the crown has ventured, and achieved, too, in many of the colonies, but always for colonial purposes.' Sydney Smith Bell, *Colonial Administration of Great Britain*, p. 404. The 18 Geo. III, c. 12 did not repeal all parliamentary duties then in force in the colonies, e.g. duties levied upon certain imports into the Province of

Quebec by the Quebec Revenue Act of 1774 (14 Geo. III, c. 88). These latter imposts long continued to form an important part of the public revenue of Canada; cf. Lord Durham's *Report,* ed. by C. P. Lucas, II, 141.

5. Margaret Marion Spector, *The American Department of the British Government,* 1768-1782, chap x. Considerations of English domestic politics help to explain the abolition of the Board of Trade and the American Department. Hertz, *The Old Colonial System,* chap. x.

6. *Parl. Papers,* 1861, XIII, report cited in note 2 above, p. 130.

7. *Review of 'The Colonial Policy of Lord J. Russell's Administration' by Earl Grey,* 1853, *and of Subsequent Colonial History,* p. 380. Merivale, *Lectures on Colonization and Colonies,* p. 585.

8. Merivale, op. cit. p. 587 n.; also *Parl. Papers,* 1861, XIII, report cited, p. 132.

9. *Parl. Deb.,* 3rd ser., CLXV, 1039-41.

10. Quoted in *Parl. Deb.,* XL, 269.

11. C. P. Stacey, *Canada and the British Army,* 1846-1871, pp. 33-4.

12. *Parl. Papers,* 1834, VI, 'Report from Select Committee on Colonial Military Expenditure,' Appendix, pp. 112-13.

13. Ibid. Report, p. iii.

14. *Parl. Papers,* 1860, XLI, 'Report of the Committee on Expense of Military Defences in the Colonies,' p. 3. By way of contrast with British colonial policy the report referred to the Dutch and Spanish colonies, which yielded surplus revenues to their mother countries. It stated that in 1857 'the surplus revenue paid by the Dutch colonies into the metropolitan exchequer, after defraying all their military and naval expenses, was 31,858,421 florins (about £2,600,000). The estimated surplus revenue from the Spanish colonies for the past year (1859) was 115,000,000 reals (about £1,150,000).' Ibid. p. 3 n.

15. *Parl. Papers,* 1860, XLI, report cited, pp. 4-5.

16. *Parl. Papers,* 1861, XIII, 'Report from the Select Committee on Colonial Military Expenditure,' pp. iv-v.

17. R. L. Schuyler, *Josiah Tucker,* p. 365.

18. Nor was this all. 'If we would know the amount of the whole [cost of colonies to Great Britain], we must add to the annual expense of this peace establishment the interest of the sums which, in consequence of her considering her colonies as provinces subject to her dominion, Great Britain has upon different occasions

laid out upon their defence. We must add to it, in particular, the whole expense of the late war [the Seven Years' War], and a great part of that of the war which preceded it. The late war was altogether a colony quarrel, and the whole expense of it, in whatever part of the world it may have been laid out . . . ought justly to be stated to the account of the colonies.' *Wealth of Nations,* Everyman's Library ed., II, 112.

19. Ibid. II, 113.

20. Ibid. II, 124.

21. Lord Shelburne was the first Prime Minister to be influenced by Adam Smith. In his *Autobiography,* written in 1801, he speaks of Smith as one whose 'principles have remained unanswered for above thirty years, and yet when it is attempted to act upon any of them, what clamor!' Fitzmaurice, *Life of Shelburne,* I, 24.

22. *Parl. Deb.,* 3rd ser., LXX, 205-7.

23. Ibid. CII, 1228; CXV, 1440-41.

24. Ibid. CIII, 1010; CXV, 1378.

25. Ibid. CXV, 1372-3. Molesworth distinguished between 'military stations,' such as Gibraltar and Malta, 'plantations or subjugated territories,' like Ceylon, and 'Colonies, properly so called.' Ibid. CIX, 669.

26. Ibid. CXV, 1401-2.

27. This document was found by Professor Paul Knaplund in the Gladstone Papers and was published in *The Canadian Historical Review,* V, 231-6 (September 1924).

28. *Parl. Deb.,* 3rd scr., CXV, 1421.

29. Richard Cobden, *The Three Panics;* Sir Robert Biddulph, *Lord Cardwell at the War Office,* p. 39; Stacey, op. cit. pp. 58-9.

30. Bell, op. cit. p. 68.

31. *Colonial Policy of Lord John Russell's Administration,* I, 18, 43. See also Keith, *Responsible Government in the Dominions,* III, 1248.

32. Grey, *The Colonial Policy of Lord John Russell's Administration,* I, 353-4.

33. *Parl. Papers,* 1861, XIII, report cited, pp. 11, 19, 278, 312 ff.

34. *The Elgin-Grey Papers,* I, 144-5.

35. Ibid. I, 217.

36. Ibid. II, 560.

37. For this dispatch, see Grey, *The Colonial Policy of Lord John Russell's Administration,* I, 257.

38. Stacey, op. cit. pp. 79, 82.
39. Grey, op. cit. I, 44. This statement of policy was not intended to apply to imperial naval or military stations.
40. *Parl. Papers*, 1861, XIII, report cited, p. 150.
41. *Parl. Deb.*, 3rd ser., CXXX, 1290.
42. Stacey, op. cit. p. 90.
43. Ibid. pp. 91-4, 102; *Parl. Papers*, 1861, XIII, report cited, pp. 308-11. It is significant that at the time of the Indian Mutiny Canada tendered a regiment for imperial service, which was mobilized and actually served; Bell, op. cit. p. 405.
44. J. B. Brebner, 'Joseph Hume and the Crimean War Enlistment Controversy,' *Canadian Historical Review*, XI; Stacey, op. cit. p. 99.
45. *Parl. Papers*, 1860, XLI, 'Report of the Committee on Expense of Military Defences in the Colonies,' p. 9.
46. Ibid. report cited, pp. 1-2.
47. The report and memorandum are printed in ibid. report cited, pp. 2-18.
48. Ibid. p. 4. Merivale, in a later edition of his *Lectures on Colonization and Colonies*, published in 1861, thus analyzed (p. 590) the purposes for which this imperial expenditure had been incurred: Defense of posts for military, convict, commercial, and other special purposes, £1,600,000; defense of colonies against foreign powers solely, £400,000; defense of colonies against foreign powers and internal disturbances, but chiefly the latter, £600,000; defense of colonies against warlike natives, £1,000,000.
49. Merivale says of the interdepartmental report of 1859: 'this paper contains a thorough political discussion of the general subject, by Mr. Godley of the War Department, and Mr. Elliot of the Colonial Office, whose opinions widely differ, and are powerfully defended.' *Lectures on Colonization and Colonies*, p. 587 n.
50. *Parl. Papers*, 1861, XIII, report cited, p. 319.
51. The report of the committee, together with minutes of evidence and appendixes, is printed in *Parl. Papers*, 1861, XIII.
52. Ibid. pp. iv-v. Gladstone informed the committee that a great part of what appeared in returns as colonial expenditure did not lighten the burden of the British exchequer but was paid 'simply by way of addition to the regular pay and allowances of the forces.' Ibid. pp. 255-6.
53. *Parl. Deb.*, 3rd ser., CXCIV, 1115-16.
54. Ibid. CLXV, 1035.

55. *Parl. Papers*, 1861, XIII, report cited, p. 257.
56. *Parl. Deb.*, 3rd ser., CLXV, 1060.
57. Todd, *Parliamentary Government in the British Colonies*, p. 393; Adderley, op. cit. p. 388.
58. *Parl. Papers*, 1871, XLVII, 'Correspondence respecting the Affairs of the Cape of Good Hope,' p. 2.
59. *Parl. Deb.*, 3rd ser., CXCIV, 1116.
60. Stacey, op. cit. pp. 118, 122. For a detailed consideration of Canadian defense during the Civil War and its aftermath of Fenian raids, see chaps. vi-viii of this work.
61. *Parl. Papers*, 1871, XLVII, 'Correspondence respecting the Affairs of the Cape of Good Hope,' p. 1.
62. Sir Robert Biddulph, *Lord Cardwell at the War Office*, pp. 249-54.
63. Ibid. pp. 26-8.
64. *Parl. Deb.*, 3rd ser., CXCIV, 1113 ff.
65. Granville to Sir John Young, 14 April 1869, quoted in Stacey, op. cit. p. 214.
66. Stacey, op. cit. p. 227.
67. Ibid. p. 228.
68. See pp. 270-71, above.
69. Quoted in Stacey, op. cit. p. 247.
70. See pp. 264 ff., above.
71. For a brief statement concerning the withdrawal of imperial forces from Australia, New Zealand, and Canada, see Keith, *Responsible Government in the Dominions*, III, 1249-56.
72. *Parl. Deb.*, 3rd ser., CCXIV, 1527-8.
73. Proceedings of the Colonial Conference, 1887, vol. II, pp. 302-3, 338. The Commission, of which Lord Carnarvon was chairman, made three reports. The evidence given by witnesses was treated as confidential and was not made public. Extracts from the reports can be found in the published proceedings of the Colonial Conference of 1887.

CHAPTER VII

1. *The Economist*, VI, 844 (22 July 1848).
2. By 1860 the last vestiges of the commercial restrictions of the old colonial system were swept away. In 1859 Canada laid protective duties on imports from Britain, and her example was soon followed by other colonies.
3. *Parl. Deb.*, 3rd ser., XXXVII, 1249.

4. W. P. M. Kennedy, *Documents of the Canadian Constitution,* 1759-1915, pp. 522 ff.

5. For an estimate of Grey as Colonial Secretary, see W. P. Morrell, *British Colonial Policy in the Age of Peel and Russell,* chap. ix.

6. In correspondence with Lord Elgin, the Governor General of Canada, Grey spoke of the experiment in responsible government which Elgin was conducting as 'our policy.' *The Elgin-Grey Papers,* 1846-1852, II, 852.

7. 'When Parliament, after a protracted discussion of many years, finally determined upon abandoning the former policy of endeavouring to promote the commerce of the Empire by an artificial system of restrictions, and upon adopting in its place the policy of Free Trade, it did not abdicate the duty and the power of regulating the commercial policy, not only of the United Kingdom, but of the British Empire. The common interest of all parts of that extended Empire required that its commercial policy should be the same throughout its numerous dependencies.' Grey, op. cit. I, 281. Grey continued to hold this opinion and deplored the setting up of protective tariffs in the colonies. In a debate in the House of Lords in 1870, he said that when the mother country relieved the colonies from the restrictions previously imposed upon their trade, 'it was not with a view that they should impose fresh restrictions founded upon the same vicious principles as those which had been abolished . . . That was, however, exactly what they had done. They [the Imperial Government] had stood by and looked on while their Colonies, in many cases, had adopted rules contrary to the whole principles of the commercial policy of the Imperial Parliament.' *Parl. Deb.,* 3rd ser., CCII, 475.

8. W. P. Morrell, op. cit. pp. 219-21.

9. This principle is usually considered to have been established when the Imperial Government declined to disallow the Canadian tariff of 1859. The essential documents can be found in *Selected Speeches and Documents on British Colonial Policy,* 1763-1917, ed. by Arthur Berriedale Keith, II, 51-83.

10. *Parl. Deb.,* 3rd ser., CVIII, 535-67.

11. Elgin to Grey, 23 March 1850, *The Elgin-Grey Papers,* II, 608-9. Elgin continued to preach the same gospel. In a dispatch written early in 1853 to the Duke of Newcastle, Secretary of State for the Colonies in Lord Aberdeen's Ministry, he urged that if there were to be further reductions in the British military forces in Canada,

they should be made quietly and discreetly. 'Let it be inferred from your language,' he wrote, 'that there is in your opinion nothing in the nature of things to prevent the tie which connects the Mother-country and the Colony from being as enduring as that which unites the different States of the Union, and nothing in the nature of our very elastic institutions to prevent them from expanding so as to permit the free and healthy development of social, political, and national life in these young communities.' *Letters and Journals of James, Eighth Earl of Elgin,* ed. by Theodore Walrond, p. 133.

12. Quoted in *The Elgin-Grey Papers,* II, 617.

13. Ibid. II, 621.

14. Grey, op. cit. I, 11 ff.; Morrell, op. cit. 521 ff.

15. W. P. M. Kennedy, *The Constitution of Canada,* p. 250.

16. Grey to Elgin, 25 January and 18 May 1849, *The Elgin-Grey Papers,* I, 286, 351-2. For further evidences of anti-imperial sentiment in the middle of the nineteenth century, see Grey, op. cit. Letter 1; Thomas Carlyle, *Latter Day Pamphlets,* No. 4; J. A. Roebuck, *The Colonies of England;* Sydney S. Bell, *Colonial Administration of Great Britain,* pp. 393, 396, 431 ff.; George Burton Adams, 'Origin and Results of the Imperial Federation Movement in England,' *Proceedings of the Historical Society of Wisconsin,* 1898, pp. 93-116; C. A. Bodelsen, *Studies in Mid-Victorian Imperialism,* chap. i.

17. '. . . no one advocates independence in these Colonies except as a means to the end annexation . . .' Elgin to Grey, 23 March 1850, *The Elgin-Grey Papers,* II, 612.

18. *The Canadian Economist,* 30 May 1846, quoted in *Select Documents in Canadian Economic History,* 1783-1885, ed. by H. A. Innis and A. R. M. Lower, pp. 347-8.

19. For a careful and full account, see C. D. Allin and G. M. Jones, *Annexation, Preferential Trade, and Reciprocity* (1912). More recent and briefer accounts can be found in Gilbert Norman Tucker, *The Canadian Commercial Revolution,* 1845-1851 (1936), chap. ix, and Lester Burrell Shippee, *Canadian-American Relations,* 1849-1874 (1939), chap. i.

20. Tucker, op. cit. pp. 6, 207-8.

21. Ibid. p. 218.

22. Elgin to Grey, 14 March 1849, *The Elgin-Grey Papers,* I, 307.

23. Same to same, 14 October 1849; ibid. II, 522.

24. Same to same, 15 November 1849; ibid. II, 548.
25. The document can be found in many publications, e.g. in Tucker, op. cit. Appendix B.
26. *The Elgin-Grey Papers*, II, 522.
27. Ibid. I, 142, 150, 224, 349.
28. Ibid. I, 256, 319.
29. Ibid. II, 534.
30. Ibid. II, 609.
31. Ibid. II, 611.
32. Ibid. II, 595.
33. Ibid. II, 720; III, 983.
34. Reciprocity encountered serious obstacles in the United States, but after prolonged and discouraging delays the Elgin-Marcy Treaty of 1854 provided for reciprocal free trade between the United States and the British North American colonies in a long list of articles which included all the exportable products of Canada. The events leading up to the treaty may be followed in Charles C. Tansill, *The Canadian Reciprocity Treaty of 1854*, or Lester Burrell Shippee, op. cit. chaps. ii-iv.
35. *The Times*, 4 February 1862.
36. *Parl. Deb.*, 3rd ser., CLXIX, 96.
37. Ibid. CC, 1818; *Spectator*, XLII, p. 868; *Proceedings of the Royal Colonial Institute*, VI, p. 37; *Fraser's Magazine*, September 1871, p. 396; *The Morning Post*, 16 March 1869, p. 8.
38. Sir G. F. Bowen, *Thirty Years of Colonial Government*, I, 209.
39. P. 168.
40. *Reminiscences*, p. 169; also articles in *Macmillan's Magazine*, March 1865, and *The Fortnightly*, April 1877.
41. Lord Edmund Fitzmaurice, *The Life of Granville George Leveson Gower, Second Earl of Granville*, II, 10; *Dictionary of National Biography*, second supplement, III, 520-23; *The Supremacy of Great Britain Not Inconsistent with Self-Government for the Colonies* (London, 1851), Appendix.
42. The idea of a statute declaring the conditions on which Great Britain would be prepared to emancipate colonies was not original with Thring; see Sydney S. Bell, *Colonial Administration of Great Britain* (London, 1859), pp. 396, 465.
43. In 1885 Bury wrote: 'It is twenty years since I published, in 1865, some volumes on the history of Colonising Nations, in which I arrived at very much the same conclusions that Mr. Forster has

arrived at now, and so for years I watched for the separation which I firmly believed would come; but instead of separation came firmer union.'

44. Stephen Gwyn and Gertrude M. Tuckwell, *The Life of the Rt. Hon. Sir Charles W. Dilke,* I, 60-69.

45. *Greater Britain* (London, 1868), I, 80, 318; II, 407.

46. Ibid. I, 79-80; II, 149-50.

47. Ibid. II, 108-10, 156-7.

48. Ibid. Part III, chap. xv.

49. Ibid. Part IV, chaps. xx and xxi.

50. R. A. Macfie, *Colonial Questions Pressing for Immediate Solution,* p. v; *Parl. Deb.,* 3rd ser., CXCVIII, 780.

51. P. 169; see also Fitzmaurice, op. cit. II, 20.

52. *Parl. Deb.,* 3rd ser., CLXV, 1033, 1042.

53. *Speeches of John Bright,* ed. by J. E. Thorold Rogers. I, 153-4; see also p. 161.

54. *An Essay on the Government of Dependencies,* ed. by C. P. Lucas, p. 324.

55. *Letters of the Right Hon. Sir George Cornewall Lewis,* ed. by Sir Gilbert Frankland Lewis, pp. 201-2.

56. *Parl. Deb.,* 3rd ser., CLXVIII, 860.

57. Ibid. CLXXVIII, 153.

58. Report from the Select Committee on Africa (Western Coast), p. iii, *Parl. Papers,* 1865, vol. v.

59. *Parl. Deb.,* 3rd ser., CC, 1900-1901.

60. Quotations from this dispatch are given by Paul Knaplund in his *Gladstone and Britain's Imperial Policy,* p. 99. In comment Professor Knaplund says that this sentence 'supports the charge that Granville was willing to cut the bonds of imperial union.' He thinks that Granville took his duties as Colonial Secretary lightly and let his subordinates in the Colonial Office write his dispatches.

61. Quoted in C. P. Stacey, *Canada and the British Army,* 1846-1871, p. 218.

62. Lord Norton, *Lord Lyons,* I, 291-2.

63. G. E. Buckle, *The Life of Benjamin Disraeli,* V, 194 ff.

64. Lord Malmesbury, *Memoirs of an Ex-Minister,* I, 344.

65. Monypenny and Buckle, *The Life of Benjamin Disraeli,* III, 386.

66. Sir William Gregory, *An Autobiography,* chap. v; see also Goldwin Smith, *Reminiscences,* p. 168.

67. O. D. Skelton, *The Life and Times of Sir Alexander Tilloch Galt*, p. 443.

68. Buckle, *The Life of Benjamin Disraeli*, IV, 476.

69. Sir Joseph Pope, *Memoirs of the Right Honourable Sir John Alexander Macdonald*, I, 273.

70. O. D. Skelton, *The Life and Times of Sir Alexander Tilloch Galt*, pp. 410-11.

71. For Buller's celebrated but very unfair attack on Stephen, see *Responsible Government for Colonies* (London, 1840), chaps. vi and vii. This pamphlet was published anonymously, but there is no doubt that it was written by Buller. It is reprinted in E. M. Wrong, *Charles Buller and Responsible Government*. For an able vindication of Stephen, see Paul Knaplund, 'Mr. Over-Secretary Stephen,' *Journal of Modern History*, I, 40-66; also his 'Sir James Stephen and British North American Problems, 1840-7,' *Canadian Historical Review*, V, 3 ff.

72. *Autobiography of Henry Taylor* (London, 1885), II, 300-301.

73. Leslie Stephen, *The Life of Sir James Fitzjames Stephen*, p. 49.

74. Caroline Emelia Stephen, *The Right Honourable Sir James Stephen: Letters with Biographical Notes* (privately printed, 1906), p. 144. The quotation given is from a letter dictated by Stephen to his wife.

75. See his *Lectures on Colonization and Colonies*, new edition, London, 1861, p. 677.

76. *Reminiscences*, p. 169.

77. *Letters of Frederic, Lord Blachford*, ed. by G. E. Marindin, pp. 299-300. Baillie Hamilton, in an article entitled 'Forty-Four Years at the Colonial Office,' referred to the attitude of the permanent officials in the Office at the time he entered it, in 1864: '. . . it would have required an exceptionally powerful and determined Colonial Minister in those days to inaugurate any new developments in Colonial affairs, and he certainly would not have received much encouragement from the permanent staff . . . when I recall the general tenour of the policy that was openly and deliberately advocated by them as the advisers of the Secretary of State, I can only wonder that we have any Colonies left.' *The Nineteenth Century*, LXV, 604 (April 1909).

78. *Letters of Frederic, Lord Blachford*, p. 425.

79. *Correspondence of Henry Taylor*, ed. by Edward Dowden, p. 200.

80. *Autobiography of Henry Taylor*, II, 234.

81. Ibid. pp. 239-41.
82. *Parl. Papers*, 1868-69, XLIV, pp. 418, 420, 422-4.
83. *The Tablet*, XXXIV, pp. 125-6.
84. *Parl. Papers*, 1870, L [C. 83], pp. 95-100.
85. Ibid. pp. 63, 196-7.
86. Ibid. No. 180, pp. 3-4.
87. *Parl. Deb.*, 3rd ser., CC, 1821.
88. See *New Zealand Parliamentary Debates*, 4th Parl., 5th Sess., VII.
89. *Parl. Deb.*, 3rd ser., CXCVIII, 457.
90. *Parl. Papers*, 1870, L, 180, p. 8; *Parl. Deb.*, 3rd ser., CC, 1820; *Spectator*, XLII, 1522.
91. *The Times*, 26 August 1869.
92. Ibid. 25 November 1869.
93. Ibid. 18 January 1870.
94. Skelton, op. cit. pp. 410-11, 449.
95. Ibid. pp. 451-2; for Galt's views as to the future of Canada, see *Parl. Deb., Dominion of Canada*, 3rd Sess., I, 139 ff.
96. Skelton, op. cit. p. 454.
97. *Spectator*, XLIII, 393; *The Tablet*, XXXV, 382; *Parl. Deb.*, 3rd ser., CC, 1820-21; Skelton, op. cit. p. 455.
98. *Parl. Deb.*, 3rd ser., CXCIX, 204-5, 208; Fitzmaurice, op. cit. II, 23-4; Sir Arthur Hardinge, *The Life of Henry Howard Molyneux, Fourth Earl of Carnarvon*, II, 17.
99. *Parl. Deb.*, 3rd ser., CXCIX, 209-10.
100. Hardinge, op. cit. II, 21.
101. *Lee at Appomattox and Other Papers*, p. 158.
102. Ibid. 157, 160; Allan Nevins, *Hamilton Fish: The Inner History of the Grant Administration*, pp. 300, 424.
103. C. P. Stacey, *Canada and the British Army*, p. 231.
104. J. D. Lang, *The Coming Event* (London, 1870), especially pp. 313-14; *Victoria Parliamentary Debates*, 1869, IX, 2264 and 2266-7.
105. *Parl. Deb.*, 3rd ser., CC, 1823.
106. *Spectator*, XLIII, 393-4.
107. Burt, *Imperial Architects*, chap. vi; *Proceedings of the Royal Colonial Institute*, I, 1-18.
108. *Parl. Deb.*, 3rd ser., CC, 1847 ff., and CCII, 460 ff.
109. See his speech to his constituents on 17 January 1870; *The Times*, 18 January 1870, p. 5.
110. *Parl. Deb.*, 3rd ser., CXCIX, 219; CCIII, 715.
111. Cf. *Spectator*, XLIII, 632.

112. For the negotiations between the New Zealand Commissioners and the Colonial Office and their outcome, see *Parl. Papers,* 1870, L [C. 83], pp. 102-4, 127; ibid. no. 298; 33 & 34 Vict., c. 40.
113. *New Zealand Parl. Deb.,* 4th Parl. 5th Sess., VIII, 17, 137.
114. *Spectator,* XLIII, 632.
115. *Parl. Deb.,* 3rd ser., CCII, 454.
116. Ibid. CCVI, 750 ff.
117. For the debate, see ibid. CCXIV, 1520 ff.
118. T. W. Reid, *The Life of W. E. Forster,* II, 100.
119. This task has been performed with a large measure of success by J. E. Tyler, in his monograph *The Struggle for Imperial Unity,* 1868-1895.
120. This article, entitled 'England and Her Colonies,' was reprinted in Froude's *Short Studies on Great Subjects,* 2nd ser.
121. Quoted in Tyler, op. cit. p. 10.
122. *Parl. Deb.,* 3rd ser., CXCIX, 1002-77.
123. Benjamin H. Brown, *The Tariff Reform Movement in Great Britain,* pp. 5-7.

BIBLIOGRAPHY

I

SOURCES AND CONTEMPORARY WRITINGS

Allen, Joseph, *The Navigation Laws of Great Britain, Historically and Practically Considered*. London, 1849.

Anderson, James, *The Interest of Great Britain with regard to her American Colonies Considered*. London, 1782.

Annual Register, The. London, 1761–.

Antigua, The Laws of. London, 1865.

Auckland, Lord, *The Journal and Correspondence of William, Lord Auckland*, 4 vols. London, 1861-2.

Barbados, Laws of, 2 vols. London, 1875.

Bentham, Jeremy, *The Works of*, ed. by John Bowring, 11 vols. Edinburgh, 1838-43.

Blachford, Lord, *Letters of Frederic, Lord Blachford*, ed. by G. E. Marindin. London, 1896.

Bland, Richard, *An Enquiry into the Rights of the British Colonies*. Williamsburg, 1766.

Bright, John, *Speeches on Questions of Public Policy*, ed. by James E. Thorold Rogers. London, 1869.

Browne, J. Houston, *The Navigation Laws: Their History and Operation*. London, 1847.

Buller, Charles, *Responsible Government for Colonies*. London, 1840.

Bury, Viscount, *Exodus of the Western Nations*, 2 vols. London, 1865.

Canada, Journals of the Legislative Assembly of the Province of. Quebec and Toronto, 1841-66.

Canada, Provincial Statutes of.

Carlyle, Thomas, *Latter-Day Pamphlets*. London, 1858.

Cartwright, John, *American Independence the Interest and Glory of Great Britain*. London, 1774.

— —, *Take Your Choice*. London, 1776.

Chalmers, George, *Opinions on Interesting Subjects of Public Law and Commercial Policy arising from American Independence*. London, 1785.

Child, Josiah, *A New Discourse of Trade*. London, 1693.

Cobden, Richard, *The Three Panics*, 3rd ed. London, 1862.

Defoe, Daniel, *A Plan of the English Commerce*, The Shakespeare Head Edition of the Novels and Selected Writings of Daniel Defoe, XII. Oxford, 1927.

Dictionary of National Biography. London, 1885—.

Dilke, Sir Charles W., *Greater Britain,* 2 vols. London, 1868.

Documents of the Canadian Constitution, 1759-1915, ed. by W. P. M. Kennedy. Toronto, 1918.

Douglas, Sir Howard, *Considerations on the Value and Importance of the British North American Colonies.* London, 1831.

Durham Papers, The, Report on Canadian Archives. Ottawa, 1923.

Lord Durham's Report on the Affairs of British North America, ed. by Sir C. P. Lucas, 3 vols. Oxford, 1912.

Economist, The. London, 1843—.

Edinburgh Review, The. London, 1802-1929.

Edwards, Bryan, *Thoughts on the Late Proceedings of Government respecting the Trade of the West India Islands with the United States of America.* London, 1784.

Elgin, Letters and Journals of James, Eighth Earl of, ed. by Theodore Walrond. London, 1872.

Elgin-Grey Papers, 1846-1852, *The,* ed. by Sir Arthur G. Doughty, 4 vols. Ottawa, 1937.

Evening Standard, The. London, 1827-1905.

Fortnightly Review, The. London, 1867—.

Franklin, Writings of Benjamin, ed. by A. H. Smyth, 10 vols. London, 1907.

Fraser's Magazine. London, 1830-82.

Godwin, Wm., *Enquiry concerning Political Justice,* 2 vols. London, 1793.

Gray, Hugh, *Letters from Canada.* London, 1809.

Greville Memoirs, The, ed. by Lytton Strachey and Roger Fulford, 8 vols. London, 1938.

Grey, Earl, *The Colonial Policy of Lord John Russell's Administration,* 2 vols. London, 1853.

Hakluyt, Richard, *A Particular Discourse concerning . . . Western Discoveries,* first published in Collections of the Maine Historical Society, 2nd series, Vol. ii. Cambridge (Mass.), 1877.

Hume, David, *Essays, Moral, Political, and Literary,* ed. by T. H. Green and T. H. Grose, 2 vols. London, 1882.

Huskisson Papers, The, ed. by Lewis Melville. New York, 1931.

Huskisson, Speeches of the Right Hon. William, 3 vols. London, 1831.

Jamaica, The Statutes and Laws of the Island of, 12 vols. Kingston, 1889.

Knox, William, *Extra Official State Papers,* 2 vols. London, 1789.

Knox, William, Correspondence of. Historical Manuscripts Commission, Report on Manuscripts in Various Collections, vi, 81-296.

Lewis, Sir George Cornewall, *An Essay on the Government of Dependencies*, ed. by Sir C. P. Lucas. Oxford, 1891.
— —, *Letters of*, ed. by Sir G. F. Lewis. London, 1870.
McCulloch, J. R., *Principles of Political Economy*. Edinburgh, 1825.
— —, *Statistical Account of the British Empire*. London, 1837.
Macfie, R. A., *Colonial Questions Pressing for Immediate Solution*. London, 1871.
Mackay, Alexander, *The Western World; or Travels in the United States in 1846-47*, 4th ed., 3 vols. London, 1850.
Macmillan's Magazine. London, 1859-1907.
Malmesbury, Lord, *Memoirs of an Ex-Minister*, 3rd ed., 2 vols. London, 1884.
Malthus, Thomas R., *Principles of Political Economy*. London, 1820.
Marx, Karl, *Free Trade: A Speech*. Boston and New York, 1888.
Mill, James, *Elements of Political Economy*. London, 1821.
Mill, John Stuart, *Autobiography*. New York, 1924.
Mirabeau, Victor Riquetti, Marquis de, *Philosophie rurale*, 3 vols. Amsterdam, 1764.
Mun, Thomas, *England's Treasure by Forraign Trade*, ed. by W. J. Ashley. London, 1903.
New Brunswick, Acts of the Legislative Assembly of. Fredericton.
Nova Scotia, Acts of the General Assembly of. Halifax.
Our Free Trade Policy Examined (Anon.). London, 1846.
Parliamentary Debates, 1803-1820, *Cobbett's*. (Beginning with Vol. XIX, this series is entitled *The Parliamentary Debates from the Year 1803 to the Present Time*.) 46 vols. London, 1804-20. Published under the superintendence of T. C. Hansard.
Parliamentary Debates, New Series, 25 vols. London, 1820-30. Published under the superintendence of T. C. Hansard.
Parliamentary Debates, Hansard's, Third Series, 356 vols. London, 1831-91.
Parliamentary History of England from the Earliest Period to the Year 1803, 36 vols. London, 1806-1820. Printed by T. C. Hansard.
Parliamentary Papers. The Sessional Papers of the House of Commons have been referred to in this book as *Parl. Papers*.
Parnell, Sir Henry, *On Financial Reform*. London, 1830.
Preference Interests, The (Anon.). London, 1841.
Price, Richard, *Observations on the Nature of Civil Liberty, the Principles of Government, and the Justice and Policy of the War with America*. London, 1776.

Prince Edward Island, Journals of the House of Assembly of. Charlotte-town.

Quarterly Review, The. London, 1809–.

Regulations lately made concerning the Colonies, and the Taxes imposed upon Them, Considered (Anon.). London, 1765.

Ricardo, David, *On the Principles of Political Economy and Taxation.* London, 1817.

Ricardo, J. L., *Anatomy of the Navigation Laws.* London, 1847.

Roebuck, J. A., *The Colonies of England.* London, 1849.

Royal Colonial Institute, Proceedings of the, 40 vols. London, 1870-1909.

Russell, The Later Correspondence of Lord John, ed. by G. P. Gooch, 2 vols. London and New York, 1925.

Schuyler, Robert Livingston, *Josiah Tucker: A Selection from his Economic and Political Writings.* New York, 1931.

Select Documents in Canadian Economic History, 1783-1885, ed. by H. A. Innis and A. R. M. Lower. Toronto, 1933.

Select Documents on British Colonial Policy, 1830-1860, ed. by Kenneth N. Bell and W. P. Morrell. Oxford, 1928.

Selected Speeches and Documents on British Colonial Policy, 1763-1917, ed. by Arthur Berriedale Keith, 2 vols. Oxford, 1918.

Sharp, Granville, *A Declaration of the People's Right to a Share in the Legislature.* London, 1774.

Sheffield, Lord, *Observations on the Commerce of the American States.* London, 1784. First published in 1783.

Sinclair, Sir John, *The History of the Public Revenue of the British Empire,* 3 vols. London, 1785-90.

Smith, Adam, *An Inquiry into the Nature and Causes of the Wealth of Nations.* Everyman's Library, 2 vols. London, 1910. First ed., 1776.

Smith, Goldwin, *The Empire.* Oxford, 1863.

— —, *Reminiscences,* ed. by Arnold Houltain. New York, 1910.

Spectator, The. London, 1828–.

Tablet, The. London, 1840–.

Taylor, Henry, *Autobiography,* 2 vols. London, 1885.

— —, *Correspondence of,* ed. by Edward Dowden. London, 1888.

Thring, Henry (Lord), *Suggestions for Colonial Reform.* London, 1865.

Times, The. London, 1788–.

Tooke, Thomas, and Newmarch, William, *A History of Prices,* 6 vols. London, 1838-57.

Tucker, Josiah, *Brief Essay on the Advantages which respectively attend France and Great Britain with regard to Trade.* London, 1749.

— —, *Four Tracts together with Two Sermons.* Gloucester, 1774.

Tucker, Josiah, *The True Interest of Great-Britain set forth in regard to the Colonies.* Reprinted in *Four Tracts together with Two Sermons.*
— —, *Humble Address and Earnest Appeal.* Gloucester, 1775.
— —, *Cui Bono?,* Gloucester, 1781.
— —, *Treatise concerning Civil Government.* London, 1781.
— —, *Four Letters on Important National Subjects.* London, 1783.
Turgot, Robert Jacques, *Œuvres,* ed. by Eugène Daire and Hippolyte Dussard, 2 vols. Paris, 1844.
Victoria Parliamentary Debates, Melbourne.
Wakefield, Edward Gibbon, *A View of the Art of Colonization.* London, 1849.
Westminster Review, The. London, 1824-36.
Wharton, Francis, *The Revolutionary Diplomatic Correspondence of the United States,* 6 vols. Washington, 1889.
Young, Arthur, *Travels in France during the Years* 1787, 1788, 1789, ed. by M. S. Betham-Edwards. London, 1900.

II

SECONDARY LITERATURE

Adams, Charles Francis, *Lee at Appomattox, and Other Papers.* Boston and New York, 1902.
Adams, George Burton, 'The Origin and Results of the Imperial Federation Movement in England,' *Proceedings of the Wisconsin State Historical Society,* 1898, pp. 93 ff.
Adderley, Sir C. B. (Lord Norton), *Review of 'The Colonial Policy of Lord J. Russell's Administration' by Earl Grey,* 1853, *and of Subsequent Colonial History.* London, 1869.
Albion, Robert G., *Forests and Sea Power.* Cambridge (Mass.), 1926.
Allin, C. D., and Jones, G. M., *Annexation, Preferential Trade, and Reciprocity.* Toronto and London, 1911.
Andrews, Charles M., *The Colonial Period of American History,* 4 vols. New Haven, 1934-8.
Beer, George Louis, *British Colonial Policy,* 1754-1765. New York, 1907.
— —, *The Origins of the British Colonial System.* New York, 1908.
— —, *The Old Colonial System,* 2 vols. New York, 1912.
Bell, Herbert C., 'British Commercial Policy in the West Indies, 1783-93,' *English Historical Review,* XXXI, 429 ff.
Bell, Sydney Smith, *The Colonial Administration of Great Britain.* London, 1859.

Bemis, Samuel Flagg, *Jay's Treaty*. New York, 1923.

Benns, F. Lee, *The American Struggle for the British West India Carrying Trade, 1815-1830*. Bloomington, Ind., 1923.

Biddulph, Sir Robert, *Lord Cardwell at the War Office*. London, 1904.

Bodelsen, C. A., *Studies in Mid-Victorian Imperialism*. Copenhagen, 1924.

Bonar, James, *A Catalogue of the Library of Adam Smith*. London and New York, 1894.

Bowden, Witt, *The Rise of the Great Manufacturers in England, 1760-1790*. Allentown, Pa., 1919.

— —, *Industrial Society in England towards the End of the Eighteenth Century*. New York, 1925.

— —, 'The English Manufacturers and the Commercial Treaty of 1786 with France,' *American Historical Review*, xxv, 18 ff.

Bowen, Sir G. F., *Thirty Years of Colonial Government*, 2 vols. London and New York, 1889.

Brady, Alexander, *William Huskisson and Liberal Reform*. Oxford, 1928.

Brebner, J. Bartlet, 'Joseph Howe and the Crimean War Enlistment Controversy between Great Britain and the United States,' *Canadian Historical Review*, xi, 300 ff.

Brock, W. R., *Lord Liverpool and Liberal Toryism*. Cambridge, 1941.

Brougham, Henry (Lord), *An Inquiry into the Colonial Policy of the European Powers*, 2 vols. Edinburgh, 1803.

Brown, Benjamin H., *The Tariff Reform Movement in Great Britain, 1881-1895*. New York, 1943.

Brown, George W., 'The Opening of the St. Lawrence to American Shipping,' *Canadian Historical Review*, vii, 4 ff.

Buck, Philip W., *The Politics of Mercantilism*. New York, 1942.

Burn, D. L., 'Canada and the Repeal of the Corn Laws,' *Cambridge Historical Journal*, ii, 252 ff.

Burt, Alfred Le Roy, *Imperial Architects*. Oxford, 1913.

Canada and its Provinces, ed. by Adam Shortt and Arthur G. Doughty, 23 vols. Toronto, 1914-17.

Carter, Clarence E., 'The Office of Commander-in-Chief: A Phase of Imperial Unity on the Eve of the Revolution,' *The Era of the American Revolution*, ed. by Richard B. Morris, pp. 170 ff. New York, 1939.

Cartwright, John, *The Life and Correspondence of*, ed. by F. D. Cartwright, 2 vols. London, 1826.

Clapham, J. H., *An Economic History of Modern Britain*, 3 vols. Cambridge, 1930-38.

Clapham, J. H., 'The Last Years of the Navigation Acts,' *English Historical Review,* xxv, 480 ff., 687 ff.

Clark, Dora Mae, *British Opinion and the American Revolution.* New Haven, 1930.

Clark, Walter Ernest, *Josiah Tucker, Economist.* New York, 1903.

Cockroft, Grace Amelia, *The Public Life of George Chalmers.* New York, 1939.

Cole, Charles Woolsey, *Colbert and a Century of French Mercantilism,* 2 vols. New York, 1939.

— —, *French Mercantilism,* 1683-1700. New York, 1943.

Creighton, D. G., *The Commercial Empire of the St. Lawrence,* 1760-1850. New Haven, 1937.

Cunningham, W., *The Growth of English Industry and Commerce in Modern Times,* 3rd ed. Cambridge, 1903.

— —, *The Wisdom of the Wise.* Cambridge, 1906.

Davidson, John, 'England's Commercial Policy towards her Colonies since the Treaty of Paris,' *Political Science Quarterly,* xiv, 39 ff., 211 ff.

Disraeli, Benjamin, *Lord George Bentinck: A Political Biography,* new ed. London, 1858.

Edwards, Bryan, *The History, Civil and Commercial, of the British Colonies in the West Indies,* 2 vols. London, 1793; 4 vols. Philadelphia, 1805-6.

Fitzmaurice, Lord Edmond, *The Life of Granville George Leveson Gower, Second Earl of Granville,* 2 vols. London, 1905.

— —, *Life of William, Earl of Shelburne,* 3 vols. London, 1875-6.

Fortescue, Sir John W., *History of the British Army,* 13 vols. London and New York, 1899-1930.

Froude, James Anthony, *Short Studies on Great Subjects,* 4 vols. New York, 1909-14.

Fuchs, Carl Johannes, *The Trade Policy of Great Britain and her Colonies since* 1860, trans. by Constance H. M. Archibald. London, 1905.

Gipson, Lawrence Henry, *The British Empire before the American Revolution.* Vols. i-iii, Caldwell (Idaho), 1936; Vols. iv-v, New York, 1939-42.

Goebel, Dorothy Burne, 'British Trade to the Spanish Colonies, 1796-1823,' *American Historical Review,* xliii, 288 ff.

Graham, Gerald S., *British Policy and Canada,* 1774-1791. London, New York, and Toronto, 1930.

— —, *Sea Power and British North America,* 1783-1820. London, 1941.

Gregory, Sir William, *An Autobiography,* ed. by Lady Gregory. London, 1894.

Gwyn, Stephen, and Tuckwell, Gertrude M., *The Life of the Rt. Hon. Sir Charles W. Dilke,* 2 vols. New York, 1917.

Hacker, Louis M., *Triumph of American Capitalism.* New York, 1940.

Halévy, Elie, *The Growth of Philosophic Radicalism,* trans. by Mary Morris. New York, 1928.

Haliburton: A Century Chaplet. Toronto, 1897.

Hamilton, Baillie, 'Forty-Four Years at the Colonial Office,' *The Nineteenth Century,* LXV, 599 ff.

Hardinge, Sir Arthur Henry, *The Life of Henry Howard Molyneux Herbert, Fourth Earl of Carnarvon,* 3 vols. London, 1925.

Harper, Lawrence A., *The English Navigation Laws: A Seventeenth-Century Experiment in Social Engineering.* New York, 1939.

— —, 'The Effect of the Navigation Acts on the Thirteen Colonies,' *The Era of the American Revolution,* ed. by Richard B. Morris, pp. 3 ff. New York, 1939.

— —, 'Mercantilism and the American Revolution,' *Canadian Historical Review,* XXIII, 1 ff.

Heckscher, Eli F., *Mercantilism,* tr. by M. Shapiro, 2 vols. London, 1935.

Hertz (Hurst), G. B., *The Old Colonial System.* Manchester, 1905.

Higgs, Henry, *The Physiocrats.* London, 1897.

Holland, Bernard, *Imperium et Libertas.* London, 1901.

— —, *The Fall of Protection.* London, 1913.

Keith, Arthur Berriedale, *Responsible Government in the Dominions.* 3 vols. Oxford, 1912; 2nd ed., 2 vols. Oxford, 1928.

Kennedy, W. P. M., *The Constitution of Canada.* London, 1922; 2nd ed., London, 1938.

Kent, C. B. R., *The English Radicals.* London, 1899.

Knaplund, Paul, *Gladstone and Britain's Imperial Policy.* New York, 1927.

— —, 'Sir James Stephen and British North American Problems, 1840-7,' *Canadian Historical Review,* V, 3 ff.

— —, 'Mr. Over-Secretary Stephen,' *Journal of Modern History,* I, 40 ff.

Knorr, Klaus E., *British Colonial Theories,* 1570-1850. Toronto, 1944.

Lang, J. D., *The Coming Event.* London, 1870.

Lascelles, E. C. P., *Granville Sharp and the Freedom of Slaves in England.* London, 1928.

Levi, Leone, *History of British Commerce and of the Economic Progress of the British Nation.* London, 1872; 2nd ed., London, 1880.

Lindsay, W. S., *History of Merchant Shipping and Ancient Commerce*, 4 vols. London, 1874-6.

Lingelbach, Anna Lane, 'The Inception of the British Board of Trade,' *American Historical Review*, xxx, 701 ff.

— —, 'William Huskisson as President of the Board of Trade,' *American Historical Review*, XLIII, 759 ff.

McCulloch, J. R., *The Literature of Political Economy*. London, 1845.

— —, *A Dictionary, Practical, Theoretical, and Historical, of Commerce and Commercial Navigation*, new ed., London, 1839.

Maitland, F. W., *The Constitutional History of England*. Cambridge, 1911.

Marshall, Alfred, *Industry and Trade*. London, 1920.

Merivale, Herman, *Lectures on Colonization and Colonies*, ed. by K. Bell. Oxford, 1928.

Mills, R. C., *The Colonization of Australia*. London, 1915.

Monypenny, W. F., and Buckle, G. E., *The Life of Benjamin Disraeli*, 6 vols. New York, 1911-20.

Morgan, William, *Memoirs of the Life of the Rev. Richard Price*. London, 1815.

Morley, John, *The Life of Richard Cobden*, 2 vols. London, 1908.

— —, *The Life of William Ewart Gladstone*, 3 vols. London, 1903.

Morrell, W. P., *British Colonial Policy in the Age of Peel and Russell*. Oxford, 1930.

Nevins, Allan, *Hamilton Fish: The Inner History of the Grant Administration*. New York, 1936.

Newton, Lord, *Lord Lyons*, 2 vols. London, 1913.

Nicholson, J. Shield, *A Project of Empire*. London, 1909.

Pargellis, Stanley M., *Lord Loudoun in North America*, New Haven, 1933.

Penson, Lillian M., 'The London West India Interest in the Eighteenth Century,' *English Historical Review*, xxxvi, 373 ff.

Pope, Sir Joseph, *Memoirs of the Right Honourable Sir John Alexander Macdonald*, 2 vols. London, 1894.

Ragatz, Lowell Joseph, *The Fall of the Planter Class in the British Caribbean*, 1763-1833. New York, 1928.

— —, *A Guide for the Study of British Caribbean History*, 1763-1834, *including the Abolition and Emancipation Movements*. Washington, 1932.

Reeves, John, *The Law of Shipping and Navigation*. Dublin, 1792; 2nd ed., London, 1807.

Reid, S. J., *Life and Letters of the First Earl of Durham*. London, 1906.

Reid, Sir T. W., *Life of the Right Hon. W. E. Forster*, 2 vols. London, 1888.

Schmoller, Gustav, *The Mercantile System and its Historical Significance illustrated chiefly from Prussian History*. New York and London, 1896.

Seeley, Sir John R., *The Expansion of England*. London, 1883.

Shippee, Lester Burrell, *Canadian-American Relations, 1849-1874*. New Haven, 1939.

Skelton, Oscar Douglas, *The Life and Times of Sir Alexander Tilloch Galt*. Toronto, 1920.

Spector, Margaret Marion, *The American Department of the British Government, 1768-1782*. New York, 1940.

Stacey, C. P., *Canada and the British Army, 1846-1871*. London and New York, 1936.

Stephen, Caroline Emelia, *The Right Honourable Sir James Stephen*. Privately printed, 1906.

Stephen, Leslie, *The English Utilitarians*, 3 vols. London, 1900.

— —, *The Life of Sir James Fitzjames Stephen*. London, 1895.

Tansill, Charles C., *The Canadian Reciprocity Treaty of 1854*. Baltimore, 1922.

Thomas, Roland, *Richard Price*. London, 1924.

Todd, Alpheus, *Parliamentary Government in the British Colonies*, 2nd ed. London and New York, 1894.

Tucker, Gilbert Norman, *The Canadian Commercial Revolution, 1845-1851*. New Haven, 1936.

Tyler, J. E., *The Struggle for Imperial Unity*. London, New York, and Toronto, 1938.

Veitch, G. S., *The Genesis of Parliamentary Reform*. London, 1913.

Vogel, Sir Julius, 'Greater or Lesser Britain,' *The Nineteenth Century*, I, 809 ff.

Wagner, Donald O., 'British Economists and the Empire,' *Political Science Quarterly*, XLVI, 248 ff.

Wallas, Graham, *The Life of Francis Place*, revised ed. London, 1918.

Walpole, Sir Spencer, *A History of England from the Conclusion of the Great War in 1815*, 5 vols. London, 1879-86.

— —, *The Life of Lord John Russell*, 2 vols. London, 1889.

Wrong, E. M., *Charles Buller and Responsible Government*. Oxford, 1926.

Yonge, Charles Duke, *The Life and Administration of Robert Banks, Second Earl of Liverpool*, 3 vols. London, 1868.

INDEX

337

Date Due